The *GAWAIN*-Poet

COUCY

barry of six vair and gules

The *GAWAIN*-Poet

Studies in His Personality and Background

By HENRY LYTTLETON SAVAGE

Chapel Hill

The University of North Carolina Press

To

ROBERT ARMSTRONG PRATT

Your worde and your worchip walkeʒ ay-quere

Acknowledgments

MY COLLEAGUES who suffered so patiently during the writing of this book will read these very inadequate words of acknowledgment with undisguised relief, as will also those one-time strangers (now my friends) whose leisure I imposed upon, and whose lives I made burdensome by wearisome cross-examination upon the minutiae of medieval days. The list of their names is a long bead-roll.

Among my colleagues on the Princeton Faculty, past and present, I have to thank the late H. H. Hudson, and the late Professor D. A. Stauffer for making transcriptions from heraldic manuscripts in the British Museum and in collegiate libraries at Oxford; F. E. Agard and the late E. C. Armstrong for assistance in the resolution of cruces in the text of Froissart's *Chroniques*; D. D. Egbert for counsel about the symbolism of the Middle Ages; W. F. Stohlman for sending me from European libraries and museums photographs of the Coucy achievement; J. R. Strayer for help in the interpretation of the fourteenth century public records published and unpublished; and C. H. Baker for the strongest kind of encouragement.

My debt of gratitude, however, transcends limitations of land and water. I am under particular obligation to Mrs. R. R. Cawley and Mrs. Tenney Frank for their kindness in consulting for my benefit genealogical and heraldic manu-

scripts in London and Oxford. I owe much to the instruction
I received *secus pedes Gamaliel,* when the deans of heraldic
lore, the late Oswald Baron, F.S.A., the Late Reverend E.
E. Dorling, F.S.A., and the late S. M. Collins, F.S.A., were
my teachers. To Anthony R. Wagner, Esq., Richmond Herald, I am indebted for professional advice and private courtesy. To his kindness I owe an introduction to M. Jacques
Meurgey, *chargé du Service sigillographique aux Archives
nationales,* who very kindly sent me a facsimile of a seal of
the Sire de Coucy in his collection. I am grateful to H. H.
Stanford London, Esq., for giving careful answers to en-
quiries that must have seemed tediously minute, and to
Hilary Jenkinson, Esq., of the Public Record Office for
kindness extended to me within and without the walls of
that Office. To our own American heraldists, Dr. Harold
Bowditch, G. A. Moriarty, and the late Pierre la Rose, it is
a pleasure to express gratitude for assistance given without
stint. I would thank Professor J. J. Parry and the late Professor W. Graham, editors of the *Journal of English and
Germanic Philology,* for permission to reprint an article that
appeared in Volume 27 (pp. 1-15), of that journal. It stands
in this book, with considerable revision, as Chapter II. I am
greatly indebted to Professor A. H. Marckwardt of the University of Michigan for advice upon the validity of the linguistic evidence used to localize *Sir Gawain.* I am deeply
grateful to the Early English Text Society for permission to
quote from the most recent and best edition of *Sir Gawain
and the Green Knight*—that of the late Sir Israel Gollancz
and Miss Mabel Day.

My thanks are due also to the officials and staff of the
Literary Search Room of the Public Record Office for fa-
cilities and courtesies during the autumn of 1937; to Mr.
Kingsford and his assistant at the Library of the Society of
Antiquaries; and to the Reference Librarian and Staff of the

Widener. Nor must I forget the courtesy and attention I have received, and still receive, at the libraries of the Princeton Theological Seminary and Princeton University. At the latter institution Dr. J. H. Hanford and Mr. Alexander Wainwright have been patient under my questions and efficacious in answering them.

For all errors I alone am responsible. They are fewer because of the patience and kindness of those named above. I should be lacking in courtesy, did I not voice my gratitude to Professor Roland M. Smith of the University of Illinois for some excellent "cathartic" criticism.

I am obliged to the American Philosophical Society, whose grant in aid of research has helped to make the writing of this book possible; and I would voice my thanks to the late Professor Capps, and to Professors Friend and Osgood, members of a quondam committee on research at Princeton University, for an earlier grant given for the same end.

Finally, I am deeply grateful to Dean Taylor and the members of the University Research Committee for a grant sufficient to ensure publication.

Contents

Acknowledgments   vii

Introduction   xv

I   "Master Anonymous"   3

II   Symbolism and Allegory in *Sir Gawain and the Green Knight*   31   P. 37, 42-46

III   A French Knight of the Garter   49

Appendices

     A   The English Estates of the House of Coucy-Guines   123

     B   Linguistic Evidence as to Place of Origin of the Author of *Sir Gawain and the Green Knight*   128

     C   The Date of *Sir Gawain*   138   P. 140-141

     D   Enguerrand de Coucy and the Order of the Garter   142

     E   The Pentangle   158

     F   Philippa Countess of Oxford   168

     G   The Meaning of *Sir Gawain*, Lines 862-71   176 ?

     H   The *Cri de Guerre* of the House of Coucy   190

     J   The Order of the Crown   195

     K   Possible Position and Status of the Author of *Sir Gawain*   206

     L   Coucy's Letter of Resignation, August 26, 1377   217

Bibliography   219

Index   231

Illustrations

The Arms of COUCY, *barry of six vair and gules*   *frontispiece*

The Arms of GUINES, *vairy or and azure*   *facing page* 189

Introduction

THE CHIEF reason that has hitherto kept the *Gawain-* (or *Pearl-*) poet from enjoying the fame which has been the lot of his more popular contemporary, Geoffrey Chaucer, has been his deliberate use of the verse medium of his native region—the poetic line which his fathers had used, a line of subtle rhythm and telling alliterative effect, written out in the dialect of Lancashire, or that of the adjacent district of Craven in the Yorkshire West Riding, a region whose local idiom was not destined to grow, like Chaucer's dialect, the Southeast Midland, into the standard speech we use and write and hear today. His "yoke" and "thorn" letters, the glottal and aspiratory sounds of his Scandinavianized vocabulary have frightened off more than one potential critic whose words might have enlightened us. So his vigorous and artistic speech, once so current and so splendidly alive, was destined to sink into a dialect that one hears now only in remote dales of Northwest England and on the trackways that connect them. I well remember that learned and sensitive medievalist, the late Oswald Barron, remarking, as he held open a copy of *Sir Gawain*, "but he's a North of England, and I'm a Southern man."

There are, of course, other reasons why the *Gawain*-poet is less read than Chaucer. His interest in the varieties and eccentricities of human character is less broad, though some

very amusing, very lovable, and very human individuals
lurk within his pages. The set of his mind is aristocratic
rather than democratic; what he says appeals to a sophisti-
cated audience, interests the few rather than the many. Yet
he and his *façon de parler* are not entirely and solely to
blame for his being less read than he should be. Had one
writer, the author of a very readable book on Chaucer,
known him better, he scarcely could have written the following words, so patently untrue:

"One [*The Knight's Tale*] is the work of a free artist, the other
[*Sir Gawain*] of a moralist—of a moralist with considerable
artistic taste, to be sure, and with a lively interest in nature, costume, armor, jewels, furniture, and the ways of the courtly circle,
but one who nevertheless conceives of art and poetry as hand-
maids to virtue and religion."[1]

To come truly to know a great poet there is no better
way than to act as the editor of one of his masterpieces, for
the truth that escapes the critic who writes *currente calamo* is
often revealed to that patient drudge who must weigh his
author's words. It is at this very slow and protracted task
that the present writer has been engaged since 1933—the
preparation of an edition of *Sir Gawain and the Green
Knight*. But as editorial work progressed, one thing slowly
became self-evident—that there was much to be said about
the writer of *Sir Gawain* that ought not to be compressed
within the covers of an edition of the poem. The present
studies, therefore, discuss the writer and the writing of that
romance in a way impossible to its editor, who must stick
to his text and cannot enjoy the essayist's privilege of ranging far afield.

I have availed myself of that privilege in the first and
second chapters of this book. In doing so, however, I have
made a strong and conscious effort not to follow the will-o'-

1. P. V. D. Shelly, *The Living Chaucer* (Philadelphia, 1940), p. 12.

the-wisps of unrestrained imagination into scholarly morasses
or into fields fenced off by logic or probability. The reader
must judge how successful that effort has been.

For the inclusion of my third chapter I owe the reader a
more precise explanation. Editorial labors had required me
to read extensively in the monastic chronicles and in the
chancery and exchequer records that covered the years of
the second half of the fourteenth century. As I read I
chanced to come upon an actual situation that bore a close
resemblance to the one the poem depicts. As I compared
more closely fact with fiction, little points of correspondence
between the two became more apparent, and differences that
at first seemed to tell against a connection between them, less
forbidding. Indeed so close was the parallelism that I wondered at times whether the poet was not hinting at a story
whose events had recently happened before his eyes. If he
was, it is likely that he was hinting at a *cause célèbre* of the
Court of Richard II—that of the Princess Isabella, aunt of
the monarch, and her husband, the Sire de Coucy.

It seemed entirely possible that in his story of the spot-
less knight, who in rejecting an amorous lady broke his
plighted oath and returned to his own country disgraced
in his own eyes, the poet might have written with the French
knight in mind—the knight who, in order to remain true
to his first allegiance, abandoned his wife and renounced
his oath.

Evidence, however, for an actual connection between the
two series of events, the fictional and the factual, is lacking.
Conceivably it might turn up. Long and patient effort might
lead to a clue now hidden in some financial account or in a
record of some grant made to a member of the royal or of a
baronial household. But up to the present there has been
little to which one could anchor the chain of inferences and
circumstantial evidence which make up my third chapter. I

can assure the reader that I have done my best to make the inferential chain strike anchorhold in some event of the late fourteenth century, but so far without success. Honesty compels the utterance of this warning, for I would have the reader at all times aware that he is following a recital of possibilities or probabilities and not one of proved fact.

I may be asked why, in this attempt to localize the occasion at which *Sir Gawain* was written, I have bothered to formulate hypotheses unproved, and possibly unprovable. I may be told that unproved hypotheses have no place in sound scholarship.

The last statement, however, is but a partial truth. Unprovable statements, as every scholar knows, can always be challenged, to their makers' embarrassment, but many of the certainties even of our daily life are based upon unproved assumptions. Indeed, "sound scholarship" itself is continuously dealing with unproved hypotheses and requires ceaseless effort to weigh and test their capability of being substantiated. And scholarship that is really sound results from repeated attempts to solve a difficulty apparently insoluble.

My third chapter, then, is one of hypotheses. Since they have been framed with discrimination and careful thought, I offer no apology for advancing them. Though they, as a group, do not explain completely each and every difficulty the poem presents, yet no previous group has met so adequately the different situations in which the hero of the poem finds himself. If at any future time we shall identify the author of *Sir Gawain*, and ascertain the locality and circumstances in which he wrote his poem, that knowledge will be attained by some such method as that employed in this study.

The *GAWAIN*-Poet

CHAPTER I

"Master Anonymous"

IN A SMALL quarto-size volume in the British Museum there are bound up, incongruously enough, two Latin tracts and four long narrative poems. A strange destiny indeed, for poetry and didacticism thus to lie cheek by jowl! Such a juxtaposition, however, was not of medieval making, but due entirely to the notions of cataloguing that buzzed in the brain of some librarian of later years. Of the four poems, written out in a "small, sharp, irregular" handwriting of the later fourteenth century, we know practically nothing. No author has inscribed his name within the opening or closing lines of any of them, or concealed it within the letters of some punning rebus or play on words. And learning the identity of the author is made the more difficult, because it is certain that the manuscript we have—and it is the only manuscript—is not the original one that the author himself wrote or dictated aloud to an amanuensis. The poems in the Cotton Nero MS A. x., for such is its imposing title, are all of them one remove, and some of them may be two or three removes, away from the author's original manuscript.[1] With an anonymous group of poems written in a handwriting that has

---

1. See J. B. Oakden, "The Scribes of the Poems of the Cotton MS Nero A.x.," *Alliterative Poetry in Middle English* (Manchester, 1930), Vol. 1, App. 3, pp. 261-63. See also *Library* 13. 188-89, and 14. 353-58. Miss Mabel Day, editor of *Sir Gawain* (EETS, Oxford, 1940), tells me that "the Gawayne text had a different history from that of the other three poems, and was probably put together with them by some collector."

been slowly fading into illegibility, and in a manuscript that is perhaps a third or fourth copy of the original, discovery of the author, or even of the time and place at which he wrote, seems about as likely as success in catching and shoeing the wind.

The task is difficult enough, but not quite so hopelessly futile as at first sight it would seem. For years, patient drudges, of whom the writer is one, have been pecking away at the poems. They have endeavored to localize the speech in which the four poems were written, and have succeeded in narrowing quite closely the geographic bounds which hem it in. By examining the poet's descriptions of armor and of clothing, they have reached certain conclusions about the time within which he wrote. Furthermore, examination of allusions to be found within the lines of several of the poems, and of scrawls on the margins of the manuscript has yielded to them the right to assert more boldly conclusions that at first were only remotely possible. We know now a good deal more than we did about these four poems, not because of any new discoveries turned up in some collection of hitherto unpublished papers, nor from any new finds made in the British Museum or in libraries at Oxford and Cambridge, but because those same drudges stuck to their uninspiring task of tracing the development of the OE y sound in the poet's writings, studying his use of the weak verb, noting his stylistic mannerisms, or writing the history of Lancashire parishes.

Such patient labors have not been confined only to the poems of our manuscript; they have also been exerted, during the course of the past twenty years, in almost every field of medieval life and thought. Those twenty years have provided more efficacious tools and instruments in the shape of editions or printings of material unpublished, of more glossaries, and a mass of learned articles of considerable value;

while during the time that these weapons were being forged and shaped to the scholar's hand, there have appeared newer and better books on the art, history, theology, and typography of the Middle Ages. We understand better, know more about, the life of that very creative and very restive time than we did, and since what is greater includes what is less, we know more about the author of the four poems of the Cotton Nero MS. The mounting mass of all that printed matter (written scholarship is self-perpetuating) has not buried him, but lifted him into clearer definition. How, then, does he appear in this sharper focus?

Of the four poems of this unknown author two of them, *Patience* and *Purity*, are narrative poems with a distinct didactic purpose; a third, *The Pearl*, is an elegy; and the fourth, *Sir Gawain and the Green Knight*, a romance.

The two homiletic poems were written, as one might suspect, to inculcate the virtues which serve as their titles. Poetry written to teach the practice of conduct is quite often apt to be poor poetry, because the writer, in his endeavor to inculcate the conduct that ought to be, is prone to forget, if he ever knew, what poetry ought to be. But to say that a poet must not write about religious matters or conduct, as so many young critics do say today, is a very illiberal and outmoded opinion. It circumscribes the scope of poetry and limits closely the range of experience. A true poet will write about whatever he wants to write about, as this poet did, irrespective of whatever petty and absurd conventions narrow-minded critics may frame. *Quidquid tetigit adornavit.* Seldom has preaching been so absorbingly interesting. The author illustrates the virtue of Patience by a most vivid and amusing account of the Prophet Jonah's lack of it. *Purity* is composed of a series of biblical episodes, with short links connecting them. In both poems the vigor of the poet's phrasing astonishes one, and the beauty and resonance of the allitera-

tive line are an unending charm. Hear him describe the
perplexity of the magicians and soothsayers as they stand
before the wall whereon the armless hand has inscribed the
mysterious words which have so terrified King Belshazzar
and which none of them is able to read:

> This cry was up-cast, and there comen many
> Clerks out of Chaldea that keenest were known,
> As the sage satraps that sorcery knew,
> Witches and valkyries[2] won to that salle,
> Diviners of demerlayk[3] that dreams could read,
> Sorcerers and exorcists and many such clerks;
> And all that looked on that letter as "lewed"[4] they were
> As they had looked in the leather of my left boot.[5]

But of *Patience* and *Purity* enough. Our task is to learn
more of the personality of their gifted author, and up to the
present time, the only means of gaining this further knowledge has been following out the clues that his writings afford
to the point where they cease and progress becomes error.

Today we can date the work of the *Gawain*-poet more
precisely than we could twenty years ago. We know, for
example, that he used the Old French version of *Mandeville's Travels* as one of the sources of his *Purity*. This poem,
therefore, could not have been composed before 1356, the
probable date of the appearance of the Travels,[6] and must
have been written sometime after that date, quite possibly
in the late sixties or early seventies of the fourteenth century. As most scholars consider *Purity* to have been written

2. Sorceresses.   3. Magic.
4. Ignorant.   5. Lines 1574-85.
6. A. Steiner ("The Date of Composition of *Mandeville's Travels*,"
Speculum 9. 144 ff.) would place the composition of the *Travels* between
1365 and 1371; M. Letts (*Mandeville's Travels*, Hakluyt Soc. 1. xxvii-
xxviii) suggests a date between 1360 and 1370; Mrs. Josephine W. Bennett (*Sir John Mandeville*, MLA of America, New York, 1954, pp. 140,
146, 151) has, however, shown that the *Travels* was composed before
1371, so that it becomes more probable that Mrs. Bennett's assumption that
1356 is the genuine date of its publication is a correct one.

early rather than late in its author's career, *The Pearl* and *Gawain* may not have been composed until the decade later than 1360.[7] A second indication as to the date at which *Gawain* was written is to be found in lines 701-2 of that poem. The poet describes the Wirral (the promontory between the Dee and the Mersey in the northwest portion of the county of Cheshire) as a place where there dwelt few who "either God or fellow-man with good heart loved." The characterization was correct; the Wirral (a royal forest, and hence the favored resort of criminals and outlaws) was a bad place—so bad that in July, 1376, it was disafforested to permit the entrance of the sheriff of the county.[8] Now a lawless condition in a particular district is apt to be a thing of gradual and progressive growth, and of slow and protracted conclusion; but since Cheshire and the Wirral became more and not less disorderly as the century drew to a close, we are safe in assuming that *Gawain* was written in the days when conditions had indeed become a public scandal. And in the last few years of Edward III and the early years of Richard II such they were.

Another indication as to the years in which the poet wrote is one derived from an alliterative poem called *St. Erkenwald*.[9] This poem is the legend of the English saint of that name (Bishop of London 675-93). It is contained in another manuscript (Harleian Collection, No. 2250) than the Cotton Nero, but it is very probable that it was written by the *Gawain*-poet. Therefore, any reasonable conclusions as to

7. *Purity*, ed. R. J. Menner (New Haven, 1920), pp. xxvii ff.

8. Disafforestation meant that the laws of the forest (a royal forest was not governed by the common law of the land, but by a particular code of its own, the "law of the forest") were repealed and that the whole area of the former forest became subject to the common law and the courts that administered it. It was because Sherwood Forest was free of the common law that Robin Hood and his men resided there. See H. L. Savage, "A Note on *Sir Gawain and the Green Knight*," *MLN* 46. 455-57.

9. *St. Erkenwald*, ed. H. L. Savage (New Haven, 1926).

the date at which it was composed provide a little more
knowledge about the chronology of the life and writings of
our author. Now in 1386 the Bishop of London issued a
pastoral letter in which he ordered the clergy of his diocese
to celebrate the day of the saint's death (April 30) and the
day of his translation (the anniversary of November 14,
1148, when his body was removed from the position where
it lay in St. Paul's to another more honorable site in that
cathedral) with the same solemnity as the day consecrated
to St. Paul himself, the patron of the cathedral. To put it
briefly, in 1386 high ecclesiastical honors were paid to the
memory and merits of St. Erkenwald, and coincident with
their establishment appears a poem, in all probability from
the pen of the *Gawain*-poet, in honor of the saint. It is far
more reasonable to suppose that the poem was not written
before this attempt to prepare a place for their former pastor
in the minds and hearts of the members of his flock, but *after*
Bishop Braybroke had begun to "boom" the saint, and while
the tide of popular devotion was running at the full. It
seems, then, as certain as anything can be without legal
proof, that the *Gawain*-poet was writing between 1365 and
1386, a period of slightly over twenty years, the later years
of Edward III and the earlier and middle years of Richard II.[10]

A good deal more can be learned about the author from
a study of the language in which his poems are written.
Scholars are pretty well agreed that he writes in a speech or
dialect of the Northwest Midland counties of England, a
speech that one might have met with in Cheshire, in the

10. I believe there is in *Pur.* 1232 a reference to the warlike qualities
of the Ottoman Turks who had in 1358 gained their first foothold on
European soil (*Camb. Mod. Hist.*, I. 67). From that date on they pur-
sued those campaigns, so destructive to the Byzantine empire and to Greek
Christianity, that led on to the final campaign and battle of Nicopolis
(1396), fatal to many of the poet's contemporaries and to some whom he
may very well have known.

Peak District of Derbyshire, in the Yorkshire West Riding, or in East Lancashire, where that county borders on the district of Craven, which is a part of that Yorkshire West Riding I have just mentioned. Of these several districts the last two seem more likely to have been the places whence the poet (some perhaps may prefer to say "scribe") might have hailed, because the vocabulary he used is nearer to that used in those two localities than it is to the vocabulary of North Cheshire or that of the Peak.[11] Where there are neither railways, newspapers, telephones, nor radios, local speech habits and individualities of expression do not change much; even between two places not very far apart as the crow flies, there exist marked differences in speech and in pronunciation.

But there are other methods of learning about the homeland of the poet than those purely linguistic. In *Sir Gawain and the Green Knight* he has described quite realistically the setting of the story. We know, for instance, that in Lancashire the sparse settlements and the great distances that separated them required the priests of a parish church to trudge or ride many a weary mile to hold services for those who found it impossible, through age, infirmity, or infancy, to come to the regular services at the parish church. Gradually through the years, small chapels were erected near isolated communities, or within a knightly or baronial castle, of which the priest, or his curate, was known as the chaplain. Now there is in *Sir Gawain* a reference (line 2107) to this very matter of the outlying chapelry, and since the number of such chapelries was large in Lancashire and Yorkshire,

11. One is on much safer ground with alliterative than with nonalliterative poetry when he draws deductions about an author's language. While copyists must at times have changed one or more of the alliterations in a particular line of poetry (sometimes, no doubt, the alliteration of a whole line), few of them could have been such "lords of language" as to have kept it up for any sustained length. Study of alliterative poetry has confirmed me in the belief that the vocabulary that a particular poet uses is his own, marked by his own preferences and idiosyncrasies.

and few in North Cheshire, and since also the poet writes of this ecclesiastical practice as if it were a very usual one, it is quite likely that he was describing conditions that he knew, and that he was either a Lancashire or a West Riding man.

But how or in what way did he live and earn his daily bread? Was he a public servant like Chaucer, or a priest of a parish, or a monk in a cloister? It is possible that in his later years he may have become a monk, if certain hypotheses which a learned nun, Sister Mary Madeleva, believes to be true, really are true. Within the neighborhood whence we believe he may have come stood the wealthy Abbey of Whalley (Lancashire), and in Northwest Lancashire, a region by no means ruled out as the place of his abode, the great Abbey of Furness. It is possible that either one may have sheltered the old age of the *Gawain*-poet. But of one thing we may be quite sure: in young manhood certainly, and probably also well into middle life, he had not taken monastic vows. He knows too much about the world and its ways; had I said "the world and his wife," I would not have been wrong either: our very own world, and all the individualistic persons who knock around in it, boisterous as Bercilak, querulous as Jonah, well-behaved as Noah.[12] He knew the practices of the Court, was familiar with the ceremonial of banquets of state, had assisted at the services in cathedrals and minsters that marked the solemn days of the ecclesiastical calendar, had waited, like a true Englishman, at covert side, until the hounds had picked up scent again. One who had entered the cloister in early life could never have described the pleasant, gay, and naughty world as he has done.

But if he were no monk, how came he to be so familiar with aristocratic life and yet at the same time to remain still a man of the shires? Country speech and courtly manners

12. Unfortunately he does not retell in his account of the Deluge (*Pur.*) the story of Noah's trifling lapse into inebriety.

do not, we have been told, go well together. There was but one way in medieval times by which a man of country stock could come to know of courts and the aristocratic way of life, and that way was by entering the service of some powerful nobleman. An aspiring or ambitious youngster made that entrée by taking service in the household of the magnate of whom his father held, or of one whom all recognized as the first gentleman of his native county. In Lancashire and Craven there was no lack of country gentry, local knights and landholders, but service in their attenuated households would never have taken one into the Court's outer purlieus. Only in the household of such a magnate could our aspiring youngster have seen that great world which lay beyond the boundaries of Lancashire and Craven.

Within the years when the *Gawain*-poet may be supposed to have been writing, there were two noblemen, both members of the royal family, whose holdings in Yorkshire and Lancashire gave them prestige and a standing in those counties, and in whose households a man could have advanced his fortunes. They were John of Gaunt, Duke of Lancaster, the "Knight in Black" of Chaucer's *Book of the Duchess*, whose domain included the lion's share of the county of Lancaster, as well as the castle of Richmond in Yorkshire and the country one could see from its battlements; and his brother-in-law, Enguerrand de Coucy, the French Earl of Bedford, who held lands in North Lancashire and also in the country where the little stream of the Ribble flows below the Yorkshire downs until it turns into Lancashire on its way to the Irish Sea. It is surmise, and not fact, that the *Gawain*-poet served either (or both) of these princes in some administrative or clerical capacity, but the surmise is far from being an unreasonable one and can safely be advanced until a better one be adduced.[13]

13. J. P. Oakden (*Allit. Poetry in ME* 1. 257-61) believes that the *Gawain*-poet was a retainer of John of Gaunt, Duke of Lancaster, that

But not all our knowledge of the *Gawain*-poet is confined to what we can glean from his writings by indirect assays. The writings themselves give us plenty of information about their author.

If the hypothesis that the poet was a member of the household of some magnate, and enjoyed his patronage, be an allowable one, there are passages in his poetry that take on a more vivid and realistic color and, by doing so, help to illuminate his career. It is worth remembering that in *Purity* (125-132) he describes a great feudal lord passing up and down between the long tables at which his guests sit, chaffing old acquaintances, greeting new ones, and generally dispensing cheer.[14] In *Gawain* the same description occurs again, but with this difference, that the host who moves among his guests is not duke or earl, but a king. In both poems the scene is painted from life. At Richmond Castle or at the Savoy thus had done John of Gaunt; at Windsor, perhaps,

---

he may have resided at the ducal castle of Clitheroe in that county and described the lay of the land near the adjoining village of Downham as the setting for Gawain's adventure at the Green Chapel. Miss M. Day in her recent edition of *Sir Gawain and the Green Knight*, pp. xix-xx, believes that the scenery described in the boar-hunt and in the encounter at the Green Chapel is much more like that of Dovedale or Wyedale. She would place the scene of Gawain's meeting with the Green Knight in the Staffordshire moorland (the nearest mountain scenery to Wirral), more specifically at Wetton Mill, Staffs. Evidence to prove or disprove either suggestion is scanty. Against Oakden's identification it may be said that the country about Clitheroe and Downham is somewhat tame, if the landscapes of the poem are painted from life and not purely imaginary. Against Miss Day's, the objection (not a conclusive one) is to be made that wherever the poet's native locality may have been, the language of the scribe of the MS. appears to be somewhat north or northwest of Staffs. See Mary S. Serjeantson, "The Dialects of the West Midlands in Middle English," *RES* 3. 327-28, and Oakden, *Allit. Poetry in ME*, 1. 85-86.

14. It is of interest to see how the poet has "modernized" the episode of the guest who wore no wedding garment (Matt. 22:7-14). The words of this offended host, more vivid and blistering in *Purity* than in Matthew's gospel, have an authentic ring, and probably echo the overheard expressions of some irritated dignitary whose banquet had been shamed by boorish presumption.

the Earl of Bedford; at Eltham or Sheen, King Edward himself. No poet can describe convincingly what he has not seen or does not know, and the descriptions I have mentioned are convincing. The poet had lived in Lancashire and in London with the *haute noblesse.* He knew their habits, manners, and diversions. Indeed, in the case of the favorite diversion of the medieval aristocrat, that of hunting, his knowledge of the habits of the quarry entitle him to very high rank in the list of great English sportsmen.[15] Most certainly he would have subscribed to the adage "manners maketh man," which Lord Chesterfield renders "being in the fashion will soon fashion you."

And he was equally familiar with a less fashionable group —the learned. In *Purity* (line 193), by a phrase thrown in almost as an aside, he tells us that he had conversed about the problem of human sin with "many high clerks," and there were plenty of them in his day,[16] and also had done considerable reading upon the subject (see line 194), almost certainly in the *Summa Theologia* of St. Thomas Aquinas, and throughout the theological treatises of the patristic writers. Few modern scholars have noticed this quiet but telling confession. In one way, indeed, it hardly tells us anything that is new. No one who reads the notes to Professor C. G. Osgood's edition of *Pearl* can fail to perceive that a very learned man is speaking. But the author's learning does not strike one on a first perusal. It is not evidenced by an

15. For particular instances of his intimate knowledge of hunting craft, see the writer's notes in *PQ* 9. 209; *PMLA* 46. 169; *MLN* 52. 36; *Med. Aev.* 4. 199.

16. To mention but a few, Bishop Bradwardine, Dr. John Wiclif, "the philosophical" Strode (whom Gollancz suspected of being none other than the *Gawain*-poet himself). The possibility that our author may have been a "clerk" would not necessarily imply that he was a man of humble origin. E. F. Jacob ("English University Clerks in the Later Middle Ages," *Rylands Bulletin* 29. 305) tells us that "there was a fair sprinkling of *generosi,* young men of high birth, in the later medieval University."

imposing body of quotation and reference; one simply follows the sustained and continuous utterance of a born story-
teller, with its quiet changes of tempo and tone, changes so
gradual and unarresting that one does not always realize how
important in the works of this poet are his occasional asides
and bits of self-revelation. The present one tells us how it
is that behind the poet's statements on theology, behind the
episodes and events of his story, there is such a wealth of
allegorical, topical, and analogical implication. There are
times when Chaucer seems to parade his learning, the number of books he has read or referred to. One becomes aware
of the range and depth of the *Gawain*-poet's reading, not
by his own recital of the books he has read, but by recog-
nizing the contribution which a Peter Lombard, a Thomas
Aquinas, or a John Mandeville has made to the thought he
expresses.

To strengthen our surmises as to the poet's origins and
his later career, other evidence from his poems is not wanting. That he was a Lancashire man, or else one from West
Yorkshire, or even South Westmoreland, is altogether likely,
and the likelihood is increased by the scenery he describes
in the four poems of his creation. In *Pearl* and *Gawain*, the
downs with their miles of moorland roll away into the distance. The roads circle around their feet, and between the
"rises" even copse and spinney seem as if they, too, were
either climbing up or slipping down hill. Rock screes, described in *Gawain* particularly, recall vividly parts of North
Lancashire about Coniston Water. The higher hills—Pendle,
Ingleborough, Skiddaw—threaten one another across many
miles of country by donning the "mist-hat," whose distant
appearance country folk believe a sure token of rain in their
own localities.[17] Even in *Purity* the Deluge itself deluges not

17. Cf. *Gawain* 2081:
     Vch hille hade a hatte, a myst-hakel huge.

the flat Sumerian plain, but the great scree-buttressed "hog-backs" and the narrow trackways that crawl beneath them and wind through the Lake district of Lancashire and West-moreland. The poet's eye is quick to notice even the wayside flora of his native heath. In the field where the disappointed Jonah "squats" after his denunciation of Nineveh,[18] one of the plants he uses to build his bower is the "ever-fern" or poly-pody (*Polypodium vulgare*), a fern which the poet had seen growing in the holes and indentations of his native cliffs or on old tree trunks, *but always in shady spots*.[19] Though he was doomed to final disappointment, the author points out that Jonah's judgment as to the site of his "booth" was good: where the "ever-fern" grew the sun would not be hot. In *Gawain* (line 526) he notes a characteristic of the later sum-mer, the early falling of the linden leaves, in a dry year a sure presage of autumn's quiet but relentless march over the landscape.[20]

One other indication of the poet's place of origin is too important to pass unnoticed. When the terrible Green Knight broke into King Arthur's hall, he held in his hand a holly branch and assured the bystanders that its presence was pledge that he passed "all in peace" and sought no fight. I had never found any allusion to this folk-custom anywhere in England or out of it, though I have searched far and wide. But one day while leafing through an old novel called *Scars-dale*,[21] of the mid-nineteenth century, whose story is laid in

18. *Patience* 437-40.
19. For information about *Polypodium vulgare* I am indebted to my friend, the late Mrs. Allan Marquand of Guernsey Hall, Princeton, N. J., whose knowledge of flowers, old and modern, wild and cultivated, was her friends' good fortune.
20. For information about the linden or lime tree, *Tilia cordata*, I am indebted to Mr. Hill, Director of the Royal Botanic Gardens at Kew (private letters of 7/26/'33 and 12/4/'39). Our poet's reference is to *Tilia cordata*; *t. vulgaris*, the lime more often seen today being then un-known in England.
21. Sir J. Kay-Shuttleworth, *Scarsdale* (London, 1860), I. 60-62.

the region whence sprang the poems of the Cotton MS., I ran upon the thing I wanted. The proprietors of a cotton spinning mill, so the story ran, were besieged by their striking workmen. (You will remember that Lancashire is today the home of an extensive weaving and spinning industry.) An emissary was sent out to the workmen from the beleaguered mill, and on his journey he carried a holly-bob as a sign of his peaceful intention, that he might not be stoned or shot. Whether the custom is to be found in other English counties I do not know. The fact that it existed for five centuries within one locality shows that it was known and practiced in Lancashire for a long time.

Residence in the feudal society of his county, varied by recourse to that of the cloister, has given to the poetry of this man its peculiar and characteristic stamp. For one thing, it is almost completely lacking in the "commercial atmosphere" that one sometimes savors in the verse of his great contemporary. Geoffrey Chaucer was, to our good fortune and his own, all his life a man of business, a man whose career can be charted through the Exchequer and Patent Rolls.[22] Legal deeds and civil appointments act as guideposts to the student of his career. And his life as businessman is reflected in his writings. Businessmen, tonsured or untonsured, crowd the *Prologue* and crop up in the *Tales*. Nay, when "business is poor" and money scant, Chaucer (no shame to him) sings to his empty purse, with the hope that his song will be overheard. As compared with Chaucer's interest in money, the *Gawain*-poet's apparent unconcern about pounds and pennies is interesting. Exact market prices for perfect pearls are not quoted in the poem of that title. In *Gawain* the best gems are those that "myȝt be preued of prys wyth penyes to bye," certainly rather a vague indication of value. Such seeming

---

22. In fairness to Chaucer, it should be said that the fact that the *Gawain*-poet is unknown prevents one from compiling from documents in the Public Record Office any record of him as a man of business.

unconcern with something that is the most important thing in life to most people, may have been due to the poet's residence in a society more feudal and less commercial than London. In the Lancashire and Yorkshire of his day there was almost no mining or manufacturing. His country was the nurse of the great flocks whose wool went south for export, and whose maintenance required not close settlement and its resultant chaffering, but the open grasslands that ended with the horizon line. Or such a seeming unconcern may have come about because he had never been compelled to undergo a life of continuous struggle for his daily bread. His praise of Poverty in *Patience* (lines 13, 31 ff.) is probably not so much praise of the material condition as of the spirit enjoined by the Beatitude, *Beati pauperes spiritu.* Where food and shelter had been provided by a generous lord, their lack would never have been felt, and the poet would never have alluded to or reasoned about the money which secured them both. Yet it is more reasonable to attribute this indifference to money to his conviction that money really was a thing indifferent. He valued it for the conveniences and amenities it could provide, as indeed his romance shows, but his fears and hopes were elsewhere.

> Bot Crystes mersy and Mary and Jon,—
> Þise arn þe grounde of alle my blysse.[23]

Of our poet as a painter of natural scenery Professor Moorman has spoken well, but not always wisely. He praises his "keen appreciation of natural form," but finds his "colour-sense . . . not specially prominent."[24] It would be hard indeed to reproach with an indifferent color-sense the artist

23. The poet's words identify the crucifix. Medieval crucifixes displayed not only the figure of the Saviour, but often those also of His Mother and St. John; see John of Gaunt's *Register 1379-82*, I. III (no. 327) where there is recorded a payment for "une croys un crucifix ovesque Marie et Johan garnisez de diverses pieres et perles."
24. F. W. Moorman, *Quellen und Forschungen* 95. 101.

who painted the brilliant flowers shading the bank where the pearl trundled down—clove-pink, or carnation, the low-lying ginger with maroon flower, the blue-gray gromwell, and the peony with its petals of deep, dark red.[25] One might, it is true, dismiss this "flower-picture" as a conventional study of "color in still life," but one could not brand as conventionalized mannerism the poet's picture of the dog-rose against its brown briar-stem,[26] or of the brilliant green of the holly-tree against the bare winter landscape.[27] But it is not only the striking colors that catch the poet's eye—the yellows, greens, reds, and blues. Grays and whites do not go unobserved either. Witness the winter landscape that Gawain sees as he journeys over the downs, and that study of the Green Knight's dale—gray rock rising over the white water of the mountain burn that "blubbers" in its channels "as though it had boiled." Witness again the third hunting morning, with the red sun rising through the cloud-bank, and the fleeting shadows which the clouds throw down as the swift wind chases them through the sky. Having failed to notice how sensitive the poet's eye was to such studies in gray—as the granite of tumbled scree and the mist-cap that thickens round the knob of some swelling "saddle-back," Moorman asks, "Did this poet really feel a sense of pleasure in such scenes of desolation as he describes?" and answers his question in the affirmative. But the question is unwarranted, for Moorman has failed to note that the poet was describing his "ain countree," and that he was in love with that gray land of crag and winds. Desolate or not, it was his home. As well blame Wordsworth for loving the same "desolate" region.

Miss Spurgeon's revealing book *Shakespeare's Imagery*[28] made me wonder whether a study of the images which the

25. *Pearl* 41-44.
26. *Pur.* 791.
27. *Gaw.* 206-7.
28. C. Spurgeon, *Shakespeare's Imagery and What It Tells Us*, N. Y., 1935.

Gawain-poet uses might not lead to some interesting *aperçus*.
My combing of his poems has not been exhaustive, but I
think that in several distinctive images that crop up frequently in all four poems (and to a lesser degree in *Erkenwald* as well) there are definite indications of the set of his
mind, of the preferences which appealed to him. Miss
Spurgeon has shown that Shakespeare held not only preferences, but antipathies as well. Certain ideas filled him with
intense disgust. As compared with Shakespeare, the *Gawain*-
poet would seem less governed by his dislikes. His humor
is never far from the surface of his narration, and at times
bobs up even in the course of an admonition to the reader.[29]
The *Gawain*-poet seems to dislike torn and tattered garments
(and, less pronouncedly, those soiled by labor or filth), but
his dislike never seems to rise to an obsession,[30] as does
Shakespeare's dislike for the ubiquity of dogs about a dinner-
table. He appears to have been too balanced to indulge himself in the luxury of obsessions.

Several images, however, recur in his poems again and
again. One is that of flowing water. To be more precise, one
might better call it the image of the overflowing water-
course, or of the mountain burn swollen by flood. It occurs
in all four poems, and in *Erkenwald* also. In *Pearl* (lines
607-8) he speaks of the ditch—not necessarily a muddy hole
—dug to carry off surface water. Christ's wound from the
spear is a well (*Pearl*, line 649), whence flows water and

29. Cf. the description of "Janglande" Jonah, *Pat.* 90, and *passim*, and
Lot's endeavors to quiet unseemly disturbance in *Pur.* 857-90. In his
account of the evening potations on St. John's Day (Dec. 27), customarily given over to deep drinking, the poet describes (*Gaw.* 1022-28)
how, at last, when it was late, the company broke up, "each one to wend
on his way who was a strong man," the implication being that those who
were not "strong" availed themselves of the assistance of pages or grooms
—or remained under the tables.

30. Some might consider that the poet's dislike of stinking smells almost amounts to an obsession, but such a reaction, always strongly expressed, is too normal for further remark. We may toss it to the psychiatrist to make what he can of it.

blood. A cry from Heaven is heard in Paradise like *flodeʒ fele leden runnen on resse*, "the voice of many waters as they run on in race."[31] In *Patience* (lines 309 ff) the streams, fed from many brooks, break the dam, a sight our poet must have often seen. Moreover, when one thinks of the meaning of *Pearl* and of *Erkenwald* too, one begins to understand how it was that this poet, whose visual perceptions were so keen, turned so often and so instinctively to the idea of a powerful force overflowing the limits and bounds erected to restrain it. The Grace of God was great enough to over-flow the philosophic dicta created to define and regulate its operation, the man-made limitations of its efficacy.

Yet the poet was impressed also by the fact that the river naturally and rightly should be running within a channel or watercourse, so that when it did overflow it was behaving in a way that violated the order and harmony of nature, the law God has set for its obedience. For the idea of law was one to which his mind often turned. Failure to abide by law or ignorance of its demands is the cause of sorrow and suffer-ing in all of the poems. Sir Gawain fails to observe a promise freely given; the dreamer in *Pearl* impatiently starts to ford the severing stream, and finds himself "out of Paradise"; the human protagonists in *Patience* and *Purity* are, many of them, sharply punished for their reckless and open defiance of divine law. The poet's language is crammed with legal-isms, "lerned out of som decree";[32] lawyers' language and phrases of court crop up again and again. The Pearl-maiden is "seised" in the high heritage of heaven, while others have to "purchase" possession of it. She warns the dreamer that he must "come to court" and while there he cannot "plete" further "þen couenaunde." In *Purity* those who bring "fals famacions and fayned lawez" may "forfeit" their bliss. In

31. For *resse* cf. OF *rasse. rase*, "water-course, (mill-) race."
32. Images derived from the law are very numerous in the poems of the Cotton MS., and my search has not been exhaustive.

Gawain the Green Knight offers to "quitclaim" his axe to anyone who grasps it. Again (line 1636), he reminds Gawain that the boar's head belongs to him (Gawain) by "fyn for-warde and faste"—i.e., by "final agreement" (an amicable agreement of a suit). One should also notice the meaning which the word *faste* has in the dialects of Cheshire, Derbyshire, Yorkshire, and Lancashire, "bound, secured by an agreement, engaged, pledged."[33]

Such expressions, and they are only several of the full number of legal terms to be found in the poet's vocabulary, indicate that he had had some legal training, or had filled some administrative post where the terminology of the law was his daily language. One must also remember that the mouth speaks only from what one has felt, seen, and done in the life he leads or has led. The legalisms on the poet's lips betray the course of his thinking in more retired hours. Every poem which he is supposed to have written seems to have grown out of the conflict in his own mind between the law (man-made or divine) and human frailty. How far were men bound by the solemn obligations that they themselves had assumed? How far did God carry his justice against those who had knowingly broken his law; how far against those who had broken it unwittingly? Did ignorance of the full meaning of an obligation excuse its violation? By the answers he framed to these questions, we can see that his personal experiences and his own observations had taught him to recognize that pardon, as much as punishment, is not only the prerogative, but also the duty, of king or justiciar. Provision had been made for its extension to the errant in the chancery of Heaven as well as in that of Westminster.

Images from hunting, while not as numerous as those derived from water in spate, are still frequent enough in the poet's language to show that it was a pastime much in his

33. See *EDD* (*Fast.* adj.). This meaning is not given in *NED*.

thought.[34] At one time the poet of *Pearl* is said to "dance as a doe" in his frustrated grief. At another, he stands paralyzed beneath it as a "dased quayle." In his endeavor to escape God's notice by taking ship to Tarsus, Jonah "to schort schote of his ame." The man in foul clothes "hurkles down" with his head, as a hare settles herself low in her "form" in a snowstorm. Before the deluge, God sees that each man has "forloyned fro þe ryȝt wayez," and *forloyne* means to leave the "field," or run off from the pack, to lose the "line" and go astray.

So much for the imagery which the *Gawain*-poet employs. One might pause at this point to formulate whatever conclusions its use seems to warrant. Certainly the author's fondness for legal terms and those derived from hunting indicates familiarity with a profession and a pastime neither of which was allowed to very cloistered religious. True it is that monastic obedientiaries did hunt, and that many of them had perforce to act as legal administrators, but such interests would be those which a secular priest, rather than a monk, would be more likely to evince, and a layman likelier still. If the poet was a monk, it seems safe to conclude, on the basis of such evidence as we now have, that he did not become one until after he had savored some of the pleasures of the world and had helped conduct some of its business.

As a metrist the author of *Pearl* and *Gawain* must stand very high. Critics of English verse have recognized, as indeed they could hardly help doing, the vigor and resonance of the alliterative line and its appropriateness to descriptions of battles or storms at sea. But I cannot at the moment remember any who have pointed out its perfect appropriateness for the expression of beauty in the color and the distances of landscape, or in the quiet changes in air or light, or for indication of the delicate nuances of speech or repartee. Com-

34. I have not classed as "hunting images" the detailed descriptions of the chase that occur in the 3rd fytte of *Gawain*.

pare, for instance, the onomatopoetic line which echoes the guttural grunts of the angry boar, alliterative verse at its rugged and resonant best,

> Ful grymme quen he gronyed; þenne greued mony;

with those, which even more than the opening lines of the *Prologue* breathe a "breath of spring uncontaminate,"

> Schyre schedeȝ þe rayn in schowreȝ ful warme,
> Falleȝ vpon fayre flat, flowreȝ þere schewen,
> Boþe groundeȝ and þe greueȝ grene ar her wedeȝ;

or with that vivid picture of the hunter's moon, a picture whose soft beauty is but the augury of storms to come,

> Til Meȝelmas mone
> Watȝ cumen wyth wynter wage;

or with the lovely lines that describe the lighting of the torches in Bercilak's hall

> Clere lyȝt þenne
> Wakned bi woȝeȝ, waxen torches
> Seggeȝ sette, and serued in sale al aboute;

or with those which tell how those two friends of the early morning hours greet one another at the last of their stolen tête-à-têtes;

> With smoþe smylyng and smolt þay smeten in-to merþe,
> Þat al watȝ blis and bonchef þat breke hem bitwene,
> And wynne.

There are hundreds of lines such as these, that evince their writer's knowledge of vowel and consonantal quality, his awareness of that elusive, but very real, nexus between sound and sense, the quickness of his imaginative powers. One runs upon them in every one of the poems attributed to this unknown poet. Keen sensitivity to the values of consonant and vowel, meticulous care in the arrangement of the alliterative

syllables—for the bad ear is even more deplorable in alliterative than in non-alliterative verse—skill in the employment of
the caesura, and in the manipulation of the double caesura
or long pause, all these exalt our author above his less gifted
brethren of the school. Nor need he dread comparison with
Chaucer as a metrist; for he seldom wrote a line lacking in
zest, or imagination, or rhythm—and Chaucer sometimes
did. To say so much is simply to say that he was past master
of his medium.

But not in metric alone did he show himself a master-
craftsman. In the planning and construction of his story, be
it homily, legend, elegy, or romance, he need not fear comparison with his great contemporary. Indeed, it is an open
question whether his two homilies, his one saint's legend(?),
his elegy, and his romance are not, in each case, better written and more vividly told than Chaucer's best attempt in
the same genre.

The saint's legend, *St. Erkenwald,* is told with as much
suspense in the telling as the tale of Chaucer's Prioress, and
its denouement is as sudden, and no less convincing or adequate. As a piece of narrative, it may, I think, take pride of
place over the *Second Nun's Tale.* Though no single episodes in *Purity* and *Patience,* except, perhaps, the vivid little
story of the Man in Foul Clothes, can rank with the swift
and powerfully told *Pardoner's Tale* as an example of homi-
letical narrative, yet it must be remembered that in writing
the two homilies their author used many stories (all of them
well told) to illustrate his main theme. He was thus working
with a larger canvas than Chaucer, who in *The Pardoner's
Tale* had confined himself to a single *exemplum.* He had set
himself a more ambitious task, *tirer la longue haleine.* It
goes without saying that the two homilies are far better
reading than *Melibeus* or *The Parson's Tale.* The greater
concentration and vividness which good verse can claim over

good prose could hardly be better illustrated than in the case of *Purity* and *Patience* on the one hand, and Chaucer's two moral tales on the other. Elsewhere I have sought to show that the *Book of the Duchess* is more skillfully written than some scholars have believed; yet as an elegy its most ardent advocates would admit that, in the skill with which it has been composed and in the intensity of feeling which it evokes, it is inferior to *Pearl*. Gaston Paris has (to general acceptation) acclaimed *Sir Gawain* as "the jewel of English medievalism." Accordingly I shall not need to labor the question of its superiority as a romance to the *Knight's Tale*. Its action is more unified and rapid; its suspense better sustained; its characterization more convincing.

Architectonic skill is, then, quite clearly manifested in every one of our author's poems, and in no one of them over any other. The planning of *Patience,* the dovetailing of its parts, the apportionment of just the right amount of emphasis to each particular incident, and the poetic justice of its conclusion, are to the good critic as marked and perceptible as the same "evidences of design" in *Gawain.* But time permits the analysis of but one work of the several penned by this master-maker of "thrifty tales," and that one shall be his best known, *Sir Gawain and the Green Knight.*

The poem falls into four divisions, the Challenge, the Arrival, the Sojourn, and the Rendezvous. The events that happen in each one of the divisions lead inevitably into those that happen in the next. When the hero accepted the Green Knight's challenge he took the first step, and every step he takes thereafter leads him to the snow-covered dell where he meets for the second time that "aghlich mayster." No challenge, no journey; no journey, no discovery of the hospitable castle in the western wilds; no discovery, no temptation; no temptation, no solution of the plot of the story. As we analyze the plot we can discover no alternative method of bringing about the denouement, no other way that would "do just as well." This story, unlike the alliterative *William of Palerne*, unlike the *Tale of the Man of Law*, is free from unnecessary episodes and useless characters; in it there is no lost motion.[35] All through 2,400 of its 2,500-odd lines runs our suspense, ever mounting as the tale moves on. And move on it does as speedily as the days of summer.

The tone of the conversations, and that of the hunting field as well, is one of cheerful good humor. The characters are gentlefolk, and conduct themselves as such. Moodiness and the abstraction caused by jealousy, apprehension, self-pity, or the contemplation of the unknown terrors of a future day, do not appear at Camelot or Hautdesert. Gawain seems always to be master of himself. Yet at times we wonder whether he ought not to be realizing what his end is to be and how near it actually is. Surely if he did, he would not be making "as merry as any man might" within Bercilak's hall. Why, in a sequence of events whose termination surely must be tragic, keep up this unconcerned tone of light repartee and merry banter? But Gawain's apparent unconcern over his fate is merely the author's device for impressing upon us that we are gazing upon a very great gentleman, a man who takes fate as it comes.

As to the outcome of the story, the author at times seems as unconcerned as his hero. There is no shaking of his hand; no hurry in his voice; all things in good time and good order; "frenkysch fare" is his literary, as it is his social, ideal. But this seeming unconcern is again merely a device for increasing the suspense of his story. How is the merry contest between the lady and her guest going to end? Surely it has naught to do with the previous pledge of Gawain to the

35. In the next chapter I have sought to show that the events of the hunting field (fytte 3, "Sojourn"), are connected in both theme and outcome with the interviews in the bedchamber between Gawain and his hostess.

Green Knight that he will meet him on New Year's Day. Or does it? Into his third fytte (the "Sojourn"), by means of those amusing scenes of solicitation by Bercilak's artful wife, the poet weaves into this rare piece of medieval tapestry some fresh strands of a different hue, and their introduction adds more color to its texture and removes some of the dark monotony inherent in the tale of a lonely wanderer, who is also a "fey" man, one fated to fall. Yet those strands of different hue are in the tapestry merely to provide contrast to the color and mode of its main theme. Death looms all the more dire beyond those brief hours of pastime and good company, of laughter, and of proffered love.

Indeed, if we study the poem deeply, we notice slight but quite definite indications that the author is quietly stimulating our sense of apprehension (or of suspense). The auditors or readers of his day caught these traffic signals of the story more quickly and were affected by their import, but we have lost the voices which came to medieval men and women through symbolism or through a liturgy that carried more than one meaning to those who heard it. Gawain departs on his quest on All Souls' Day, on whose morn the three masses are offered for the souls of the faithful departed and *Dies Iræ* is sung. We are to consider him a dead man, one as good as gone. Reynard, after the habit of dog-foxes in the breeding-season, breaks covert to draw the hounds away from a vixen who lurks therein, and eventually, like Sir Gawain, falls victim to his desire to shield a lady. Reynard escapes one death by an almost instinctive movement of avoidance of Bercilak's uplifted and descending blade; but this very movement, in its quick swerve, carries him into the jaws of a hound. A day later we see again the shimmer of uplifted steel, and the quick instinctive movement of avoidance. Sir Gawain rides off to the Green Chapel on the Day of the Circumcision, one of the days when Christ shed his blood for man.[36] The medieval man would remember the day as one of the effusion of blood, and would, at first thought, expect no other outcome than the death of the hero. His second thought, if he had one, would tell him that the blood-shedding would not be unto death.

One cause alone has hindered the wider appreciation of this very great artist, the difficulty of his language. His sense is more obscure than that of Chaucer because he wrote in a speech that did not have the good fortune to become the standard speech of English. There are in Chaucer's lines more words whose spelling and pronunciation are easier for us to understand than there are in the lines of the *Gawain*-poet, and Chaucer's mellifluous verse is far more free from alliteration with its memory of Teutonic stress rather than of Latin quantity. Lacking also in Chaucer's lines are those Old Norse consonantal sounds which clatter and rattle in the speech of the West Riding and Lancashire. Yet the *Gawain*-poet has a keener sense of the nuances of words, and, I think, a more accurate recognition of *le mot juste*. His less gifted brethren of the alliterative school were often forced to let the necessity for an alliteration dictate the word they used. I have found no case where one can enter that charge against the *Gawain*-poet. True, the language of his poem requires of the reader more dictionary-searching and more word-weighing than does that of Chaucer, but I do not think it unfair to say that by such study and such a process of verbal evaluation the reader is more richly repaid for his pains. One who opens the glossary of an edition of one of the four poems of the Cotton MS opens it to differ with an editor's limited or unimaginative interpretation of a particular word, because the poet has charged that word to its fullest connotative power. In the case of that particular word, one will

36. Cf. Wiclif: *Sermons*, ed. T. Arnold (Oxford, 1869), I. 336 (Gospel on New Year's Day: "Men seien þat Crist þries shed his blood for man: first in circumcision of þis tendir membre," etc.

often find, after study of its derivation and etymology, that connotations which influence our judgment of the poet's meaning spread out from it, as do the ripples from a pebble cast into some tarn amid his native hills. Nothing intimidates him: he can turn a rare Latin sense, dredged up from one of the early Church fathers, into current Lancashire, and when he can find no such English equivalent, he coins what he needs.[37] His ability to do so without any jar to our aesthetic sense is the best attestation that he is indeed "lord of language."

Whether purposely, by his own wish, or through the inadvertence or carelessness of copyists, the *Gawain*-poet remains to us today the *Gawain*-poet, an anonymous author. He is known only by the work he did, by the art he called into being. I, and my betters, have sought, without any striking success, to discover, by prying back into old dead days, more about the life and personality of this gifted artist. There is, as you have seen, more to be found, and I believe that more will be found in days to come. But if "þurghe sum lant goste lyfe of hym þat al redes,"[38] he should speak to us, I am sure that he would bid us look, not back to him and his past, but forward to our own future, the preservation of what Macbeth calls "mine eternal jewel," the soul. For the darkness has not fallen, and there is work to be done in the vineyard (you will remember that the poet uses the parable of the Vineyard to illustrate the inadequacy of man's working efforts, and the generosity of God's grace), and as yet we cannot cross those "mereʒ" which separate us from that *urbs coelestis, urbs beata*, and "rapely þerinne" we are

37. Cf. the word *pretermynable, Pearl* 596 and annotation thereon in ME bibliographies. Professor Rettger of the staff of the *Middle English Dictionary* in Ann Arbor, Michigan, writes me, 7/3/40, "Our dictionary experience has given us a profound respect for the sense-stretching audacity of the Gawain-poet."

38. *Erkenwald* 192: "Through some spirit granted life by Him who plans all."

"restayed." Days still remain to us in which to labor. But while we labor we have Heaven's own promise of the rainbow, which God gave to Noah, the promise that we shall have about us all the beauty of the changing seasons, and all the hope of days to come.

> Sesounez schal yow never sese of sede ne of hervest,
> Ne hete, ne no harde forst, umbre ne droȝþe,
> Ne þe swetnesse of somer, ne þe sadde wynter,
> Ne þe nyȝt, ne þe day, ne þe newe ȝerez,
> Bot ever renne restlez.

CHAPTER II

Symbolism and Allegory in
Sir Gawain and the Green Knight

I HAVE OFTEN wondered why the author of *Sir Gawain and the Green Knight* should have recounted the hunting exploits of the lord of the castle with such a wealth of description. Some 280 lines of the poem are devoted to the hunting scenes, and some 370 to the interviews between Sir Gawain and the lady. While vivid descriptions are characteristic of the *Gawain*-poet, he rarely digresses for the sake of mere description, or pads a narrative with episodes or details that are extraneous to his main theme. The accounts of the chase in the poem certainly warrant our regarding their author as a keen sportsman, a worthy ancestor of "John Peel," Baker, Selous, and Baillie-Grohman; but does not their apparent importance in the mind of the poet mean that they are more closely connected with the events going on all the while at the castle than we, perhaps, have realized? The poet has indeed bound together the events taking place indoors with those going on out-of-doors by means of the "forwarde" that the lord and his guest shall exchange with each other what they have captured during the day. But is it not possible that an even closer nexus between the hunting scenes and the happenings at the castle may be found? Certain facts about the animals which formed the quarry of the medieval huntsman, to be found in the hunting treatises of the time, and certain popular beliefs about their habits and tempers promulgated by the bestiaries and by the practices of heraldry, will, I believe, enable us to see that the two series of events are linked not only by the "forwarde," but also by a certain parallelism in their situations which would probably be quite apparent to the lady or gentleman of the fourteenth century.

The key to an understanding of the *raison d'être* of the hunting scenes lies, I believe, in the attitude of the medieval hunter and herald towards the several beasts whose chase the poem records. Let us examine first the treatises in which the rules and practices of venery are set forth. The mind of the Middle Ages loved order and the relegation of the individual to his proper inclusive class, and the practices and customs of hunting well exemplify this trait. Game animals were classed as either "beasts of venery" or "beasts of chase."[1] To the first class belong the stag and hind (male and female of the red deer, *Cervus elaphus*), the wild boar, and the wolf; to the second, the buck and doe (male and female of the fallow deer, *Cervus dama*), the roe deer (*Capreolus caprea*), the marten, and the fox. This division had small legal significance and meant little more than that certain beasts were hunted in one way and certain others in another.[2] It is possible that a higher prestige or distinction was attached to the pursuit and slaying of the animals of the first class, because we find them also listed as "beasts of the forest," i.e., beasts that were protected by the law that governed the royal forests, while they lived on the land that formed part of the forest domain; whereas the animals of the second class, while they lived in a chase (enclosure), were protected only by the common law. It is probable that, at the time at which the *Gawain*-poet was writing, distinctions between the

1. Cf. *Le Venery de Twety*, ed. Wright and Halliwell in *Reliquiæ Antiquæ* (London, 1841), 1. 150; *Boke of St. Albans*, facsim. reproduction and introd. by William Blades (London, 1881), fol. e₁. See also the article on "Forest Laws" in *Encyclopaedia Britannica* 10. 644-45.
2. Cf. *Select Pleas of the Forest*, ed. G. J. Turner, Selden Soc. 13 (London, 1901), cxiv-cxv.

two classes, apart from the difference between the penalties incurred by a poacher, according as he killed in a royal forest or in a chase, were nil; and that any early differences in the manner of hunting the various beasts tended to disappear with the passage of time. Certainly we find Bercilak hunting hinds (females of the red deer) and does (females of the fallow deer) at one and the same time, with no difference of method because of the difference in category. The animals hunted on the first two days, the two species of deer and the wild boar, were favorites among medieval hunters because of the good "runs" they gave, "runs" which were varied by the red deer's habit of taking to water,[3] and by the wild boar's habit of turning frequently to bay.[4]

But if the red deer, the fallow deer, and the boar were favorites, there was no such feeling of admiration for the fox. It is quite clear that at the time at which our author wrote the fox was regarded as vermin to be hunted out and destroyed.[5]

The words in which Bercilak replies to Gawain's inquiry as to the success of his third day's sport allow us to see that the hunter took little pride in that day's quarry:

> For I haf hunted al þis day, and noȝt haf I geten
> Bot þis foule fox felle, þe fende haf þe godeȝ![6]

Mr. Baillie-Grohman's note (pp. 65-66) in the chapter on

3. See line 1169. For more detailed discussion of this habit, see *The Master of Game*, written by Edward, 2nd Duke of York. Ed. W. A. and F. Baillie-Grohman (New York, 1909), pp. 32-33.

4. See *Gaw.* 1450. Cf. *Master of Game*, pp. 50-51.

5. Though the fox was regarded as a noxious animal, it might appear as though some grace were to be extended to him, for William Twici (*The Art of Hunting*, ed. A. Dryden, Northampton, 1908, p. 31) tells us that the fox-hunting season opened on the day of the Nativity of Our Lady and extended until the Annunciation. The period of closed season, however, which covers roughly the present season, as observed by the best English and American packs, probably existed more for the convenience of the hunters, whose revenues depended on the crops during the closed season, than for the ease of the fox.

6. Lines 1943-44.

the fox in *The Master of Game* makes it quite clear that Bercilak's attitude toward the victim of his third day's sport was the ordinary and usual one among medieval hunters:

Our MS. only gives this one chapter on the fox, while Gaston Phœbus has another: *Comment on doit chassier et prendre le renard.* In this he gives directions as to earth-stopping, and taking him in pursenets, and smoking him out with "orpiment and sulphur and nitre or saltpetre." He says January, February, and March are the best months for hunting, as the leaf is off the trees and the coverts are clearer, so that the hounds have more chance of seeing the fox and hunt him closer. He says that one-third of the hounds should be put in to draw the covert, and the others in relays should guard the boundaries and paths, to be slipped as required.[7] Although this is a Frenchman's account of fox-hunting, we have no reason to believe that the fox was treated at that period better by English sportsmen, for until comparatively recent times the fox was accounted vermin, and any means by which his death could be encompassed were considered legitimate, his extermination being the chief object in hunting him, and not the sport. Even as late as the seventeenth century we find that such treatment was considered justifiable towards a fox, for, as Macaulay tells us, Oliver St. John told the Long Parliament that Strafford was to be regarded, not as a stag or a hare, to whom some law was to be given, but as a fox, who was to be snared by any means, and knocked on the head without pity.

Corroboration of the existence of this attitude is not wanting. In his catalogue of the "beasts of the chase" Twici refers specifically to the rough treatment which Reynard must expect from the hunters:

> And ther ben othyr bestis. v. of chase;
> The buk the first, the do the secunde,
> The fox the thryde, *whiche ofte hath hard grace,*
> The ferthe the martyn, and the last the roo.[8]

7. This is the manner in which the fox is hunted in the poem. In lines 1712-15, 1727, Reynard runs into just such relay stations.
8. *Art of Hunting*, p. 150. The italics are my own.

That this opinion of the fox found expression in the laws governing the administration of hunting preserves, such as royal forests, chases, parks and warrens, is eloquent testimony to its widespread prevalence.[9]

Such an attitude toward *Canis vulpes* was probably due in large measure to the reputation for cunning and duplicity which he has always held.[10] *The Master of Game* informs us that "she [the fox] is a false beast and as malicious as a wolf,"[11] and goes on to say that "they are so cunning and subtle that neither men nor hounds can find a remedy to keep themselves from their false turns."[12] When the fox eludes his pursuers by going to earth, "then men may dig him out and take him."[13] Certainly the hunters in our poem recognize their rufous opponent as a tricky and wily fellow, deserving of much opprobrium because of his "false turns" and underground habits:

> Here he watȝ halawed when hapeleȝ hym metten,
> Loude he watȝ ȝayned with ȝarande speche,
> Þer he watȝ þreted and ofte þef called.[14]

Let us now turn to the story of our poem. Bercilak rouses on the first day of his hunting large numbers of deer, of both red and fallow species. These he hunts in approved manner, being careful to slay no stags or bucks, which were then under

9. For the status of the fox in law, see *Select Pleas of the Forest* (ed. G. J. Turner), pp. cxiv-cxv, cxxix, cxxx, cxxxi. Turner (p. cxxxii) gives some evidence that the fox was legally held to be a beast of warren. If such were the case, it is almost certain that the fox was regarded in the eyes of the law as a beast of vermin.

10. It is probably because of this reputation for cunning and duplicity rather than for its notorious reputation as a poultry thief that the animal was regarded as a pest. The wolf was far more destructive to man and domesticated animals (cf. *Master of Game*, pp. 59, 61, 62), yet it was not regarded as a beast of vermin. Men hated it, but their hate was mingled with a hearty respect, bred of its ferocious nature.

11. P. 64.

12. P. 67.

13. P. 65.

14. Lines 1723-25.

the protection of the closed season.[15] On the second day a huge boar is roused, which leads the hunt a rigorous chase, and afterwards turns finally and fiercely at bay, where he is slain by the lord. On the third day a fox is started. Reynard provides great sport, and is brought down immediately in front of Bercilak's horse. So close is he to the lord, that Bercilak strikes at him with his weapon, but misses, because the fox at that instant dodges. His dodge avails him nothing, however, for a hound seizes him at the moment that he avoids the descending blade, and the whole pack falls on him at once.

Now during the first day's hunting while her husband is pursuing the hinds and does, the lady is seeking to tempt Gawain. Her attempt, however, is unsuccessful. She finds herself, like her husband, pursuing "noble game." The amenities and decencies that mark the conduct and pursuits of gentlefolk are preserved both in forest and castle. On the second day she is no more successful. Like her husband in the forest, she has again roused noble game.

On the third day, however, Bercilak routs out a beast of vermin, a creature of craft and duplicity. And it is upon that very day that Gawain breaks his "forwarde," and thereby incurs the guilt of being false to his knightly word and deceitful to a generous and trusting host. While it is true that the pressure of his hostess makes it difficult for him to refuse her gift of the green lace (belt, girdle), yet the deciding factor that prompts his acceptance of it is fear for his own neck. Thus fear for his life has led him to avail himself of a "false turn."[16] On the third day, then, a false beast is roused

15. Lines 1156-57:
> For þe fre lorde hade defende in fermysoun tyme
> Þat þer schulde no mon meue to þe male dere.

The adjective "fre" is indicative of Bercilak's reputation for good sportsmanship.

16. Fear of his life leads Gawain to commit a base action. Cf. *Master of Game*, pp. 65-66, for an account of certain base vulpine habits that are revealed when Reynard is hard pressed by the greyhounds.

in the forest, and a false man revealed in the castle; a sly
fox is caught in the wood, a "sly fox" in the castle.

But the parallelism between the last day's hunting in the
wood and the events of the day in the castle may be worked
out to an even closer degree of correspondence. Attention
was called above to the rapid series of actions which led to
the death of the fox. I shall allow the poet to tell his own
story:

> Renaud com richchande þurȝ a roȝe greue,
> And alle þe rabel in a res, ryȝt at his heleȝ.
> Þe wyȝe watȝ war of þe wylde and warly abides
> And braydeȝ out þe bryȝt bronde and at þe best casteȝ;
> And he schunt for þe scharp and schulde haf arered,
> A rach rapes him to, ryȝt er he myȝt,
> And ryȝt bifore þe hors fete þay fel on hym alle
> And woried me þis wyly wyth a wroth noyse.[17]

In the endeavor to avoid the danger from the lord's blade,
Reynard "shunts," and attempts to reverse direction, but his
very shift carries him into the jaws of his enemies.

The correspondence between the case of Reynard and
that of Sir Gawain is very close. In the endeavor to avoid
the fate which threatens him, the fox resorts to a bit of
trickery, and that bit of trickery is the very cause of his un-
doing. The position of Gawain is the same: in his desire to
avoid death from the impending blow, he resorts to trickery,
and his recourse to duplicity proves the sole and only cause
of his disgrace. Thus the two situations closely resemble
one another. Before closing our discussion of the evidence
afforded by the hunting treatises, a further correspondence
between the details of Reynard's death and the conduct of

17. Lines 1898-1905. Some of the words of Sir Thomas Cockaine,
author of *A Short Treatise of Hunting, compyled for the Delight of
Noblemen and Gentlemen* (London, 1591) explain Bercilak's action
(quoted in Badminton Library: *Hunting*, p. 30): "Every huntsman his
part is to hew (=shout?) him, or backe him into the covert again when
he offereth to breake the same."

Gawain should be noted. The theatre of events, as far as the human actor is concerned, is not now at the castle, but at the Green Chapel. There, as on the day before, is the up-lifted blade and the instinctive movement of avoidance.[18]

In tracing the parallelism between the two series of events, we have relied almost entirely upon the evidence to be garnered from the hunting treatises of the time, but we must not neglect another field that may be gleaned, I believe, with good results—that of popular heraldry. The hunting treatises do, indeed, tell us that such animals as harts, hinds, and boars are to be classed together, because their pursuit is more elevating and noble than that of the fox; they do differentiate between "beasts of venery (or forest)" and "beasts of chase"; but they do not tell us what were the qualities that entitle us to place beasts that possessed them in the higher of the two categories last mentioned. We can see why it is that the hart and the boar are regarded more highly than the fox, but we can *not* see just what qualities in the hart and the boar led to their being listed as "beasts of venery." The two animals are characterized by attributes that would seem to mark them off as unlike; what is the trait, or traits, that prompted the medieval Nimrod to place them both within a single class, and that the most elevated? To learn the peculiar attributes which differentiated these beasts in the minds of their pursuers, we must turn to heraldry.

For in heraldry, as M. Gevaert tells us,[19] there is to be

18. Similarity between the two situations is to be found even in their phraseology. Cf. line 1902 (account of the death of the fox) with lines 2267-68 (description of Gawain's instinctive movement of avoidance).

19. "D'une façon générale, l'empreinte de cette morale mondaine se reconnaît sur toute l'héraldique" (E. Gevaert, *L'Héraldique*, Paris, n.d., p. 32.). Gevaert's words on the allegorical meaning of certain of the more familiar beasts deserve quotation with reference to previous discussion of the fox: "Tandis que les figures exprimant l'orgueil individuel et affirmant la force sont fréquentes, on ne rencontre guère, dans les armes, l'agneau qui représente la douceur, le chameau, image de l'humilité, de la soumission et de l'obéissance, ou le boeuf qui figure la patience. Leur rareté est égale à celle du lièvre, image de la peur, ou à celle du renard dont la ruse est incompatible avec l'honneur militaire" (p. 32).

found the imprint of the common ideas and the popular opinion. The books on hunting assume a familiarity with this common notion or popular idea of the animal, as *The Master of Game* allows us to see;[20] hence in them we shall probably not find much discussion or analysis of those qualities or traits in which the brute creation would seem to resemble man.

The day of heraldry is past, and modern zoology has told us, whether rightly or wrongly, that we ought not to attribute to animals the spiritual, emotional, or mental qualities of which we ourselves are conscious. But when the author of *Sir Gawain and the Green Knight* wrote, heraldry was still instinct with meaning for those who wore its insignia. The fourteenth century would probably not have objected to the phrase which a modern writer has taken for the title of his book on natural history: *The Minds and Manners of Wild Animals*,[21] for to the men and women of that time wild animals had both minds and manners. Hence the appearance of a particular beast or bird upon crest or shield was sometimes (though not always) sign and warrant to the world that the particular family which had assumed it had in time past chosen to associate itself with, or become typified by, that particular animal or avian charge. The reason for the assumption may have been a resemblance, real or fancied, between the qualities exhibited by one or several of the early ancestors of the family and the traits for which the beast or bird was famous or notorious. Or it may have been an aspiration to acquire or display those spiritual virtues which the bestiaries declared the beast or bird exemplified. Or it may have been nothing more important than a desire to pun upon the family name. But eventually at least something of the

20. Cf. p. 23: "The hart is a common beast enough and therefore me needeth not to tell of his making, for there be few folk that have not seen some." Cf. also pp. 46, 64 where boar and fox are introduced in practically identical phraseology.

21. William T. Hornaday, *The Minds and Manners of Wild Animals; a Book of Personal Observations*, New York, 1923.

"character" of the four-footed or two-footed charge stuck to the family which bore it. Knights and noblemen, by common voice or vulgar reputation, were given attributes, and even natures, which as individuals they may never have possessed, because of a household badge embroidered on the tapestries of their halls, or the rampant attitude of some four-footed charge blazoned on their surcoat or carved over the arch of their gatehouses. For proof of what has just been said, we may cite the practice of a contemporary of our poet, the unknown author of the alliterative poem *Richard the Redeles.* This cautious moralist scolds his captive monarch, the unfortunate Richard II, for his past misbehavior and mistakes, but preserves himself from the possible consequences of unintentional indiscretion by employing the badge of a particular nobleman of his day, or one of the supporters of his shield, instead of his name, when referring to him. It was safe to scold Richard by name, for he was imprisoned behind bars; to allude to his nobility, who now ruled the roost, a more cautious and indirect way of reference was advisable.

Of the hart, or stag of the red deer, John Guillim, the learned herald of the late sixteenth and early seventeenth centuries has the following words to say in connection with the shield of Jones of Monmouthshire: "Nature having denied this Beast other Securities, hath indued him with two excellent Favours above others; the One, exceeding quickness of Hearing, to foreknow his Hazards, and so the sooner to prevent them (for which Cause the Stag is among the Emblems of the five Senses, representing the Hearing); the other exceeding Speed of Foot, to fly from the Danger when it approacheth";[22] and he remarks relative to the hart of the

22. John Guillim (*A Display of Heraldry*, London, 1724; 1st ed. 1610), p. 156. Though Guillim wrote in the days of decadent heraldry, when treatises on armory, written with much learning and little sense, were accounting for heraldic practice by extravagant analogies and a scholarship that could only with difficulty be more erroneous than it actually was, he seems to have kept his sense of discrimination more successfully than most

Holm family (upon the authority of Upton) that the "Hart born in Arms . . . betokeneth sometimes one skilful in Musick, or such an one as taketh a Felicity and Delight in Harmony: Also, a Man that is wise and politick, and well foreseeth his Times and Opportunities; a Man unwilling to assail the Enemy rashly, but rather desirous to stand on his own Guard honestly, than to annoy another wrongfully."[23]

The two quotations given above enable us to see that to a person or family whose arms bore a stag, or stags, there had come to be attributed great caution and discrimination in knowing what to avoid and when to avoid it. Furthermore, such a person or family would be regarded as one in which there existed great tact in the observance of proper times and seasons, great ability to avoid embarrassing situations, great skill in knowing the proper thing to say and the proper time to say it.

Now it is precisely this sort of tact that Sir Gawain displays in his first interview with the lady of the castle. His conduct throughout his early morning conversation is hit off exactly by the phrases which occur in the two quotations from Guillim: "exceeding Speed of Foot, to fly from the Danger when it approacheth," "a Man that is wise and politick, and well foreseeth his Times and Opportunities, a Man unwilling to assail the Enemy rashly, but rather desirous to stand on his own Guard honestly, than to annoy another wrongfully."

of his fellow theorists. But whatever his reputation, we need not fear to accept the applications to humanity that he draws from aprine and cervine behavior. Their truth and validity, verified in the hunting-fields of the Middle Ages, had long been blessed by tradition to the usages of heraldry.

23. *Display of Heraldry*, p. 156. Corroboration of Guillim's statements as to the significance of the stag in blazonry is to be found in *L'Arte del Blasone* (Venezia, 1756) of Marc' Antonio Ginanni. I quote Ginanni's remarks upon that animal: "Egli è un'Animale nobilissimo di somma velocità, che si vuole non abbia fiele, e che viva centinaja d'anni; onde è contrassegno d'antica Nobiltà, e di Prudenza militare in chi lo prese per Insegna, ovvero che fosse inclinato all'esercizio della Caccia, che è una guerra innocente, e'l divertimento proprio de ' Principi, e de'Signori di qualità" (p. 54).

One trick of the deer, that of lying low in covert until it is absolutely necessary to break out,[24] is well portrayed at the very opening of the interview between knight and lady on the first morning:

Hit watʒ þe ladi, loflyest to be-holde,
Þat droʒ þe dor after hir ful dernly and stylle,
And boʒed to-warde þe bed; and þe burne schamed,
And layde hym doun lystyly and let as he slepte.
And ho stepped stilly and stel to his bedde,
Kest vp þe cortyn and creped with-inne
And set hir ful softly on þe bed-syde
And lenged þere selly longe, to loke quen he wakened.
Þe lede lay lurked a ful longe quyle,
Compast in his concience to quat þat cace myʒt
Meue oþer amount,—to meruayle him þoʒt;
Bot ʒet he sayde in hym-self, 'More semly hit were
To aspye wyth my spelle in space quat ho wolde.'
Þen he wakenede and wroth and to hir-warde torned
And vn-louked his yʒe-lyddeʒ and let as hym wondered,
And sayned hym, as bi his saʒe þe sauer to worthe,
           with hande.[25]

All during the interview the reader cannot fail to be struck with Sir Gawain's skill in parrying off remarks that are, indeed, more than pointed. In tactful discrimination, in ability to skate over the thin ice of an exceedingly awkward situation,

24. Cf. *Master of Game*, pp. 30-31: "An old deer is wonder wise and felle (cunning) for to save his life, and to keep his advantage when he is hunted and is uncoupled to, as the lymer moveth him or other hounds findeth him without lymers. . . . And he will abide still, and if he be alone and the hounds find him, he shall go about his haunt wilily and wisely and seek the change of other deer, for to make the hounds envoise (go off scent), and to look where he may abide. And if he cannot abide he taketh leave of his haunt and beginneth to fly there where he wots of other change and then when he has come thither he herdeth among them and sometimes he goeth away with them. And then he maketh a ruse on some side, and there he stalleth or squatteth until the hounds be forth after the other (deer) the which be fresh, and thus he changeth so that he may abide."

25. Lines 1187-1203.

the knight is perfection itself. One phrase of Guillim's "a Man unwilling to assail the Enemy rashly, but rather desirous to stand on his own Guard honestly, than to annoy another wrongfully," is particularly worthy of a moment's notice as illustrating Gawain's gentlemanly attitude. The hero of the poem carefully refrains from all bitterness or severity of utterance, although it is quite apparent that the lady has taken a great liberty.

Guillim tells us that the "Bearing of the Boar in Arms betokeneth a Man of bold Spirit, skilful, politick in warlike Feats, and One of that high Resolution, that he will rather die valorously in the Field, than he will secure himself by ignominious Flight. He is called, in *Latin, Aper* (according to *Farnesius*) *ab asperitate*, because he is so sharp and fierce in conflict with his Foe. And this is a special Property in a Souldier, that he be fierce in the Encountring his Enemy, and he bear the Shock or Brunt of the Conflict with a noble and magnanimous Courage; *Miles enim dura & aspera perfringit animi & virium robore.*"[26]

One who studies carefully the speeches between the knight and the lady on the second day will perceive, I think, a difference between the tone of the conversation on that day and that of the day before. On the first day the conversation is lighter and happier in spirit; jests fly faster,[27] particularly jests about the embarrassing plight in which Sir Gawain finds himself.[28] Gawain does indeed, as the poet tells us, "fare

26. *Display of Heraldry*, p. 165. Of the boar Ginanni (p. 56) says: "Ei rappresenta il Soldato pien di coraggio, per cui restano superate le più ardue intraprese."

27. Cf. line 1212: "Al laȝande þe lady lauced þo bourdeȝ"; line 1217: "And þus he bourded a-ȝayn with mony a blyþe laȝter"; line 1290: "Þenne ho gef hym god day, and wyth a glent laȝed."

28. Cf. line 1211: "I schal bynde yow in your bedde, þat be ȝe trayst," and Gawain's answer (lines 1215-16);
    For I ȝelde me ȝederly and ȝeȝe after grace,
    And þat is þe best, be my dome, for me by-houeȝ nede.
Cf. also lines 1220-21.

with defence," and "fete ful fayre," but his defensive meas-
ures are Parthian; he wheels away from the lady's intent in
a light and elusive way. Grace and delicacy of movement are
the order of the day.

More restrained and severe is the tone of the second
day's conversation; indeed, for a brief moment, the talk
plays with the idea of force and violence. To a certain slight
degree this is due to the increasing petulancy of the lady,
irritated that her efforts to win over the knight are not more
successful. She upbraids the unresponsive knight, not unduly,
but still with a certain mild asperity. Once, indeed, toward
the end of the interview she would seem to have lost either
patience or temper, and we see, for a moment, the claws
glide out from their velvety cushion:

> Why! are ʒe lewed, þat alle þe los weldeʒ,
> Oþer elles ʒe demen me to dille your dalyaunce to herken?[29]

But it is to the speeches of Gawain that we must look if we
wish to find out the true reason for this more noticeable directness and tensity of tone which seems to characterize the
interview of the second day. On that day his conduct shows
the resolution and directness that characterize the boar. He
puts on no pretence of sleep, feigns no surprise at the visitor
or the early hour of her visit, does not make the sign of the
cross, but meets the lady as she comes, face to the front, as
the boar is to meet her husband later on that very day.[30]
His manner is never impolite—that, of course, goes without
saying, but it is less evasive and more curt than on the day
before. Once he asks point-blank what the lady means,[31]

---

29. Lines 1528-29.

30. The reader should note the force of the phrase "on fyrst," in line
1477: "Sir Wawen her welcumed worþy on fyrst." The phrase, "as an
initial step," might well translate it. It implies that Sir Gawain is aware
of the possibility of a visit, and that he is not going to be taken by surprise as he was on the day before.

31. Lines 1487-88:
> "What is þat?" quoþ þe wyghe, "I-wysse I wot neuer;
> If hit be sothe þat ʒe breue, þe blame is myn awen."

and his rebuttal of several of her pleas is at times most direct
and altogether complete.[32]   Once, indeed, his phraseology
carries a meaning that reflects upon the lady's manners and
actions, one that may very well have made her blush or
wince inwardly:

> Bot to take þe toruayle to myself to trwluf expoun
> And towche þe temeȝ of tyxt and taleȝ of armeȝ
> To yow þat, I wot wel, weldeȝ more slyȝt
> Of þat art, bi þe half, or a hundreth of seche
> As I am oþer euer schal, in erde þer I leue,
> Hit were a fole fele-folde, my fre, by my trawþe.[33]

That Sir Gawain's tactics are different on the second day
from what they were on the first, is, I think, quite apparent.
The question of the reason for that difference remains to be
answered. To me the only explanation possible is one which
takes into account the differences in physical and mental
characteristics that exist between the two heraldic animals—
the hart and the wild boar.[34]   The first beast is the soul of
honor, but elusive, shy, and ready to flee from any attempt

32. Cf. lines 1492-94:
> "Do way," quoþ þat derf mon, "my dere, þat speche,
> For þat durst I not do, lest I deuayed were;
> If I were werned, I were wrang, iwysse, ȝif I profered."

which answer the lady's plaint that he does not kiss her; and lines 1498-
1500:
> "Ȝe, be God," quoþ Gawayn, "good is your speche,
> But þrete is vnþryuande in þede þer I lende,
> And vche gift þat is geuen not with goud wylle,"

which answer the lady's suggestion that he might use force, if he were
fearful that she would refuse his kiss.

33. Lines 1540-45.

34. Some might believe that Gawain's more direct and curt manner
on the second day's visit is due to a growing irritation at the lady's in-
trusion, but one would expect to see that irritation reflected in the conversation of the day that follows the visit, whereas line 1560: "Þe lede
with þe ladyeȝ layked alle day," and the happenings of the interview on
the third day show us that no such irritation seems to have arisen in the
knight's mind. It is interesting to note that it would always have been
possible to have fastened the door, but that Sir Gawain never takes that
precaution; cf. line 1233: "Þe dor drawen, and dit with a derf haspe."

at capture; the second is one that tries to elude his natural enemies, it is true, but one that will also face his pursuer, watch his movements, and resist, with tusks that tear and lacerate, all attempts to harm him.

About the fox Guillim is practically silent, and one who glances through his pages will find few shields that bear him as a charge.[35] The reason is quite obvious: Reynard's reputation with the nobility and heralds is none too savory. While it is true that one finds him here and there among armorial lists, the reputation which hunting treatise and *vox populi* gave him furnish the reason for the statement of Woodward and Burnett that "the fox is an animal seldom met in British Heraldry."[36]

We have now come to the point where we must tread warily. For it will be said that such an attempt to account for the order of the hunting scenes is pushing the allegorizing tendency too far; that it is reading too much into the story; that imaginative interpretations are dangerous. And we shall be reminded, not without reason, that the author of *Gawain* and *Pearl* has too frequently fallen a victim to the imaginations of his critics or devotees. Making, then, every effort to steer a middle course between the Scylla of the superimaginative mind, which finds too much in a certain situation, and the Charybdis of the unimaginative mind,

35. He does, however, compare the two foxes on the shield of Kadrod-Hard of Wales to two crafty and deceitful lawyers (p. 196).

36. *A Treatise on Heraldry* (Edinburgh and London, 1892), 1. 230. A.C. Fox-Davies [note the name] (*The Art of Heraldry*, Edinburgh and London, 1904, p. 138) takes issue with the statement quoted from Woodward and Burnett: "A *Fox*, which from the similarity of its representation is often confused with a wolf, is said by Woodward to be very seldom met with in British heraldry. This is hardly a correct statement, inasmuch as countless instances can be produced in which a fox figures as a charge, a crest, or a supporter." While the remark of Woodward and Burnett may need some qualification, it is, nevertheless, quite evident that, in comparison with the frequent occurrence in heraldry of other animals, such as the lion, stag, or boar, the fox is to be found only rarely. Woodward and Burnett (1. 230) tell us that "abroad, it is somewhat more frequently found."

which sees too little and is content to go only upon surface appearance, let us try to test this apparent relationship between the two series of situations by what we know of the poet's cast of mind. A certain correspondence between the two rather remote series of events in the story does exist. Does the fact of that relationship between the several situations mean that the poet worked consciously and purposely, or is it merely fortuitous and undesigned? Our answer to that question will be largely determined by what we know of the *Gawain*-poet's method of writing, his employment of allegory, his fondness, or dislike, for subtle literary liaison.

It is just here that we are upon more certain ground. If it be granted that the author of *Gawain* also wrote *Pearl*, and there are few, if any, who would deny that asumption, a satisfactory reply is not far to seek. The *Pearl*-poet delights in symbolism and allegory. Like Spenser, he is fond of storing up behind the situation or picture that he paints a wealth of secondary meaning, which is to be found only by those who are willing to seek it out. Whether one believes that *Pearl* is a record of actual personal loss, or that it is an allegory pure and simple, it is indisputable that the poet is a lover of symbolism.[37] Its richer significance and its deeper meanings are revealed only to the reader who keeps an eye open to the allegorical vein that runs through it.[38]

The question as to whether the order of the hunting scenes in *Gawain* is the result of mere chance grouping or of design on the part of the author can receive, in all proba-

---

37. See J. B. Fletcher, "The Allegory of the Pearl," *JEGP* 20. 1-21. The allegorical content of the poem is also treated in a most interesting and suggestive, if not an entirely convincing, way by Sister M. Madeleva in *Pearl: A Study in Spiritual Dryness*, New York, 1925.

38. As with *Pearl*, so also with *Gawain*. While the claims of Isaac Jackson (*Angl.* 37, 393-423) that *Gawain* is to be connected with the foundation of the Order of The Garter are excessive, his article brings to light much that would seem to stamp that romance as an "occasional" poem; cf. Gollancz's discussion of this question in *Pearl* (1921), pp. xxxv-xxxvi. See also the next chapter of this book, and Appendix D.

bility, no definite answer. Yet where so much depends upon the nice adjustment of part to part, upon the fusion of separate incidents into unity, and upon the dovetailing of elements that are diverse where they are not actually discordant, one is inclined to see purpose rather than accident. For art is the creation not of chance, but of design.

CHAPTER III

A French Knight of the Garter

I

On May 8, 1360, there was signed in a little chateau of the village of Brétigny (eight miles southeast of Chartres) by plenipotentiaries of the dauphin of France and of the Black Prince the treaty which takes its name from that small town.[1] Then, as in our own day, France had been forced to drain a bitter cup. By the terms of the treaty the King of England now added to his hereditary possessions in Gascony and Guienne vast stretches of territory which an earlier attempt at peace—the second Treaty of London (1359)—had not given him, and, more important still, to his exchequer a ransom of three million gold crowns paid to redeem the royal captive of Poitiers (1356), Jean le Bon, now free to return to his country and his throne.

Three million gold crowns (*écus d'or*) was a gigantic sum, about forty million francs in the currency of modern France, and possibly seventy-two million, if one attempts to allow for the purchasing power of medieval French money—

---

1. It would be more nearly correct to say that the document signed at Brétigny was only a draft of conditions for a peace between France and England. Definitive form was given to those agreements by formal documents dated from Calais Oct. 24 of the same year; see the art. "Hundred Years' War" by A. Coville, in *Camb. Med. Hist.* 7, 340-67. But the agreements reached at Brétigny have been, and are still, so frequently characterized by historians as a treaty, that it would be pedantic to refer to them under any other title.

in our own money $1,836,735.00.[2] It had to be raised from
a country whose fields had been devastated and industry
wrecked by the intermittent warfare of some twenty-three
years. Payment in a single lump sum would have been an
impossibility: even the first installment, it was recognized,
could not be paid entirely in cash. In lieu of the cash that
was wanting, the French King was allowed to deliver over
to his captors "la ville, le chateau et les fortresses de la Ro-
chelle," "les chateaux, fortresses et villes" of the county of
Guines, and, as guarantees of his word, forty hostages chosen
from among the greatest lords of the kingdom, among them
the hero of this story, the Sire de Coucy.[3] And now, enough
of King Jean's ransom! It interests us only because it was
the cause of our hero's appearance at the English court. But
he still remains unintroduced. Unlike Harry Bailly, I
should make a poor "marchal in an halle." In the case of
a high born nobleman of the fourteenth century one should
know straightway of the place and lineage whence, in medieval parlance, he "bore name and arms."

Some thirteen to fifteen miles southwest of Laon there
rises a wooded hill, above whose treetops the great donjon,
the "Merveille," of the Château de Coucy once soared up-
wards, overlooking the small town of the same name in a
protecting, if somewhat patronizing, manner. I say "once
soared," for the wanton destruction of the donjon by the
Germans in 1917 has robbed civilization of one of the
marvels of medieval architecture. The "Merveille" rose to

2. For the computation of the ransom of King Jean II in terms of the
modern French franc, see R. Delachenal, *Hist. de Charles V* (Paris, 1927),
2. 204, note 2. Delachenal's calculations are based, however, upon the
mean valuation of the franc in 1909. My appreciative thanks are due
to Professor C. R. Whittlesey of the University of Pennsylvania for com-
puting the value of the sum in dollars.

3. Of the forty hostages sixteen, who had been captured with the
King at Poitiers, were by the terms of the treaty exempt from the payment of any personal ransom. The Sire de Coucy, as we shall see later,
was not among those sixteen. See Delachenal, *Hist. de Charles V*, 2. 204-5.

the unusual height of 176 feet, and was 305 feet in circum-
ference. The other buildings enclosed within its spacious
bailey were on a similar scale of magnitude and extent.

To dilate upon the antiquity of the Coucys or to chron-
icle their importance would be wasted labor, mere proof of
the obvious. *Sirerie* is equivalent to "principality," so that
by common repute the Sire de Coucy would rank as a prince.
The dignity had been lost, however, when the title passed to
the house of Coucy-Guines, descendants of the original family
in the female line. But all during the years in which they
flourished, whether they stemmed from main or from the female line, the Sires de Coucy were ranked as barons, which
meant that they held their principal seigneury (whence they
bore their title) *in capite,* i.e., directly from the king, with
all the legal privileges that such holding entailed.[4] Thus,
knowing no suzerain other than the Majesty of France, ruling as monarchs themselves within their own domains, and
increasing their wealth and prestige by brilliant marriages,
the lords of Coucy consolidated their power and spread their
renown as the medieval centuries unrolled. Of their fame
let their *devise,* at once modest and proud, bear witness:

> Je ne suis roy, ne comte aussy,
> Je suis le sire de Coucy.[5]

4. See Jean du Tillet, *Recueil des Rangs des Grands de France* (Paris,
1618), p. 11: "Le Mot de Barons, estoit anciennement general, adapté
aux Princes du sang, Ducs, Marquis, Comtes, & autres de la Noblesse de
France, tenans leur Seigneuries principales, immediatement de la couronne
en tous droicts, fors le souueraineté et hommage." Below on the same page
du Tillet informs us that at the "bed of Justice" held by Charles V (Dec.
9, 1378) against Jean de Montfort, Duke of Brittany, the Sire de Coucy
was ranked as a baron. Eustache Deschamps applies the title twice to the
subject of this paper in his *Balade Faisant Mencion de la Mort de Monseigneur de Coucy* (*Oeuvres complétes,* ed. le Marquis de Queux de Saint-
Hilaire, Paris, 1878-1903, 7. 206-8, lines 8, 46).

5. Various versions of the *devise* occur, some of them quite manifestly
wrong; see le Prince de Ponts-Asnières, *Eclaircissement Critique sur la
Devise de Coucy* (Paris, 1845) for a study of its probable form in the
Middle Ages.

No augmentation of titles could make the family more distinguished than it was. Throughout their long succession the Sires de Coucy would seem to have valued activity and ability more than office-holding or the mere attainment of higher rank. Thus the reputation and importance of the house died away only with the demise of its last representative. And of the long line of lords who held Coucy, Marle, la Fère, and Oisy, this last representative was the most able, attractive, and famous. Let us lose no further time in making his better acquaintance.

II

The exact date of the last Sire de Coucy's birth is unknown. Several dates have been suggested, but the best opinion ventures no further than the cautious "about 1340."[6] The place presumably was the Château de Coucy. The child was the only offspring of Enguerrand VI and of Cathcrine, daughter of Leopold VII, Duke of Austria (that Leopold who was defeated by the Swiss at Morgarten in 1315), and granddaughter of the Emperor Albert I. Thus he had royal blood in his veins.[7]

Of his boyhood we know nothing. His escapades, his precocity, his distastes and preferences, all remain unchron-

6. "About the year 1339" (Mary A. E. Green, *Lives of the Princesses of England*, London, 1851, 3. 199); "vers 1340" (Henri Lacaille, *Étude sur la Vie d'Enguerran VII, Sire de Coucy*). An abstract of Lacaille's *Étude* was published in *Positions de Thèses Soustenues par des élèves de la promotion de 1890*, École Nationale des Chartes, Macon, 1890, but the original manuscript, returned by the authorities of the school to the author (since dead), was never printed, and has now disappeared. Much research on original documents has therefore gone for naught. One cannot help wondering at the seeming carelessness of the *École* about the promotion and diffusion of knowledge! But whatever the sins of past directors may have been, I can only be grateful to the director of 1937, Mons. Clovis Brunel, who has courteously answered my inquiries as to the whereabouts of Lacaille's thesis. My quotation is, of course, taken from the abstract.

7. According to Jean de Noyal (*Fragments inédits de la Chronique de Jean de Noyal*, Soc. de l'Hist. de France, 1883, p. 251) Enguerrand VI and Catherine of Austria were married in 1336.

icled. In manhood he was a favorite with women, loved and followed by his subordinates, trusted and honored by kings and princes. He must, therefore, have been an attractive youngster, for what buds in youth blossoms in manhood. At the Château de Coucy the customs and practices of good manners the boy was taught would not be those of a free and easy provincial aristocracy, but those inculcated in the most distinguished households or at the courts of royalty itself. And being a Coucy meant that every detail of those practices and customs, and of the elaborate training which the aspirant for knighthood underwent, would have been insisted upon. At all events we do know that as a minor he was under the guardianship of his mother and of his uncle, Raoul de Coucy, Sire d'Havraincourt, and that the latter, if the historian A. Mazas is to be trusted, was something of a disciplinarian.[8] Some historians, notably Mazas, say Enguerrand was handsome, and probably he was, but all are agreed about the charm of his personality and the grace of his bearing. Froissart, who may have been somewhat prejudiced in his favor by benefits received, says that it well suited him to do all that he did.[9]

It seemed, however, that all those aristocratic accomplishments were not destined to embellish France, Enguerrand's native country. True enough, he did in 1358 display a promptitude and energy in stamping out in his own province of Picardy the peasant rebellion of the *Jacquerie*, thus impressing the regent, the future Charles V, very much in his favor. But his days in France were numbered, for it had been written in the treaty that he was to serve as one of the

8. Of Raoul de Coucy, Alex. Mazas says, "il observait les lois de la chivalerie avec une ferveur toute particulière" (*Vie des Grands Capitaines Français du Moyen Age*, Paris, 1838, 3. 5).

9. J. Froissart, *Chroniques*, ed. Kervyn de Lettenhove (Brussels, 1870), 1. 344-45. Froissart certainly received gifts of money from Coucy after Coucy's English sojourn was over, but he had also known him at the English Court, and probably profited financially from that acquaintance.

numerous hostages who were to remain at the English court
as pledges for King Jean's observance of the Treaty of
Brétigny.[10]

Though due in England in 1360, Enguerrand did not
appear there until some time in the spring of 1363. The fact
is important, for almost every author who has written on his
career has transported him to England in the year 1360. Possibly the reason for his nonappearance in England in 1360
was that he was still under twenty-one years of age. But
the evidence of the records makes it more likely that his
later arrival was caused by diplomatic bickerings between the
French and English courts, his departure being deferred
until one side or the other had won the particular round in
which his name had been bandied to and fro.[11]

The lot of a hostage at the court of Edward III was far
from being an unpleasant one. Each captive nobleman, Froissart tells us, brought his own menage and "held good estate,

10. The list of hostages, Coucy's name among them, is contained in
Art. 15, 16 of the Agreement at Brétigny. The treaty of Calais did not
change that list. See Delachenal, *Hist. de Charles V*, 2. 205, 251.
   11. The date of Coucy's arrival in England can be fairly closely
determined by several writs and letters issued by both the French and
English kings that are printed in vol. 6 of *Rymer's Foedera*, London,
1708. On p. 405 a letter from King Jean (Mar. 13, 1363, from Ville-
neuve-les-Avignon) addressed to King Edward suggests the substitution
of Coucy for one of the following: the Dukes of Orléans, Anjou, Berry,
and Bourbon. Another on Mar. 16 notifies those four dukes that Edward
had not consented to the substitution. On the date last mentioned Coucy
was then probably still in France. On p. 411 a letter contains the pledges
of a number of French lords, Coucy among them, to go to England as
hostages for the four dukes (and others). Place and date of this letter
are lacking through some injury to the substance on which it was penned.
On pp. 414-15 a writ of Edward III dated from Westminster on May 26,
1363, states that Enguerrand de Coucy and others had renewed their
obligations *de tenir ostage*. On or before May 26, then, Coucy was on
the point of going to England, if indeed not already there. It is well,
however, in any discussion about the dates on medieval administrative
documents, such as letters patent or writs, to remember that the date written on the document was not necessarily the date on which it was sent
out to the person or persons to whom it was directed; see J. F. Willard,
"The Dating and Delivery of Letters Patent and Writs in the 14th Century," *Bull. Instit. of Hist. Research* 10. 1-11.

grand and noble":[12] in other words, he brought his esquires and varlets, tilting armor, his hounds, palfreys and coursers, and his falcons. The king allowed them "to come and go, ride out (*chevauchier*) and disport themselves (*esbattre*), hawk and hunt throughout the realm of England." Moreover, Edward showed them the favor of his countenance, feasted them, made them welcome, and asked them what was new with them.

Indeed, King Edward might well afford to show his generous and kindly side. To do so came naturally to him, but recent events had certainly prompted his natural inclinations. His armies had only yesterday won the brilliant victory of Poitiers; he was at the height of his prestige and power: and his better angel, Queen Philippa, was at his side. A group of handsome children surrounded the royal couple, whose comings and goings, and prospective or possible marriages, aroused popular affection and excited popular expectation.

It is probable, however, that one shadow might have darkened the joy of the royal couple in their handsome children. Their eldest daughter, Isabella, was thirty-three years old and still unmarried, an advanced age indeed for a medieval princess to have been going about in maiden meditation fancy-free.

The Princess would appear to have been born on June 16, 1332, at Woodstock.[13] Through Wardrobe Accounts and Household Rolls we catch glimpses of her progress from baby- to maidenhood. She was her father's child. His were her impulsiveness, her love of finery and display, her sudden changes of mood or purpose, her lavish generosity, and her perennial need of money. The *Patent Rolls* show the King's

12. *Chroniques*, ed. Kervyn, 6. 300.

13. Mary A. E. Green, *Lives of the Princesses of England*, 3. 164. The date of Isabella's birth was ascertained from the *Wardrobe Accts.* by Mrs. Green. Her "Life" of the princess is based upon the study of the documents of the PRO, many of which still remain unprinted. The article in *Dict. Natl. Biog.* (29. 67) is largely based upon her book.

affection for his daughter, or her ability to wheedle him around her little finger. From the time that she had arrived at the "spending age," before she had a separate household of her own, and then throughout the years of that independent status[14] and all through those of her marriage up to the year of her father's death, the *Patent Rolls* report a succession of grants of manors, wardships, and hard cash from the King to his eldest daughter. It is probably true that her father's affection had somewhat spoiled her.

One of her critics, Miss Blanche Christabel Hardy, basing her judgments upon Isabella's behavior in the several marriage proposals that her parents arranged for her, is probably too severe.[15] What Isabella did is fact, and facts stand, but the reasons why she acted as she did, the purposes and motives of her action are far more difficult to ascertain. Miss Hardy may be right in her judgment of Isabella, but she may equally well be wrong. Let us look for a few moments at what those marriage proposals were, and how she reacted to them, and then determine whether, on the basis of what is known, the Princess deserves so severe a judgment.

Match-making plans in aristocratic or royal households began with the appearance of the child, and Isabella's case was no exception. At three there was discussion of a marriage between her and the young Pedro of Castile.[16] For-

14. See T. F. Tout, *Chapters in the Administrative History of Medieval England* (Manchester, 1920-33), 3. 253, note 1. Isabella appears not to have had an independent establishment on July 3, 1349 (*Cal. Pat. Rolls 1348-50*, p. 340). She would appear to have had one before Nov. 20, 1356 (*Cal. Pat. Rolls 1354-58*, p. 473).

15. *Philippa of Hainault and Her Times*, London, 1910. In speaking of the separation between Isabella and her husband, the Sire de Coucy, Miss Hardy (p. 309) says "nor is de Coucy's rather extraordinary action to be accounted for otherwise than by his wife's conduct and all but impossible temper. It will be remembered that he was some years younger than herself, and there is no reason to suppose that her selfish, vain, and overbearing character had been materially altered by marriage."

16. Subsequently known as Peter the Cruel, dramatically slain by his half-brother Henry of Trastamara at Montiel.

tunately for the child that project came to naught. The first serious attempt to bring her into the holy and blessed state of matrimony, a proposed union with the young Count of Flanders, may have left its psychological effect upon her thinking and behavior.

Both England and Flanders had found amicable and friendly relations mutually advantageous. The Flemings were the biggest buyers of English wool, because England was their best and cheapest source of supply. Whoever else fought, English kings and Flemish administrators were firmly resolved to remain at peace. It is not surprising, then, to find that in 1346-47 the idea of a marriage between Isabella and the young Count of Flanders was first discussed by Edward and the civic corporations of Flanders, and then planned. The chief obstacle appeared to lie in the unwillingness of the prospective groom to be married. Deputations of his nobles and citizens waited upon him, to urge all the advantages that would accrue to them and to their lands by his prompt espousal of the English princess. The zeal of his faithful subjects to see him married in the right quarter, however, carried them to the length of placing guards about him, so that there should be no possible outcome of the matter than the one they desired. Finally the young man weakened. Surveillance and the restriction of his pleasures and freedom brought him round, and he gave his consent to the proposal. "The delighted Flemings communicated the tidings to King Edward and his Queen, who were gratified by their zeal and success, and declared that "the Flemings were a very good sort of people."[17]

One day, subsequent to the betrothal (March 14, 1367), the young Count went hawking. He managed to ride somewhat ahead of his faithful subjects, galloped hard after the falcons who were manoeuvring about a heron, and did not

17. Mrs. Green, 3. 182-83.

pull rein until he had crossed the French border, leaving behind him his attendants, his pledges—and his bride.

To imagine what Isabella's feelings must have been is no
difficult matter. Her trousseau had been prepared, and she
herself, whatever her private judgments of her intended and
his intentions, evidently expected the wedding day to dawn.
But, like the rest of us who are disappointed, she evidently
made the best of a bad situation, and tried to forget the blow
to her *amour propre* by interesting herself in other matters.[18]
Several years later, however, the question of her marriage
was up again, the proposed bridegroom being a son of the
powerful Gascon nobleman, the Lord of Albret.[19] But these
nuptials, for reasons we do not know, were broken off, not
by the groom but by the bride. Did she avenge on Bernard
Ezi the slight that had been put upon her?[20]

And now what shall we say of this girl whose behavior
might seem to mark her as one of the "new type" of women
who appear at the end of the fourteenth century? Her interests, like those of Valentine Visconti, Duchess of Orléans,
or Isabelle of Bavaria, Queen of Charles VI, were other
than mere domesticity. Whether she really was of the new
type is doubtful. Probably the inheritance of her father's
nature best explains her. She wished very much to be an active mover of events, to take part in what was going on, to

18. Before passing judgment upon Isabella or the Count of Flanders, it
should be remembered that Louis' flight was probably more dictated by
his political sympathies than any personal aversion to the proposed bride.
His subjects were drawing him to the altar with ropes. Nor was Isabella
herself quite free to accept or reject her suitor; medieval princesses seldom
enjoyed such freedom. Probably neither had ever laid eyes on the other
before they met, and the Count's mind must have been made up long
before that meeting. Agnes Strickland (*Lives of the Queens of England*,
London, 1844, 2. 332-33), goes so far as to say that Isabella connived at
the Count's escape, but cites no evidence to support her statement.

19. The wedding was apparently to be held in Gascony; see Mrs.
Green, 3. 190-91.

20. Mrs. Green (3. 193) informs us that Bernard Ezi, "weary of the
world, in which his hopes had been thus blighted, retired forever from it,
and immured himself within the walls of a cloister."

be the hammer that shaped and not the anvil that received. Not for her, her mother's quiet (but none the less efficient) ways. With her father's energy and directness she must have inherited also some of his faults: his thoughtless generosity, his lack of foresight, his blindness to the meaning of the word "consistency" and to the obligations which a man's plighted word imposed upon him. Still, as Edward's child, she must have inherited (and documents at the Public Record Office bear this out) his open nature, his lavish generosity, his zest for the pride and pomp of courtly life, his love for fine actions and those who performed them. All of which is to say that both father and daughter had charm, possessed the power of winning from men and women devotion and love. The tragedy of both is that they could not always recognize the beauty of moral integrity. With Philippa dead, Edward III sank into the senile playfulness of his last years with Alice Perrers; while Isabella's tragedy was to find herself mated to a man who placed honor and a good name above all she could do or get for him.

But tragedy was yet far in the future. In 1363, even at thirty-one years of age, Isabella, the darling of her royal father, and somewhat freed from her royal mother's disapproving eye by the possession of an independent household, must have been the source of much of the animation and gaiety that made the English court so renowned throughout Europe. Despite her prodigality and a dash of inconsequentiality, she must have been a very lovely lady. If, like her father, she took gaily whatever lot fortune sent her, she was probably really eager for the right man to appear. And unknown to her, fortune had decreed that she was not to wait long for him.

III

In the summer of 1363, Enguerrand was welcomed at the English Court, and his own accomplishments and personality soon made that welcome warm into popularity and regard. At the return of his sovereign, King Jean of France, to London in January, 1364, he exerted himself particularly to make the hours pass pleasantly and gaily, and did so with success, excelling all others in the songs and dances of the carole.[21] During the year that followed, with its round of caroles, jousts,[22] hawking and hunting parties, he evidently became a general favorite, for Froissart tells us he was so agreeable among the ladies that he had quite a reputation, and was a welcome addition to companies of lords and ladies everywhere.[23] The chronicler's terse remark that it well suited the Sire de Coucy to do all that he did[24] telescopes into a phrase that is all too brief much of the gaiety of days long past, but, coming as it does from the lips of one who knew the *haut monde* of his day, it carries a ring of finality.

Of these years so important in Enguerrand's career few indeed are the details and Froissart is their only reciter. He is, it is true, as already suggested, hardly an unprejudiced historian.[25] Yet his prejudice in favor does not necessarily

---

21. Froissart (ed. Kervyn, 6. 392) tells us that between the hour of the King's arrival at Eltham palace and supper, there were "grans danses et grans caroles, et là estoit le jones sires de Couci qui s'efforçoit de bien danser et de canter quant son tour venoit."

22. Coucy was a practiced jouster. Froissart (14. 22) tells us that at the marriage of Charles VI (1389) he "s'i porta grandement bien, et durèrent les joustes fortes et rades jusques à la nuit que on se départy."

23. "Le sire de Coucy etoit fort aimable pres des dames, qu'il en avoit la reputation, & qu'il etoit tres bien—vu des seigneurs and dames par-tout." Quot. fol. ed., Lyon, 1561, 3. 304.

24. Froissart, 6. 392-93: "trop bien li afféroit à faire quanqu'il faisoit."

25. In *Le Joli Buisson de Jonece*, 278-81 (*Oeuvres: Poesies*, ed. A. Scheler, Brussels, 1871, 2. 9); and in *Le Dit dou Florin*, 442-44 (p. 233 of same vol.), he acknowledges gratuities from Coucy.

As with Froissart, so with Eustache Deschamps. It can be charged that he too is prejudiced in Enguerrand de Coucy's favor. He avows himself Coucy's servant ("beneficiary") in the clever little acrostic entitled *Sur les noms du Sire de Coucy et d'Eustache Deschamps* (*Œuvres Complètes*, ed. De Queux de St. Hilaire, Soc. des Anc. Textes Fran., 4. 114); prays for his safe return from the Barbary expedition of 1390 (*Sur l'expédition de Barbarie*, 4. 266); mourns his loss and that of his comrades in *Pour les*

mean that he gives us a distorted or wrong view of his benefactor's nature when that benefactor first appeared on the
English scene. St. Paul urges the Philippians to take a prejudiced view of "whatsoever things are lovely, whatsoever
things are of good report," and Froissart probably praised
Coucy in the very spirit of that injunction: because it would
have been difficult not to praise one whom all were united
in praising.

But, prejudiced or not, the testimony of other contemporary historians who recount Coucy's later career does not
belie the Flemish chronicler's report. They describe, it is
true, a Coucy who was not dallying at court, but winning
laurels in the field, and gaining, as the counsellor of kings
and the negotiator of treaties, the reputation of a very astute
and practical diplomat. But whether in England as a bache-
lor, or in France or Italy as soldier and statesman, the man
is one and the same throughout. Froissart's praise of the
young knight and courtier is echoed in the words in which
his contemporary Aretino,[26] Pope Gregory XI,[27] and the
author of the *Livre des Faicts du Mareschal Boucicaut*,[28]
paint the experienced general and astute administrator. What-

---

Français morts à Nicopolis (7. 77); and, finally, lays upon his tomb his
touching memorial wreath, *Faisant Mencion de la Mort de Monseigneur
de Coucy* (7. 206). The reason that justifies Froissart's "prejudice in
favor of," justifies that of Deschamps as well.

26. Leonardo Aretino (*Hist. Florentini Populi Liber*, 9. Muratori, 19.
pt. 3. 237), speaking of the French contingent which was sent in 1384 to
aid the Duke of Anjou in Naples, says, "ducebat vero Enghiramus quidam
gallus, vir domi potens et militia clarus."

27. See Henri Lacaille, "Enguerran de Coucy au service de Grégoire
XI," *Ann. Bulletin de la Soc. d'Hist. de France* 32. 203 ff. See particularly the letters in which the Pope congratulates Coucy on his military
successes and extols his foresight and generalship, pp. 195, 203, 205.

28. Published in *Collection des Memoires Relatifs a l'Hist. de France* 6.
Though Coucy and Boucicaut had differed sharply at the council held just
before the battle of Nicopolis, the author of the *Livre* has naught but
praise for the former (460-61): "Là estoit le vaillant seigneur de Coucy,
chevalier esprouvé, qui toute sa vie n'avoit finé d'armes suivre, et moult
estoit de grand vertu."

ever he did, be it singing, dancing, planning or fighting, was done with grace and distinction.

Given a woman charming in her own right, irrespective of all those other advantages which she derived from her position as princess royal, and a young man distinguished not only by rank but also his charm and ability, and bring both together often in one of the most brilliant courts of the Middle Ages—and the probable result will be matrimony. And matrimony it proved to be.

The marriage took place at Windsor on July 27, 1365.[29] It must have been a splendid affair, for the chroniclers who usually record passing events in the most laconic fashion, assure us that it was celebrated with due pomp and appropriate ceremony.[30] As to the details of the nuptials the *Issue Rolls* are slightly more informative, recording payments by the Exchequer to the Queen for the purchase of jewels *ad opus Isabella comitissae Bedford pro maritagio suo;*[31] to the Queen for the purchase of jewels for Isabella as a gift from her parents, brothers, and sisters.[32] That the

29. Froissart (ed. Kervyn, 17. 422) says that the marriage was "made" (*fait*), that Coucy was "quit of his faith and prison," and that he then went to Prussia, to return the summer after for the "espousal" at Windsor. As we shall see, Coucy was at Prague in Jan., 1370, but English records do not tell that he left the country before his wedding. Froissart's chronology is probably confused. His statement that Coucy was "quit" of his obligations of hostageship before July 27, 1365, certainly seems to show imperfect apprehension of the order of events; see discussion below.

30. Malverne's continuation of Higden's *Polychronicon*, 8. 365 (MS A), Rolls Ser. 41, reads: "Dominus de Coucy de Francia, qui diu in Anglia pro redemptione regis Franciæ erat obses, vicesimo septimo die mensis Julii apud Windeleshoram cum maxima solemnitate duxit in uxorem Isabellam filiam regis Angliæ, quae solum prae amore sibi voluit desponsari." To the same effect (minus the last few words) run the *Continuatio* of *Murimuth* (ed. T. Hog, London, 1846, p. 201), Walsingham (*Hist. Angl.* 1, 301 R.S. 28), and the author of the *Chronicon Angliae* (p. 56, R.S. 64).

31. Money granted to the amount of 1273/6/4, *Issue Roll* (unpublished E403/429/41E3, Michaelmas (abbreviated Mich.).

32. In the amount of 2370/10/4, *Issue Roll* (unpubl.) E403/425/40E3, Mich. In this note and the preceding my reading of shillings and pence differs from the amount given by Mrs. Green (*Princesses of England,*

royal pair spared no expense is shown by a record of payment to divers minstrels at Windsor, present at the marriage
of Isabella, the King's daughter, Lady de Coucy (*sic*), in
money paid to them of the King's gift, 100 pounds.[33] Finally there was executed a formal document dated on the
day of the wedding, sealed by Enguerrand de Coucy and
delivered to the appropriate officers of the King in which he
declares "en pure verite, de nostre Fraunche et agreable
volunte, and sans aucune constrainte" that as a hostage he
had been "honestement traicties et demeanez and selonc
nostre Estat" by the king and his people, and that he had
now been given "congie de partir hors de son dit povoir."[34]
Coucy thus had been discharged of any obligations as hostage
and granted his personal freedom, for which he would otherwise have had to pay a heavy ransom. There was thus about
the marriage no savor of a "shotgun" affair. Indeed, there
is no reason for viewing the marriage in any other light than
that of a love match. Whatever other interests it served,
whatever difficulties it raised, no obstacles seem to have occurred to the principals. Nay, their action was carried out in
the face of difficulties of interest, nationality, and allegiance.
Solum prae amore . . . desponsari.[35]

---

3. 202 and note 3 on that page). I think I am correct, but am willing to
admit that I may have read the roll wrongly. The handwriting is not
always clearly legible. Whether the Queen's present (preceding note)
was included in the present of the "whole family" I do not know. Mrs.
Green believes it was.

33. F. Devon, *Issues of the Exchequer* (London, 1837, Mich. 40E3),
p. 188. Expenses of the wedding and trousseau were evidently not cleared
up until some time afterwards, for E403/427/40E3, June 9, records a
payment of 200.1 to the Countess of Bedford *pro maritagio suo.*

34. *Foedera* (1708 ed.) b. 472: *recognitio Engerrani Sire de Coucy,
quod bene tractabatur, dum fuit obses in Anglia.* It is amusing to note
that the document is dated the day of the wedding: one wonders whether
Edward was determined to have no repetition of the affair of the Count
of Flanders.

35. Between the bride and groom there was a disparity of age. At the
time of her marriage Isabella had just completed her thirty-third year,
and Enguerrand was just entering his twenty-seventh; see Mrs. Green, 3.

Yet other subsidiary interests were served by the marriage. Mrs. Green says that the English chroniclers, "surprised at the honours conferred upon the young stranger ... spoke of him as 'a certain magnate from transmarine parts, commonly called de Coucy, but whose other name is unknown.' "[36] But if the chroniclers and others of the King's faithful subjects so thought of Enguerrand de Coucy, such were not the thoughts of Edward III and his most intimate advisers. They were under no illusions as to the importance of the Sire de Coucy, one of the most powerful lords in Northern France. Were he to adhere to the English side, or even to preserve a benevolent neutrality, Edward's path to the French crown would be a smoother one. To win over an important Picard lord to English interest, and thus to destroy a reservoir of French military strength, would have been no mean step on the road to that diadem. It is true that the problem of allegiance lay in the way, but allegiance had not sat heavily upon the conscience of the good knight Sir Guichard d'Angle, who had left the French and espoused the English cause a few years before, and was to die Earl of Huntington and Knight of the Garter. Perhaps Enguerrand de Coucy would prove as sensible and adaptable. Edward resolved to win his son-in-law over.

To assure and establish his position at court, and then throughout the country at large, was the first step in the King's plan. He gave his daughter what he thought would be an income ample enough to maintain her estate by an annual grant of 1000 marks.[37] As it turned out, either the

203. Despite the disparity, however, marital affection (at least until 1376-77) seems never to have grown cold.

36. P. 202. I have not run upon any such statements in an examination of most of the chronicles of the Rolls Series. But the quotation from Malverne does seem a little apologetic: "only true love" could force the princess royal to throw herself away upon a mere count and a French count at that!!

37. See *Issue Roll*, Mich. 1365 (E403/425/40E3). A. Duchesne (*Hist. Généalogique des Maisons de Guines, d'Ardes, de Gand, et de Coucy,*

royal father's estimates of what would be sufficient were too
close, or the royal daughter's ability to "live of her own"
nothing worth, for this grant, despite the fact that several
previous grants remained uncancelled and others were added
to it in later years, never seemed to be enough. Meagre or
not, however, it seems to have been regularly paid at the
Exchequer up to 1377, the year in which Coucy broke his
English connections.[38]

Paris, 1631, 266) gives the figure as 4000 livres. This, with the livre
tournois equal to 3 shillings, tuppence, is exactly 1000 marks (the mark
being 13 shillings, 4 pence).

38. Information as to the income from English sources received by the
Sire de Coucy and his lady comes largely from unpublished material at
the Public Record Office. In 1937 I succeeded in inducing academic su-
periors to grant a half year's leave of absence that would allow me to
obtain thence more information on Coucy's career in England. I had,
before starting off, culled out from the printed *Calendars of Close, Fine,
and Patent Rolls* a number of items about the Sire and Lady de Coucy.
The brief time at my disposal could, therefore, be devoted wholly to unprinted records or those of which there were brief abstracts in catalogues
accessible only in the Record Office. I found that the *Wardrobe Accts.* (my
search was not an exhaustive one), which I had hoped would prove revealing, gave me some new, but little important, information about the
two principal figures of my search. The *Series of Deeds, Ancient,* particularly Series A (catalogued), AS and WS, yielded a few interesting
items, but none of particular note. Most informative of all were the
Issue Rolls. These supplemented the information from the printed Calendars about the movements of lord and lady, their territorial possessions,
the wardships assigned to them, by giving information as to their annual
income from the Royal Exchequer. Since time did not allow for complete
examination of all the rolls covering the years 1363-77, it seemed best
to examine those at the beginning and end of Coucy's English connection,
Exchequer Nos. 403/421, 403/422, 403/425, 403/427, 403/428, 403/429,
403/431, 403/433, 403/438, 403/460, 403/461. These show that partial
payments on the following grants made at the time of Isabella's marriage
or slightly before it are quite regularly discharged by the Exchequer:

(a) 524 (or 534)/15/2 "as an aid in sustaining her estate." The
amount of cash payments made on this grant were diminished by de-
ducting the value of Isabella's share of the returns from the estate
of Thos. de Courtenay, whose heir was a minor in her wardship.

(b) 200/0/0.

(c) 100/0/0.

In E 403/460/50E3 full payments of (a) and (b) were made. On
(a) the escheators showed commendable activity in getting out money for
the princess, which, under ordinary circumstances, the death of her
Courtenay ward might have tied up for some time. They made a full

To assure his daughter and her spouse of an adequate income was but half the picture. Enguerrand de Coucy, if the King's plans were to meet with success, must take his place among the feudal nobility of the land, "be raised," to use Mrs. Green's pious and naïve phraseology, "to the dignity of an English peer." On May 11, 1366, Parliament being assembled, the chancellor declared to the peers, lay and spiritual, and the faithful commons that it was "fitting that the King should enhance and increase him (Coucy) in honour and name, and make him an earl, and thereupon he requested their advice and consent." Parliament replied meekly that it agreed with the King, and since the King was not then advised of what place to make him earl, the matter might be deferred to the King's good pleasure.[39] Edward lost little

---

payment of 435/18/15 in that roll. Since that year—1376—was probably the very one in which Enguerrand was pondering over whether he should cut his English ties, it looks very much as if Edward had issued orders that he should have no cause for complaint over money matters. I have not cited several grants that would seem to have been made on special occasions or for special purposes, viz. to cover indebtedness to tradesmen or foreign merchants. I should add that I have occasionally examined only one of the two *Issue Rolls* of a particular regnal year.

39. *Rolls of Parl.* (Record Comm.) 2. 290b. See also *Parl. History of England* (London, 1762), 1. 319-20, where a Mr. Tyrrel observes that it is noteworthy that Edward did not ask the advice of the Commons before creating a peer, "all the Charters of their [dukes' or earls'] Creations being granted by the King alone, and the Consent of the Parliament not at all mentioned in them." Whatever the correctness of Mr. Tyrrel's statements may be, the reference from *Rolls of Parl.* shows that the Commons were present when the chancellor asked for an expression of opinion ("Prelatz, Ducs, Countes, Barons, Grantz, and Communes esteantz en la Chambre Blanche"), and that the "nobles, each for himself, and the Commons, with one assent, agreed," etc. Princely prerogative and parliamentary procedure aside, it was obviously tactful of Edward to win for his son-in-law the good will of all estates, even the third. That he preferred to swim with the tide rather than against it is to be deduced from his movements in securing Enguerrand's earldom. Knighton (quot. T. F. Tout, *Admin. Hist. Med. Eng.*, 3. 253, note 2) tells us that Coucy was created Earl of Aumerle (Albemarle), and later historians have repeated the statements. It would seem quite fitting that he should have borne that title for the Earls of Aumerle were lords of Holderness and Wight, then held by Isabella. Edward, in all probability, had planned to give him that very title, but subsequently learned that he might offend

time in making that "good pleasure" known. A charter dated on the very same day (May 11, 1366) created *Ingelramus dominus de Coucy* Earl of Bedford, and granted to him, his spouse and their heirs male that 1000 marks whose payment the *Issue Rolls* record, and also 30 marks annually from the returns of the county of Bedford.[40]

That the marriage was a thing near to Edward's heart can be read from the official records of the reign. Even before the two principals were wedded the King was showing his young hostage particular marks of royal favor. And one evidence of his favor had, as we shall see later, an important bearing upon the story of the Earl's English years.

Edward's task in transplanting a French house to English soil was made somewhat easier in that the same French house had had in the past English affiliations. Enguerrand's great-grandmother, Christina de Lyndsay, cousin of King Alexander III of Scotland, had inherited numerous estates and holdings in the counties of Cumberland, Lancashire, Westmoreland, and Yorkshire, all or most of which comprised a moiety of the barony of Kendal. At this point I must digress briefly to explain how and why much of the Lyndsay inheritance came into the possession of the Earl of Bedford.

Christina de Lyndsay had married Ingelram de Guines, Enguerrand's great-grandfather, whose chief estates lay in the Pas de Calais, and since she had been an heiress (without brothers to inherit those lands), her estate passed into the family of Guines. Enguerrand's father, grandfather, and great-grandfather were of that family, but since his great-great-grandfather had married Alix, the heiress of Ingelram, third Sire de Coucy, his grandfather, William, accord-

---

other claimants of the Fors succession by its bestowal, and abandoned his plan (see quot. from Tout above).

40. *Cal. Chart. Rolls* 5. 193. The full text of the grant is found in *Rot. Parl.* (Rec. Com.). 2. 290. See also *Report on the Dignity of a Peer*, 1829, 5.54.

ing to common practice, had preferred to take the name of Coucy, the name of a house whose social prestige was greater. His great-grandfather, Ingelram de Guines (d. 1323), lived most of the time upon his wife's estates in Westmoreland and Lancashire, going only occasionally to France. Thus the North Country had grown to recognize the Guines coat-of-arms, and come to regard the family as one that had begun to take root in local soil. But with his son and successor William all was changed. He had become heir of the French estates of Guines and Coucy, but had chosen to reside in France rather than in the remote Northwest, and had even dropped his paternal name and arms to assume those of Coucy. Matters were complicated a little more by the fact that this William's brother, Robert de Coucy, had espoused the cause of the "King's enemies in France," so that portions of the English inheritance which his father or his elder brother (William) had given him, escheated into the hands of the King. One might remark, with the hope of condensing a good deal of tedious legal information, that the descendants of great-grandfather Ingelram appear to have been canny folk. One member of the family seems to have stayed in France and taken up arms for his French overlord whenever hostilities broke out between France and England, while another remained quietly in the possession of the English heritage.[41] The net result of such happenings was that the

41. Thus, *Cal. Inquis. post Mort.* 9. 457 (no. 675) shows us that on July 21, 1351, the knight's fees of Wm. de Coucy, and of Ing., son of Ing. de Guines (?) had escheated to the King by their deaths, those of Robt. de Coucy by war. Again, *Cal. Pat. Rolls* 1334-38, p. 494. informs us (under date of Aug. 22, 1337) that although the King had "lately" taken over estates of Frenchmen, he restored the family lands to William de Coucy (d. 1343), son of grandfather William and uncle of Eng. de Coucy VII. In 1342 the lands of Ingram de Gynes were escheated because of his support of the French enemy (*Cal. Close Rolls* 1341-43, p. 452). But the next year a preliminary grant, one that covered only the pasturing rights over the family's (former) estates in Westmoreland and Lancashire, was made to him (*Cal. Pat. Rolls* 1343-45, p. 36). If all these cullings from administrative records present to the reader a blurred picture, let him

county escheators and their royal master seemed always to be uncertain whether both Coucys (or Guines) were going to be "bad" or only one of them, and, consequently, in doubt whether the whole Coucy inheritance ought to be escheated into the royal hands, to be granted out again to loyal Englishmen, or the "good" Coucy rewarded at the expense of the "bad" one.

To present to his new son-in-law the vast mass of manors, messuages, advowsons, wardships, fisheries, and "parks" which his great-great-grandmother had once possessed was Edward's intention. Many reasons spoke for his resolution. The possession of those English estates might perhaps incline their new feudal tenant to take less interest in his French ones. With an income derived from his English lands assured him, the Earl of Bedford would be less of a charge upon his father-in-law's exchequer. And last, but perhaps not least, the repossession of the ancestral estate, would give him "local habitation and a name." Upon them he might grow into the life of the country, come to love Lancashire or Cumberland more than Picardy, and thus gradually become more of an Englishman and less of a Frenchman. The house of Coucy was the dominating political factor in Northern France. Picardy would probably follow Coucy's lead, and if the house of Coucy was English, so much smoother, King Edward thought, would be his path to the French throne.

Getting those ancestral estates into his son-in-law's possession seems to have been no easy matter. The several sequestrations had brought them into the King's hands again, and Edward's need of ready cash had induced, or compelled, him to re-grant them to others for longer or shorter periods of time. But in September, 1365, Edward seems to have

remember that it seems to have been no less blurred to county and exchequer officials. To clarify the discussion of the Coucy-Guines landed inheritance in the text, and statements made in this footnote as well, see the Genealogical Tree in Appendix A.

made a determined effort to achieve his purpose, for an inquiry was made as to the lands, etc., of William, son of
William de Coucy.[42] The jury could not have been a very
bright one, for it found (quite erroneously) that that William had died without heir in 1335, and that he was "a man
of the kingdom of France." Whether the jury reported as it
did for fear of arousing the ire of those local magnates who
were then seised of part of the former Coucy inheritance,
is not known. The return they made would justify continued
possession by those "on the ground" and would pass to the
King the task of proving that William de Coucy had not
forfeited his estates and that he himself had not granted
them out again to the possessioners. It is a fair assumption
that the royal wrath must have made itself felt in the proper
quarters, for in the next year another jury proved more
pliable and obliging. It discovered that William had died
holding the lands under question, not in 1335, but in 1341-
42, that he had an heir, and that that heir was Ingram (i.e.,
Enguerrand) de Coucy, Earl of Bedford, son and heir of
Ingram, son of the said William.[43]

These two Chancery inquisitions show quite clearly that
Edward went roundly to work in the attempt to have Coucy
hold what Coucy held. Indeed, his procedure in cases where
his protégé's interests appeared to be blocked by legal difficulties seems in several instances amusingly gauche.[44] In the

42. *Vict. Hist. of Lancs.,* 7. 303, note 47. That Edward had made the
attempt to get the lands which his son-in-law's family had formerly held
into Coucy's hands even before the marriage is proved by two *Close Roll*
entries of 1364, *Cal. Close Rolls* 1364-68, pp. 59-60.

43. *Vict. Hist. of Lancs.,* 7. 303, note 47.

44. On occasion of a contest (1364) between Coucy and Robert de
Haulay (Hanlay?) about a church at Thornton (Yks.?) the King wrote to
the justices commanding that the Lord de Coucy should by no means be
foreclosed of his right, if he had any, and that they should help him to the
utmost in their power (quoted by Mrs. Green, *Princesses of England,* 3.
200, note 5, Privy Seal Bills 39E.3.

On another occasion one can quite clearly detect the workings of Edward's hand. Because of adherence by the Coucys to the French interest

main, the King's efforts were successful. Once, when he was unable to get into his son-in-law's hands portions of the Lyndsay lands that he himself had granted out to John de Coupland and Joan his wife, he succeeded in getting Joan's (she was then a widow) tenancy of the Lancashire, Westmoreland, and Yorkshire lands limited to the duration of her life.[45]

But whatever we may think of Edward's motives, his intentions were quite apparent: he was bent upon building up in the Northwestern and Northwest Midland shires a powerful house, devoted to the throne and able to mold county opinion by virtue of its ability to reward its adherents and followers. *Patent, Close,* and *Issue Rolls* certainly show that the Earl and his countess were not niggardly in giving, as they indicate as clearly that mercantile, official, and social England was well aware that the Bedfords were to be courted and cultivated. And for us it is important to notice that within the region where formerly the Guines or Coucy family had held sway, grants of privileges and of land were being made from time to time by the new magnate and his dame. The people of Cumberland, Lancashire, Westmoreland, and Yorkshire were probably having it more and more impressed upon them that their new lord, who had become

---

the moiety of the Manor of Ulverston was granted by a charter of 1357 to John de Coupland and his wife Joan for life, with reversion to the Abbot of Furness. After the appearance of Enguerrand in England an attempt was made to put aside the charter with its provision of reversion to the abbot, on the ground that the abbot had stated falsely that William de Coucy had "no heir." See *Vict. Hist. of Lancs.*, 8. 349, note 18.

45. John de Coupland received his grant some time before May 21, 1355, Ingram de Coucy, the previous holder, having forfeited his rights because of adherence to the French cause, cf. *Cal. Pat. Rolls* 1354-58, p. 222. Coupland had captured King David of Scotland at the battle of Neville's Cross (1345). *Vict. Hist. of Lancs.*, 7.302n[46], is in error in stating that Joan de Coupland died in 1365. She was alive on July 24, 1369, for a latter patent, dated then from Westminster, informs us that she had done fealty to the Earl of Bedford for those lands (*Cal. Pat. Rolls* 1367-70, p. 295). For record of E. III's action regarding Joan's tenancy, see *Cal. Close Rolls* 1364-68, pp. 59-60.

a member of the royal family, was not so much a transplanted foreigner as a shoot of their own growing. In him the needs and wants of men and women of the Northwest would find the willing ear, the open hand. His brother- and sister-in-law, the Duke and Duchess of Lancaster, alone excepted, what better patrons could the local poets, the poets of their own alliterative school, have sought than the Earl of Bedford and his lady? To him and his countess, the "makers" and minstrels of his native region would have endited and sung. After his departure from England his Lancashire and Yorkshire inheritance remained in his wife's possession, and after her death, in the possession of their daughter Philippa, Duchess of Ireland and Countess of Oxford. So that even when his shadow fell no longer upon English ground, the Northwest would have had some reason to remember and memorialize him.

IV

Of Coucy's sojourn in England, particularly in the years that followed his marriage, we have little information. Indeed, we are better acquainted with the occasions when he left his adopted country on visits to the continent than with his days of business or relaxation in it. We do know that he was given permission to cross over to France in the spring of 1365 before his wedding in July of that year.[46] But he

46. *Cal. Pat. Rolls* 1364-67, p. 105, dated West. June 1. Notation upon an official document dated in June (before 20th day of that month) from Hotel St. Pol. mentions him as having served on a commission empowered to negotiate a treaty with the King of Navarre (No. 225A of *Mandements de Charles V* (Doc. Inéd. sur l'Hist. de France, V. 35, ed. L. Delisle, p. 111). The French King who thought highly of Coucy's abilities and must have sensed Edward's attempts to win him over, probably took the opportunity of the Navarrese negotiations to recall him to his allegiance or to make him feel his obligations to his rightful sovereign and native country. H. Lacaille (*Étude*, p. 83) does not mention this trip. E. Dewick (*Coronation Book of Charles V of France*, London, 1899, plate 11) suggests that Coucy may have been present at the sacring of Charles V at Rheims (May 19, 1364). The suggestion is made on the strength of the depiction of a figure who wears a red *cote-hardie*, blue

was soon back in England to be married, and there he spent the first four months of his union. However, his obligations to his tenants and the care of his estates must have weighed upon his mind, for toward the end of the year (1365) he sought and received permission to visit his ancestral estates in France. The letter patent in which the permission is granted goes on to record that all children of either sex born to the pair at any time abroad shall be considered capable of inheriting lands in England.[47] Such phraseology suggests that the Countess of Bedford was known to be enceinte.[48]

The medieval men and women of Edward's court and of Coucy's household enjoyed one advantage over us that all the improvements of which we now boast cannot rob them of: they knew just about when Isabella's child was expected. The first record that I have been able to find of little Mary de Coucy (we can be sure that it is long *after* the event) is an *Issue Roll* entry of August 1, 1366, in which a part payment of 66/13/4 is made to Isabella's man-of-affairs Sir Thomas Tyrrell, who brought the news of the child's safe arrival.[49] The family must have returned to England shortly

---

hood, blue hose, and a garter of cloth of gold around his right knee (the garter of Edward's famous order, then as now, was of blue and worn on the left knee). It is possible that Coucy may have attended the coronation, but to have done so, it would have been necessary for him to have procured a safe-conduct from Edward III (he would have been in 1364 still a French hostage), and the English official documents record none as asked or granted. Furthermore, in 1364 he had not received the Garter. Either Dewick's identification is a wrong one, or the artist, knowing of Coucy's close association with the French King in later years, has purposely permitted himself an anachronism. The strict observance of chronological correctness was not important to the medieval artist.

47. *Cal. Pat. Rolls* 1364-67, p. 190 (dated Nov. 26); see also Mrs. Green, *Princesses of England*, 3. 203.

48. The suggestion is further supported by entries in *Issue Rolls* (E403/427/E3 April 18, 1366; E403/427/E3 Aug. 1, 1366; E403/428/E3 Aug. 1, 1366) of payments made to a John Fitz Eustace, styled "Val. domini de Coucy," or "Val. comitissae Bedeford," for coming to the king with letters "de partibus ffranciae" and returning with the royal letters.

49. E403/427/40E.3. Payment is made "pro grato rumore idem Thom. attulit domino regi de nativitate comitis et comitissae Bede-

after it was deemed safe for mother and child to make the journey. Early in the year 1367 at the palace of Eltham, Isabella gave birth to a second daughter, whom she called Philippa after her mother.[50]

Edward seems never to have weakened in his determination to bind his son-in-law to his interests and plans, and soon an opportunity presented itself to create on Enguerrand's part another obligation. A fellow hostage of his, Guy, Count of Blois, evidently must have been anxious to procure his liberty and return to his native country. Mrs. Green informs us that King Edward offered to release him on condition of his selling the county of Soissons, which he held, to Edward's new son-in-law.[51] Guy accepted the offer, disburdened himself of the county, and Enguerrand became 17th Count of Soissons,[52] a territory that marched with his own ancestral

---

ford." Note that while "valets" such as John Fitz Eustace (see note 48) are deemed worthy to come and go with news of Isabella's condition and evidences of parental solicitude, the privilege of announcing the birth of the infant (and the reward that would go with it) was granted to (or sought by) a gentleman of name and arms. Mrs. Green (*Princesses of England*, 3. 205) gives the child's birth as of April, 1366, but cites no authority for the statement.

50. Mrs. Green, *Princesses of England*, 3. 206.

51. *Princesses of England*, 3. 207. Lacaille (*Étude*, 83-84) gives a different interpretation: "son influence à la coûr lui permet de faire délivrer un de ses compagnons de captivité, Guy de Blois, qui lui fait don à cette occasion de son comté de Soissons, le 5 juillet 1367." How freely Guy gave up the county is, perhaps, a question. It is worthy of remark that in later years Enguerrand de Coucy combined with the King of France and his brother, the Duke of Orléans, in a rather shabby attempt to force Guy to sell some lands which Orléans coveted. Even Froissart, his great admirer, blames Coucy for his share in this complot: "le sire de Coucy . . . fut moult coulpable de ce fait" (ed. Kervyn, 16. 71).

52. *L'Art de Vérifier Les Dates*, 17. 251 ff., especially pp. 266-67. The king's gift to Coucy allowed his finance officers to make some interesting adjustments. *Issue Roll* E403/433/42E3, Jan. 22, 1368, shows us that the Exchequer valued the county and dependencies at 500 mks., and deducted that sum from the annual grant of 1000 mks. paid to Coucy and his wife. The same roll also informs us that the grant was made only until the king could provide lands whose returns made up a valuation of 1000 mks., a detail that is lacking in the roll that first records the grant. An entry in a patent roll (*Cal. Pat. Rolls* 1367-70, p. 16. West. Oct. 1, 1367) explains, perhaps, the insertion of this proviso in the *Issue Roll*

estates. Information as to how the Earl and Countess busied or amused themselves after their return from France is sparse, but we do know that Enguerrand was a successful petitioner for a pardon for Richard Pye of Laycock for an "accidental" murder.[53] He was evidently showing himself the *grand seigneur*, open of access, and willing to lend an ear, and a hand as well, to the unfortunate.

The year 1368 saw Coucy again departing from England. A Patent Roll entry records permission for him to go beyond sea with thirty men and thirty horses—quite a large train.[54] The size of the train can be accounted for by the fact that Isabella and one (or both) of her children accompanied him. Their departure may have been in January of the new year, but, as we shall soon see, could not have been later than some time in March (or early April), and their first objective was

of 42ndE. 3. The entry informs us that to the King's annual grant of 1000 mks., 30 mks. out of the issues of the County of Bedford were regularly to be added, so that after the gift of the County of Soissons 530 mks. were owing to the Earl and Countess. Lands whose returns amounted to 300 mks. were granted them by this letter patent, so that the remainder, 230 mks., was, perhaps, satisfied for the year 1368 by a payment of 142/16/11 (see *I.R.* cited above). I am indebted to my colleague, Professor Joseph Strayer, for assistance in the analysis of this financial problem. He suggests that the discrepancy between the 230 mks. and the actual payment recorded in the *Issue Roll* may have been wiped out by returns from the lands higher than their valuation recorded in the *Patent Roll* entry. A French document which cites a letter from Edward to Guillaume Blondel, Maitre des Requestes de l'Hotel du Roi de France, consenting to the transfer of the county from Guy to Enguerrand, and according him special power for the execution of the French writ that records the transfer, is dated June 6, 1367, from Senlis (*Lettres des Rois, Reines, et Autres Personnages* (Doc. inéd. sur l'Hist. de France, ed. Champollion-Figeac, Paris, 1847, 2. 173-74). It should, perhaps, be said for the reader's information that the transfer of the County of Soissons would have to originate in the Chancery of the French King, and that Edward's interest in it would be purely a financial one. The date of the French document informs us that the business of the transfer must have been in train in the early months of 1367.

53. *Cal. Pat. Rolls* 1364-67, p. 389.

54. *Cal. Pat. Rolls* 1367-70, p. 75, dated West. Jan. 8, 1368. Whether Coucy had departed by Jan. 8 is, of course, unknown. The writ simply authorized his departure.

probably the Château de Coucy. In April, as Froissart tells us,[55] Enguerrand and Isabella were in Paris to assist in the welcome which the French King gave to Isabella's brother Lionel, Duke of Clarence, on his wedding journey to Milan, a journey from which he never returned. Enguerrand certainly welcomed his brother-in-law in a dual capacity: as an English peer who had married the Princess Royal; as a French nobleman of ancient lineage, the trusted confidant of King Charles V. One wonders whether on that ceremonious occasion he wore his English Garter on his knee. In August he was probably *chez lui* at Coucy-le-Château, as we learn from a document printed by Duchesne.[56]

Sometime later than August, Enguerrand was off on what might be correctly called a business trip.[57]

His destination would seem to have been Prague, then the capital of the Emperor Charles IV. It is almost certain that his business was to lay before the Emperor a claim whose denial seems to have rankled. At least, if it did not rankle, it quite evidently possessed the power of moving him to vigorous action. From his mother, Catherine of Austria, Enguerrand had inherited in chief certain allodial lands situated in Switzerland and Alsace. These, his cousins, Al-

55. Ed. Kervyn, 7. 247.

56. A charter (August, 1368), exempting the inhabitants of "la terre et Barronie de Coucy" from "mortemain et de fourmariage"; A. DuChesne, *Histoire généalogique*, p. 415.

57. Coucy had started sometime between April and September 30, 1368, for a messenger was sent in haste to him by the French King, and the document recording that fact (dated Sept. 30) informs us that he was then in Germany (*Mand. de Charles V*, 236 No. 469). It is almost certain that he missed a personal interview with the Emperor who left Prague for Italy on April 2, 1368. He may have carried on his business with some authorized deputy, but information from the English rolls would indicate that he awaited the return of Charles IV (after midsummer 1369), for *Cal. Pat. Rolls* 1377-81, pp. 375-76 shows him to have been in Prague on Jan. 14, 1369, and V. H. Galbraith's ed. of the *Anonimalle Chron.* (Manchester, 1927, p. 71, citing *Mem. Roll. K. R.* 13R2) allows us to see that he was there in January, 1370.

bert and Leopold, dukes of Austria, were detaining.[58] Earlier representations as to his rights apparently remained unheeded, and Coucy eventually must have decided to force a show-down with his recalcitrant cousins. The motive for his journey to Prague was probably to lay his case before the Emperor and obtain, if not his assistance in the prosecution of his claim, at least his approbation of it, or his benevolent neutrality. Froissart informs us that Coucy had many times complained to the Emperor,[59] who recognized well enough that there was justice in his plea, but found it inconvenient to move in the matter "against those of Austria."[60] Lacaille tells us that Enguerrand's efforts went as far as the enrollment of troops and an advance into Alsace, but adds that further activity ceased when Charles V recalled him to France in November of the year. I surmise that the reason for the King's action was his feeling that France's relations with the English monarch seemed rapidly to be drifting to a state where war seemed inevitable.

58. See Lacaille, *Étude*, p. 84. For an explanation of how there came to be two dukes of Austria ruling at one time, see *Abrégé de la Vie d'Enguerrand VII du Nom, Sire de Couci, Memoires de Litt. de l'Acad. Royale des Inscriptions et Belles-Lettres* (Paris, 1759), 25. 168 ff. The *Abrégé* also makes it clear that Enguerrand's claim could only have extended to the allodial lands of his grandfather situated in Alsace, Switzerland, and Swabia. According to the *coutume du pays*, fiefs could be partitioned among males only, but females were allowed to inherit allodial lands, *i.e.*, lands possessed in hereditary propriety, upon which no feudal due could be charged. Coucy, then, claimed only "les biens mobiliers et allodiaux" which his maternal grandfather had possessed in *haute Alsace*, the Aargau, the Hegau, Turgovia, Austria, and Swabia; see Baron Zurlauben, "Abrégé de la Vie d'Enguerrand VII du Nom, Sire de Couci," *Bibliothèque Militaire, Historique et Politique* (Paris, 1760) 2. 183-235. The term *Abrégé* when used hereafter refers to this volume and not to the *Memoires de Litt. de l'Acad. Royale*, cited above.

59. Froissart (ed. Kervyn, 17. 422) speaks of a journey made to Prussia before his wedding, but he has possibly confused this journey with the later one here discussed. We have seen above that Coucy was occupied by business in France in the June preceding his wedding (July 27, 1365).

60. Duke Albert had married the Emperor's daughter; see Zurlauben, *Abrégé*, p. 246.

War between France and England, the native and the adopted country, would have proved most embarrassing to Coucy, as, indeed, it eventually did. It would raise the problem of the protection of his French lands and the safety of his vassals who dwelt upon them; would test severely the affection and loyalty of the Princess Isabella: was she to live in France or England, think and feel as her father's daughter, or as her husband's wife? And whatever decision he might have to take in the interest and for the welfare of his tenants and his wife, must necessitate a prior decision about his own conduct and ways of life. How far must he allow the welfare and safety of others to force upon him a course of conduct that as a free agent he would not follow? Should self-interest or obligation guide him in the choice he would have to make, and if the latter, what were his obligations? Were they those feudal bonds with which he had arrived in England, or those he had newly incurred there? Or was there a middle way that cut even between the right hand and the left, by which one might avoid offending either father-in-law or natural sovereign? But be the choice right, left, or middle, certain it was that by the outbreak of the war his career would be complicated, the tenor of his way disturbed.[61] By August, 1369, war had broken out; Lancaster's army was raiding Picardy. A decision, even though it were a decision not to take sides, was imperative for Enguerrand de Coucy. He was ready for the embarrassing situation, and believed that he had discovered a *via media* that would relieve him from the embarrassment of drawing his sword against Edward or Charles V, one that had also the further ad-

61. *Cal. Close Rolls* 1369-74, p. 61, writ dated Dec. 24, 1369, recording an order to Coucy to make preparations within the holdings he had upon the Welsh border, and elsewhere, against outbreak of war with France, gives an idea of the anomalous position in which hostilities would place him.

vantage of allowing him the chance to win the military prestige for which he must have yearned.[62]

Even before his brother-in-law's invasion of France, Enguerrand had left England. He was present at Ghent on June 19, 1369, at the marriage of Marguerite of Flanders to Philippe le Hardi, where, according to Froissart, his presence added much to the festivities.[63] Thence he proceeded to the court of his cousin, the Duke of Savoy, where or whence he is almost lost from sight.[64] A document dated September 13, 1372, allows us to learn that the Pope had instructed one of his cardinals to negotiate with Coucy with a view to securing his services in the war against Bernabo Visconti.[65] Into the campaigns waged by the Pope against his rebellious children, the Visconti, in that stormy and disturbed Italy, we have no call to enter. It is sufficient to say that the Pope's flattering letter of dismissal (January 23, 1374), issued in response to Enguerrand's request to be relieved, is eloquent witness that he had won not only the military reputation he so much desired, but also high estimation as a diplomat by those who were the best judges of diplomatic proficiency, the cardinals of the Papal Curia.[66]

62. Zurlauben, *Abrégé*, 241: "Enguerrand avoit marqué dès sa plus tendre jeunesse un desir extrême de se signaler à la guerre."

63. Ed. Kervyn, 7. 319-21.

64. Wherever he was, he had not forgotten his wife and English ties, for an entry in the *Issue Roll* of Thos. de Brantingham (ed. F. Devon, 1835, p. 493) of April 3, 1370, records payment of 2/o/o to John Tipet, King's valet, for his expenses, among which were the costs of going to Dover and returning thence to bring Havekin Barbour, valet of the Earl of Bedford, payment made by direction of the King, and by order of the chancellor, treasurer and council. Another entry (p. 407) of Dec. 4, 1370, records payment to Alan Joce, valet of the Earl of Bedford, "for carrying letters of the said Earl to the Lord the King" in aid of his expenses in going and returning.

65. See H. Lacaille, "Eng. de Coucy au service de Grégoire XI," *Ann. Bull. Soc. de la Hist. de France* 32. 189.

66. See *ibid.*, pp. 205-6. The Pope's letter would seem to have re-echoed some of the phraseology employed in the letter of Coucy which evoked it. It acknowledged that Coucy's affairs had long lacked his personal attention and that war had raged around and about his terri-

Arrived again upon his estates,[67] Enguerrand must have been gratified to find that very little, if any, damage had been done to them, though armies had marched, lances had been broken, and pillage carried on, north, south, east, and west of them.[68] Edward III seems never to have ceased striving to win over the son-in-law, who gave him freely respect, affection, gratitude, but never complete allegiance.[69] As we should expect, Enguerrand seems to have held aloof from state affairs in France, while war continued, though it is nc hazardous guess to assume that he did what he could tc dispose the warring monarchs and their councillors towards a peace. His wife, who had all to lose from war, and all tc gain from peace, may have been influential in winning over her father to agree, if not to peace, at least to a cessation of hostilities.[70] But, whether urged by the Sire and Dame de

tories, and admitted that he had long been absent from his wife and children. The statement of fact in the last sentence seems to me evidence sufficient against the supposition that there had been any quarrel or disagreement between Enguerrand and Isabella. There seems no evidence for believing that he had gone to Italy because he had tired of her. The reason that sent him off was obedience to the stock medieval injunction that one should avoid slothful inactivity by leading the life that led to honor. The Pope's letter now shows us that as late as Jan., 1374 (if no later), he was missing his wife and desirous of seeing her again.

67. I have not been able to find out where Enguerrand spent the time between his return and the truce of 1375. Froissart (ed. Kervyn, 8. 369) indicates that after his return he had been establishing closer relations with Charles V. If so, he probably abode in France. Isabella might or might not have returned to her father's Court when hostilities seemed imminent. Coucy found her eager to meet him and resident at Saint-Gobain, in his own territories.

68. Froissart, ed. Kervyn, 8. 20-21, also 17. 498, 544.

69. The pressure upon Coucy to change his allegiance must have been embarrassing and sustained. It had been too much apparently for the knight whom he had named governor of his lands during his absence in Italy, Thierri de Robertsart (called "le Chanoine de Robertsart"), who at the outbreak of hostilities "tourna englès" to Edward's delight (Froissart, ed. Kervyn, 7. 325, also 418). Edward's delight was doubtless heightened by the hope that the master would follow the example of the man.

70. A letter (Mar. 27, 1375) from Gregory XI to the Countess of Bedford, among other matters, begs her "pacemque inter Franciae et

Coucy or not, a truce was agreed upon on June 27, 1375.[71]

Upon the conclusion of the truce Enguerrand came promi-
nently into the public eye. We have noted his eagerness to
establish his claim to the allodial possessions belonging to his
mother in Alsace and Switzerland. Time and the hour
seemed to favor action in support of that claim. With the
cessation of war there was no need on the part of the English
or the French for the services of the free companies or mer-
cenary troops whom they had employed, and those companies
had been making their presence felt throughout France.
They were making, in Froissart's words, "too much of evil
in the kingdom of France." The obvious remedy was to get
rid of them, have someone lead them out of the country, as
Du Guesclin had led them into Spain in 1366, and such was
the remedy to which Charles V had resort. What better ex-
pedient could have been devised for getting them out than
to have Coucy enroll them and march them off to take what
he claimed with the strong hand? By obeying this behest of
his lawful sovereign, he would be serving France as well.
Nor could King Edward interpose any serious objection to
a plan on which his son-in-law seemed so set, and whose
successful outcome would enhance that son-in-law's reputation and increase his resources. Indeed, Edward's hand had
been called. The French King had loaned or given Coucy
60,000 francs for the expenses of the expedition,[72] which was
being launched almost entirely under French auspices. In
order to show his good will (he probably had no money to
spare), Edward allowed all his subjects who desired to go, to
enroll under Coucy's banner, and seems even to have sent
to the aid of his daughter's husband Thomas Holand II
Earl of Kent. But in the contest to win over his son-in-law,

Angliae reges promoveat"; see *Lettres Secrètes et Curiales du Pape Grég.
XI*, ed. Mirot et Jassemin.

71. See *Camb. Med. Hist.* 7. 365; Zurlauben, *Abrégé*, 254.

72. Froissart, ed. Kervyn, 8. 372.

as in many another contest in the wider fields of politics and diplomacy, the English King found that he had been out-manoeuvred by the crafty Charles V.

To narrate in detail Coucy's campaign in Switzerland is no part of the story of Enguerrand's English years,[73] and may be rapidly summarized: mustering his forces sometime after the conclusion of the truce of Bruges, by September 23 he was in Alsace.[74] Winter saw him in Switzerland with his marauding bands, and winter drove him out again. He had failed to capture by the strong hand all that he claimed; yet the vigor of his campaign had evidently scared his cousins into ceding to him the towns and seigniories of Buren and Ni-dau in the Argau. His invasion of Switzerland had not been the utter failure that historians of that country would like to make it.[75] Froissart tells us that before Easter (how long before is unknown) he was at the French court and in attendance upon the person of Charles V, and that after Easter he departed, "et madame sa femme et tout leur arroy," for England.[76] For Coucy it was the last time that he was to see

73. See the writer's "Eng. de Coucy and the Campaign of Nicopolis," *Speculum* 14. 428 ff.

74. A document addressed to Strasbourg, Colmar, and other imperial towns of Alsace bears that date. In it Enguerrand, ever tactful, calls himself Count of Soissons and Earl of Bedford, a graceful acknowledgment of his indebtedness to his father-in-law; see Zurlauben, *Abrégé*, 255, 258.

75. An agreement between Coucy and his Austrian relatives, by which he obtained possession of the towns and seigniories mentioned above was concluded Jan. 16, 1376 (Lacaille, *Étude*, p. 85).

76. Froissart, ed. Kervyn, 8. 378. "Et se tint en France dalés le roy . . . et tantost apriès Paskes il eut congiet dou roy de France d'aler jeuer en Engleterre et de y mener sa femme." My colleague, Professor J. Q. Stewart, informs me that in 1376 Easter fell on April 13 (O.S.). La-caille (*Étude*, p. 85), says that numerous bands of the survivors of Coucy's army re-entered France, and that Coucy and other lords put themselves into their pursuit (Feb.-May). It is possible that Coucy did not leave France immediately, "apriès Paskes," but later in the spring. A historian like Froissart, who paints on a broad canvas, is not to be reproached because he fails of legal accuracy in minor details. There is also the possibility that Lacaille may be wrong.

the country of his adoption where he had passed so many happy hours.

The final visit of 1376 forms the fifth act of this drama of divided loyalties, of personality alternately disguised by an English or a French mask. It is brief, but like most fifth acts, the most stirring and arresting of the whole play. When the curtain falls upon it, the culmination of the story of Enguerrand's English years, we are thrilled, recognize its inevitability, yet, like all good playgoers, wonder whether, with another character as its protagonist, it would have ended differently.

V

The reader who has patiently followed the fortunes of the Sire de Coucy in England and out of it, cannot fail to have noticed his growing intimacy with his own monarch, the French King. Upon his return from Italy, Charles V "was induced, by the fame of his achievements, to offer him the *bâton* of a marshal of France, if he would join the French standards," but his scruples about the duality of his position made him decline it.[77] We have seen that the French exchequer financed his expedition to Switzerland, and that, though he had done his country and monarch a good turn by marching off with the companies, yet when all had been done, the benefits he had received were greater than those conferred. Upon his return from Switzerland he had gone to the French court, and almost certainly must have been made aware by Charles V and his intimate advisers of their fear that hostilities would recommence at the expiration of the truce signed a little less than a year past—whose time had almost run out. He would also have realized that honor and duty would eventually force him to declare openly his intention of fulfilling in the most complete and active way his obligations as a vassal of the French King. From what we

77. Mrs. Green, *Princesses of England*, 3. 211.

know of his character, we can believe that he would reach a decision, albeit regretfully, of his own mind, uninfluenced by threats or bribes, however politely conveyed or alluringly veiled. At all events, he must have had a perfect understanding with the King, and was in no doubt what to do if war should come.[78]

Enguerrand and Isabella left France casually, as though bent on nothing more than an extended visit to the court of their widowed parent.[79] Yet Enguerrand carried with him an informal request from the French that the English king and his council would inform them how and upon what terms "one might find peace and accord between them and us." Charles V justified his right to the title of "Le Sage" when he chose Enguerrand as his "unofficial" emissary to the English king. Both Enguerrand and Isabella had a definite interest in the desire of the French King and his ministers for the maintenance of peace, and with Edward both could do much. Their influence might succeed in inducing him or Gaunt to lend a less willing ear to the clamors of the war-party then so vociferous in Court and Parliament. It is not an unlikely surmise (though only a surmise) to believe that as a last resort Enguerrand was resolved to play his trump card, and announce his determination, so regretfully arrived at, to devote his last services to the monarch who had received his earliest vows.

Long perusal of the public records only proves what one would naturally infer, that Coucy was welcome in England, or that at least the English wanted him to feel that he was.

78. Froissart, ed. Kervyn, 8. 378: "eut adonques aucuns trettiés secrès entre lui et le roy de France, qui ne furent mies si tost ouvert." See also, p. 380: "li sires de Coucy . . . se commença-il à ordonner et estre tout françois . . . car il estoit françois de nom, d'armes, de sang, et d'extraction."

79. Froissart, ed. Kervyn, 8. 376-79: "il eut congist dou roy de France d'aler jeuer en Engleterre . . . dalés le roy son signeur [Edward III], qui li fist bonne chière et à sa fille ossi." Queen Philippa had died Aug. 15, 1369.

If anything is certain about the years he spent there, it is the constant and persistent efforts of the King to win him, and the King's example must have been noted and followed by courtier, minstrel, and poet. It is certain that Edward and his advisers lent a receptive ear to what he told them of the desire of Charles V for peace, and it seems just as certain that, diplomats as they were, they perceived that it was by peace, and peace alone, that they could retain the Earl of Bedford as an ally of the English King. It was probably quite unnecessary for Enguerrand to play, or even to display, his trump card. His friendly opponents knew that he had it and that, whatever they might gain by war, they would certainly lose him.

Speculation about the true inwardness of historical facts is always dangerous. But I do not think it a dangerous surmise to suppose that Coucy's unofficial and informal pourparlers and pleas had the effect of prolonging discussion and postponing hostilities. The truce agreed upon on June 27, 1375, lapsed on June 27, 1376. Enguerrand de Coucy was in England before May 12, 1376.[80] June 27, 1376, came and went; discussion still continued, and envoys wrangled on, at Bruges, Montreuil-sur-Mere, and Boulogne, until the summer of 1377.

Issue and *Patent Rolls* for 1376 and 1377 give details that make one speculate about Coucy's aims and intentions in the matter of his English lands and protégés, and Edward's aims and intentions towards him.

Issue Rolls show that grants made to him and his wife in previous years were being paid to them or their agents in

---

80. He was personally present at the drawing up of an order dated May 12, Westminster directing the royal escheator in Essex to take action (the actions directed not germane to our discussion); see *Cal. Close Rolls* 1374-1377, p. 379. A privy seal order (April 4) informs us that robes were prepared for Coucy against the Garter celebration (April 23) of 1376; see G. Beltz, *Memorials of the Order of the Garter* (London, 1841), p. 10.

1376, even after he had left England for the last time.[81] *Patent Rolls* show for the years 1376-77 a number of cases of *"Inspeximus* and *Confirmation"* of previous grants made by Coucy and authorized by Edward for payment by his own exchequer.[82] Why so many of these confront us in the last days of Enguerrand's sojourn we do not know, but we can guess pretty safely that they are down on parchment because authority either knew or feared that the Sire de Coucy would go for good. They confirm grants previously made of small sums of money to faithful servants. Either one of two reasons could explain them. Edward III may have been endeavoring to show his son-in-law that all his wishes and requests, even the slightest, would be satisfied and granted if he would "remain an Englishman." Or Coucy, resolved on resigning his English possessions and severing the bonds which bound him to the island kingdom, was, in generous and thoughtful manner, asking his father-in-law to reward English retainers who had served his interests well. Such an action would have been thoroughly true to the generous and gracious nature that all men, high and low alike, praised in him.

If the entries in the *Patent Rolls* are Enguerrand's "farewells" to servants and retainers, those to the members of the royal family were, so Froissart tells us, of a more ceremonious nature. He declares that Enguerrand paid farewell visits to the Black Prince then lying gravely ill in London,[83] to John of Gaunt, Edmund, Earl of Cambridge, and Thomas

---

81. The money due him at Michaelmas on the original grant of 1000 mks. made in 1366 was paid, probably to his wife, after he is known to have departed from England for good; see E403/460/E3.

82. *Cal. Pat. Rolls* 1374-1377. For cases in 1376, see p. 396; for those in the following year, pp. 429, 430, 476-77.

83. The Black Prince died July 8, 1376. Coucy was, therefore, not in England after July. *Cal. Pat. Rolls* 1374-77, p. 301, records payment (July 25, 1376) of money advanced by an Italian (?), Gilbert Aymeryk, to Coucy and Isabella. It must have been paid to his wife or to an agent, since he was no longer in the realm.

of Gloucester, to the young prince Richard and his tutor, Sir Guichard d'Angle. In brief, as Froissart says, "il prist congiet à tous et à toutes," and leaving behind him his wife and younger daughter, "puis s'en retourna en France."[84] Had he veiled his intention of espousing the cause of his own sovereign, he would not have taken such a ceremonious farewell.

Farewells said, and England left behind, it would be only natural to suppose that Coucy would return and report to his sovereign the results of his English mission. This he seems to have done. The King, quite correctly, judged that he could add no better qualified or abler member to the commission that was wrangling away with an English commission at Bruges. I have previously declared that I believe Coucy to have had a good deal to do with the decision of both governments to continue discussions after the date of the expiration of the truce (June 27.) But whether this belief be correct or not, negotiations were resumed in November, and continued, according to Froissart, "tout l'iver."[85]

While negotiations dragged on, we catch occasional glimpses of Enguerrand. On February 27, 1377, there is a record of letters of safe-conduct granted to Jean Cauchon to

84. Froissart, ed. Kervyn, 8. 379. Mrs. Green (3. 216) gives an account of events somewhat different from that of Froissart. She does not mention Coucy's being charged with any mission of peace to England, and believes that Isabella did not accompany her husband when he set out upon it, but had left France before him. According to her, Isabella was asked by him to exert "her gentle influence" to reconcile the king "to this change of policy" on his part. She adds that "in this delicate point she appears to have been successful."

85. Froissart, ed. Kervyn, 8. 380. C. Cosneau (*Les Grandes Traités de la Guerre de Cent Ans*, Paris, 1889, pp. 69-70) declares that negotiations went on at Bruges, Nov., 1375, at Montreuil-sur-Mer, and at Boulogne, Dec., 1376. As a result of them the truce was prorogued successively to April 1, then to May 1, finally to June 24, 1377. Meetings may not have been continuous during the fall session of 1376, or Coucy may have been only an intermittent attendant, for Delisle (*Mand. de Charles V*, p. 662, no. 1276A) prints a letter dated Nov. 11, 1376, written by Charles V in his own hand, requesting the Countess of Artois to receive the Duke of Burgundy and Sire de Coucy as emissaries specially charged to make known his will.

proceed *versus dilectum filium Regis Comitem Bedeford, in negotiis ipsius Comitis,* with two valets, three horses, and six greyhounds *in comitiva sua,* and the harness for them, to tarry with the Earl, and then to return before June 1.[86] Cauchon, it is a good guess, was sent over with letters in the endeavor to induce Coucy to change his mind, and he may also have brought routine papers for Coucy, as an English magnate, to disapprove or seal. Perhaps such letters or papers might recall ties and obligations in the land he had left,[87] and incline his mind towards rejoining his wife. Other confidential messengers followed hard upon the heels of Jean Cauchon. The *Patent Rolls* by an entry of April 12, 1377, West. inform us that a safe-conduct was granted Jean Potier, *servientum et nuncium Isabellae filiae Regis* . . . "for certain urgent matters touching the daughter of the King aforesaid"; and by another entry of June 19, 1377, West. that similar grant had been made to Enguerrand's attorneys,

86. Quoted by Mrs. Green, 3. 216 (Append. VI) from the *French Roll* (51E3.m.6). Mrs. Green reads the name of the grantee as "Cauchoiz." A later entry as "Cauchon" in the same roll, with the addition of *clerico,* and mention of a John Cauchon as Isabella's chaplain in the *Cal. of Pat. Rolls* 1374-77, p. 252, establish his identity. He was a Frenchman who, unlike his master, elected to remain in the household of the Countess at the outbreak of war (*Cal. Pat. Rolls* 1377-81, pp. 8, 12; see also John of Gaunt's *Register* 1379-83, Camden Soc. 1. 117.) He held the livings of Thornton (Yks.) and Warton (Lancs.). In all probability he carried letters from Edward and Isabella to the obstinate Enguerrand, and may have been instructed to file his own tongue to persuasive speech. The two couples of greyhounds (generally leashed in threes) may have been two of his own that the Earl wished brought to him, but the phrase *harnesis suis* leads to the belief that they were a present from the King. If Cauchon returned by June 1, he tarried not long in England, for *French Roll* (*Cat. des Rolles Français* 2. 120, Rot. F. 51E3.m.1) shows that he had another safe-conduct granted June 19. West. *eundo versus partes Franciae in negotiis Ingelrami de Coucy . . . et uxoris filiae Regis.* It is not an unreasonable surmise to suppose that the letters he carried on this second visit were of the same tenor as the previous ones, and that he himself may have had to repeat before Coucy the same arguments or pleas.

87. One grant by letters patent was actually sealed by Coucy in Paris on Mar. 25, 1377; see *Cal. Pat. Rolls* 1374-77, pp. 476-77.

Boniface Morice and James de Parmes, *in negotiis ipsorum Comitis et Isabellae.*[88]

But the negotiations in whose prolongation Coucy had been so influential (if my belief be correct) were nearing their inevitable, as well as their legal, end. Presumably both sides had been talked out by June 24, and after that date war would be the *ultima ratio regum.* Could it still be averted? Where tempers are frayed and differences many, chance happenings tip the scale towards the more rigorous or violent solution. On June 21, 1377, three days before the expiration of the truce, Edward III died. Within two years England had lost her only competent military leaders, and a child of ten sat on the throne. Charles V saw that his chances were good, and that it was time to strike. He declared war.

The die had been cast, and Coucy's role was plain. He would, as his lord's liege vassal, draw his sword against his nephew and his wife's brethren. We of today cannot know whether he had talked over all the contingencies of this bitter quandary previously with his wife. It seems unbelievable that he did not do so. Possibly Isabella had not sensed the firmness of his purpose. Had she realized it, she would hardly have sought and received permission from the new sovereign to journey beyond the seas.[89] Apparently she was bent on making one last effort to preserve her husband and her home.

But her efforts were unavailing, and she returned to her

88. Printed in Mrs. Green, 3. 216 (Append. VI). Dates of entry on the roll do not necessarily indicate dates of departure. The date of the last entry is two days before the death of Edward III. It is not an entirely unwarrantable assumption to suppose that the old King, up to the very end of his life, was earnestly trying to help his daughter hold her husband.

89. A royal order (dated June 26, 1377) to the Earl of Cambridge, Constable of Dover and Warden of Cinque Ports, to permit Isabella and her *ménage* to sail from "one of the said ports," is printed in *Foedera* (1728) 7. 153.

native country. All the difficulties that arose from Enguerrand's possession of English lands and revenues, all the embarrassment caused to him and to his fellow-companions by
his membership in the Order of the Garter, were removed by
the beautifully worded letter in which he returned to Richard II all that he held from him in faith or homage, and
begged that another might sit in his Garter stall. Five hundred and sixty years later, almost to the day of its penning,
the writer stood beside the glazed lectern beneath which that
letter was exhibited in the Museum of the Public Record
Office. A little faded, but still perfectly legible, it reads
escript le XXVI jour d'Aoust, and carries in a state of perfect preservation the pendant seal displaying the arms then
used by the Sire de Coucy. One wonders what emotions lay
behind its graceful, yet formal, phrasing.[90]

VI

If there is anything remarkable or strange in the life of
Enguerrand de Coucy it is the separation from his wife at
the outbreak of hostilities in 1377. I suppose we shall never
know why husband and wife who had, to all appearances,
made a love match, seem, after the passage of twelve years,
to have agreed (?) that each should remain on the other
side of the English Channel—permanently, or until the warfare between their respective nations had ceased. If human
experience has value, it is certain that a devoted and loving
woman follows her lord wherever he may go. If the Princess
Isabella were a devoted and loving wife, why did she not do
so? Such separation between lord and dame smacks, to all
outward seeming, of *opéra bouffe*. One might suppose it
another example of that crack-brained quixotism, or that
hyper-emotional loyalty, so rife in the days of chivalry, unless there lay behind it reasons of a deep personal or private
nature.

90. For a transcription, see Appendix L, below.

To one writer the separation is to be accounted for by just such reasons. Miss B. C. Hardy asserts that Coucy's action was the result of "his wife's conduct and all but impossible temper."[91] She believes that disparity of age might have had something to do with the parting, but goes on to surmise that "her selfish, vain and overbearing character" had not been "materially altered by marriage." These are heavy charges, if true. Are they warranted by the evidence that can be culled from contemporary documents?

The answer to that question is a decided negative. Evidence that throws light upon the bearing, moods, or idiosyncrasies of historic personages who played their hour on the stage of medieval English or French history is hard to come by. Biographers like Joinville are few and far between. But it can quite safely be said that on the basis of accessible evidence there is no ground whatever for believing that Isabella possessed or displayed such unfortunate and unpleasant traits.

Mrs. Green calls our attention to the princess' "propensity to extravagance," but the charge seems not serious enough to cause the Earl and the Countess of Bedford to bid one another a final farewell. *Issue Rolls* and *Wardrobe Accounts* might indeed support a charge that Isabella was extravagant, but generosity or "largesse" was counted as a virtue in the society in which she moved. If she received much, she probably also gave away much, and ranked the higher in popular estimation for doing so.[92] I know of no records to show that she received grants of money from her husband's exchequer, though it is possible that they exist in

91. *Philippa of Hainault*, p. 309. If by the phrase, "his wife's conduct," Miss Hardy would have us believe that Isabella was unfaithful to her husband, there is no evidence that I have been able to find that warrants such an assumption.

92. It seems unnecessary to warn the student against drawing deductions from the fact that Isabella might appear as a recipient a number of times on an annual issue roll. Most of the entries would simply record installments of money due from grants previously made to her.

French archives. English exchequer and chancery records show Coucy only as a recipient, and never as a donor who drew on his own revenues. When he rewarded English retainers, it was with money drawn from his father-in-law's exchequer. Both in England and in France he was praised for his generosity. If Isabella had an extravagant household, her husband's presence did not make it less so. That she was an extravagant wife to her husband remains to be proved.

Thus the charges against the Princess fall to the ground. Since her husband's conduct has not been blamed or censured by historians of his own or later times, we have still to seek for a reason why they went their separate ways. Let us look, then, at the facts of the parting—they are few—and strive to make out of them what fairly and honestly we can.

VII

We have seen that Isabella's journey ended unsuccessfully. How long she tarried at Saint-Gobain or at the Châteu de Coucy, what arguments or entreaties she used, whether there were scenes of a distressing nature, how and in what circumstances they parted, these things we know not. Isabella was back with her dolorous news before the end of August.[93] Official records enable us to catch a glimpse of Isabella, though a very fleeting one. By a writ dated November 5, 1377, West. all Coucy's lands and holdings, and all those of his lady as well, and all property or possessions which he may have had, or left, in England, were seized by the royal officers.[94] The effect of this seizure would eventually have reduced the Countess of Bedford to penury, may

93. *Cal. Fine Rolls* 9. 11, contains an order dated August 30, 1377, West. to the escheators of Yks. and Westmoreland to take over the lands occupied by Joan Coupland (with reversion to Coucy and then to the King). It will be remembered that Coucy's letter of renunciation is dated Aug. 26. See also *Pat. Rolls* 1377-81, p. 22, Sept. 10, 1377, Chiltern Langley, for appointment of Bishop Courtenay of London and three others as custodians of those same lands.
94. *Cal. Fine Rolls* 9. 31.

even at the moment have straitened her somewhat.[95] To prevent such a catastrophe, Isabella petitioned her nephew that manors, rents, castles, farms, etc., belonging to her husband and now in the king's hands, be given over to her. In it she speaks of herself as a daughter of Edward III, "vostre ael [aieul]" and as the king's "povre cousyn," and points out that she was alone: "ele feust sole come son seigneur et mary le sire de Coucy" was away.[96] There is some danger of drawing from the formalized language of an official document deductions that do not describe accurately personal situations or feelings. Isabella's clerks would put into the petition, we may be sure, whatever would tell most in her favor and incline her nephew's ear towards her plea. The legal term *femme sole*, as opposed to *femme coverte*, describes a woman who could hold property in her own right, and her claim to be in exactly that situation was what they wished to establish.[97] But we should note that they were careful to level

95. It is difficult to believe that between Aug. 30, and the end of the year 1377, she could have been in any dire need. Still "need" is a relative term, meaning one thing to commoners like us, and another to a princess. The officers of her receipt certainly recognized the meaning of the royal actions, and doubtless had their mistress present the petition we are about to discuss.

96. *Ancient Petitions* 9/95/4710. I neglected to copy the day and month of this petition from the vellum strip on which it is written. It is quite safe to say that it was presented after Aug. 30 and before Nov. 27, 1377, the date when it was answered. One would be on less certain ground in narrowing down the interval, but the attempt to do so is worth while. As we have seen above, on Nov. 5 all lands and goods belonging to the Earl and Countess, and all the Earl's personal possessions, were seized into the royal hands, so that it is quite probable that the Countess' petition was presented between the 5th and 27th of November. Yet one must remember that the order to the Yks. and Westmor. escheators dated Aug. 30 may have appeared to Isabella's clerks a handwriting upon the wall, and prompted them to get their petition ready soon after its promulgation.

97. After their marriage, nearly all grants of money or lands made to the Earl and Countess were made out to "Ingelram and Isabella." Isabella could not legally receive the returns from their estates until her new status had been formerly and legally recognized. Her plea that she was "alone" brought that new status to the attention of the legal and fiscal officers, and probably is one of the reasons why she offered it. Yet had there been any matrimonial quarrel, the petition could have been easily written up in a

no charge against the absent Earl, and the entire absence of any uncomplimentary reference to her husband's behavior in English official documents or literary productions, implies —and implies strongly—that the princess would not have had it otherwise. It is not reading too much into the petition to believe that its failure to mention that the Earl had cut finally his connections with England, implied that the petitioner at least had not given up hope of his eventual return on some happier day. In short, I see almost no evidence whatever for believing that Isabella had not loved her husband, or that she did not love him after they had parted. The belief that her temperament or expensive habits were responsible for the separation rests, as we have seen, solely on inference or suspicion; the charge that her affection for her husband had grown cold rests on no firmer basis.

Indeed, the initiative in the matter of separation would appear to have been Coucy's. His resolve to remain what he had been—a true Frenchman—must have brought to an end a situation which had forced his wife to pass many anxious hours. But not only does the resolution appear to have been his; his also seem the steps that converted it into fact.

How the parting was effected or under what circumstances it took place is not quite clear. One manuscript of Froissart tells us that Enguerrand sent his wife back to her native land, and this is the account that most subsequent historians have followed. Another, however, tells us a story that seems less brusque and more creditable to Enguerrand's sense of tact, according to which Isabella remained in England, with her younger daughter, as her lord left it for the last time.[98]

---

very different way. Coucy could have been described as a rebel and a traitor, who had adhered to the adversary of France. It is worthy of remark that, instead, he is described as "being away"; with naught said about the unlikelihood or impossibility (?) of his return.

98. Both in Froissart, ed. Kervyn, vol. 8. The first version, p. 380; the second, p. 379.

We have seen that, as far as the meagre evidence carries, the blame (if blame there be) for what happened rests
not upon Isabella but upon her husband. The question, then,
arises: How far are his actions ascertainable, understandable,
or pardonable?

Some motives ascribed for his action are by no means
creditable to him. Their reality is questionable, however,
since they have been advanced by Duchesne, the seventeenth-
century historian of the House of Coucy and some of his
successors. Duchesne's words are quite charming in their
naïveté: "having seen that his majesty (Charles V) loved
him and was favourable to his interests, he resolved to remain
thenceforward a good Frenchman. For this reason he sent
back his wife Isabella to England, where she died later."[99]
Dom Toussaints du Plessis tells us that Enguerrand swore
complete fidelity to his prince, and to give unequivocal proof
of that fidelity, "il renvoia en Angleterre la princesse Isabeau
sa femme."[100] To believe that the Sire de Coucy, in order to
gain the favor or allay the suspicions of administrative Jacks-
in-Office, would have been willing to dishonor his wife, in
so public a fashion, as these historians have twisted poor
Froissart into implying—to believe this, I say, is flying in the
face both of likelihood and of fact.

Enguerrand de Coucy's reputation for courtesy, tact, and
honor stood too high among his contemporaries for us to be-

99. A. Duchesne, *Histoire Généalogique*, p. 267: "ayant recognu que
sa Majesté l'aimoit, & fauorisoit ses affaires, il resolut de demeurer de
là en auant bon François. A cet effet il renvoya son espouse Ysabeau en
Angleterre, où elle mourut depuis."

100. *Hist. de Coucy* (Paris 1728), p. 87. Two later historians go on
to the same effect. M. Melleville (*Hist. de la Ville et des Sires de Coucy*,
Laon, 1848, pp. 109-10), informs us, with complete solemnity, that as a
pledge of the sincerity of his oath, he did not remain content with returning to the successor of Edward III the insignia of the Garter, but *sent back
his wife as well* (italics mine)! No less delightful is the wording of the
Chevalier de l'Epinois, *Hist. de Ville et de Sires de Coucy* (Coucy-aux-
Ruines, n.d., p. 179): "afin de donner . . . une preuve éclatante de sa
fidélité, il renvoie . . . la princesse Ysabeau, sa femme."

lieve that he would have treated any high-born dame, least of all his own consort, in so sordid a fashion. Furthermore, had he done so, we can be quite sure that some of the events of his later career would never have shaped themselves as they did. As a French commissioner he would never have been *persona grata* to the English in the negotiations of 1380, 1381, and 1382,[101] and we may be quite sure that he was appointed to these several French peace delegations, not only because he was a skillful negotiator, but also because his former countrymen saw him gladly, knowing that nowhere else was there a Frenchman so familiar with their aims and so favorably inclined towards them. Nor would his second wife, Isabella of Lorraine, have been chosen as an attendant upon Isabella of France when she travelled to England as the fiancée of Richard II.[102]

Were you and I, reader, to pick up these ravelled skeins which history has left us, and try to weave them again into the garment that clothed human feeling in the fourteenth century, we should certainly shape it into one of more sober color and less extreme form. For the actions of this husband and this wife can, perhaps, be placed in a more understandable light without resort to scandal or a low view of human nature. Both were so splendidly alive in their day that it seems something less than fair to surrender them after death to the psychiatrist.

It requires no particularly keen sensitivity to imagine with what feelings the Sire and Lady de Coucy saw the war cloud that had always lurked on the rim of the horizon grow greater until it threatened to blot out the brightness of their life. We have seen that Enguerrand de Coucy had striven

101. *Cat. des Rolles Français* II. 131 gives (*anno* 3 R 2), "salvus cond. ambassatoribus Franciae, vid . . . Ingueram Sire de Coucy." Two other safe-conducts (*Anno* 4 and *Anno* 6 R 2) to French embassies (Coucy being a member) are printed on p. 137.

102. See *Chron. de Traison et Mort de Richart Deux*, ed. B. Williams, (London, 1846), p. 165, note 1; see also Mrs. Green 3. 228, note 1.

his utmost to avert it by influencing the several conferences which he attended to discuss and explore each and every possibility of peace as long as any possibility remained—and that the later conferences had continued their discussion and exploration even after the final possibility had gone glimmering.[103]

And when war came, what a future lay before husband and wife! Perhaps, had Isabella been of lower rank, they might have "carried it off." But she had been reared in her father's Court, the very central point of anti-French feeling. The proclamation of her father's claim to the French throne, his institution of the Order of the Garter, his quartering of the French fleur-de-lis with his own leopards, all these were her background, part of the predispositions and judgments on which she had grown up. To change them, to force herself to think in new ways because she had gotten a new name, would have been impossible; nor was the princess one who would seek to make the effort. Had she tarried in France, only loneliness and sorrow of spirit would have been her lot. It seems quite likely that her husband saw, if she did not, what her future would have been, and insisted in kindly fashion that she return to the life she knew, in which familiar events and faces could occupy hours that else would have been empty in his absence. No doubt he believed the hostilities would be of no long duration, or interrupted by long periods of truce. His own campaigns in Italy and Switzerland had not been long-drawn-out affairs. Time would restore the loved one from whom it was now parting him.

Some such explanation as this just given seems more in conformity with what we know of the Sire and Lady de Coucy, and of the political situation that existed when they

103. The attempts of Coucy to prevent war are themselves evidence that tends to clear him (and his wife also) of scandalous or selfish motives for separation. In their discussion of what prompted the break, historians hitherto have overlooked this point.

parted. If it were thus with them, then the decisions they made in their perplexities seem not so much quixotic or bizarre, as endeavors to reconcile the claims of duty with those of desire, attempts to choose wisely and well in that conflict between impulse and obligation, between one's duty as parent and husband, and one's duty to the state. Yet however reasonable this interpretation may appear, it is supported only by circumstantial evidence, not by fact. Why the Earl and Countess of Bedford parted we can guess at or infer, but we cannot know. Whatever the reason, part they did —as chance would have it never to meet again.[104]

104. The subsequent career of the Countess of Bedford can be briefly told. We have already seen that her finances had been affected by her husband's departure, and have commented upon the petition she laid before her nephew's council, begging for more generous treatment. It was answered favorably, and all manors, hamlets, honors, domains, towns, lands, tenements, which she and her lord had formerly held, were delivered into the hands of the Archbishop of York, the Bishops of London and Salisbury, and four other commissioners, to appropriate the entire revenues of them to her use "quod, quamdiu ipsa, infra dictum regnum nostrum Angliae moretur" (grant printed in full by Mrs. Green 3. 443-49, Append. VII; see also *Cal. Pat. Rolls* 1377-81, p. 174). The council's reply makes it explicitly clear that should the Countess rejoin her husband; or be persuaded or compelled by him to leave the kingdom; or send out of it to him any part of that revenue; or meet him in Richard's domain in France without permission; she would lose the income paid her. How far one is justified in seeking to discover intention behind the generalized and impersonalized jargon of the law is dubious, but Mrs. Green (3. 219-20), a careful student, believes it possible that whoever directed the drafting of the document knew of Isabella's "tenacious affection" for her husband.

I agree with Mrs. Green that the express stipulation that the Countess reside in England is evidence that the separation was the result of the difficult political situation, and that husband and wife never ceased to care for each other. It is noteworthy that the Countess continued to impale her husband's arms after the separation (see F. Sanford, *Genealogical Hist. of the Kings of England*, London, 1677, p. 178).

Documents that might inform us more precisely of the financial situation of the Countess are lacking at the present time. It would be interesting to know what money adjustments the parting necessitated. Coucy, by his renunciation of fealty, would have lost every penny of income he received from English sources, though I have the suspicion that he turned over his English revenues to his wife to spend. As far as I can ascertain, he never seems to have paid her any income from his French lands: in July, 1376, when she was in France, her half-yearly income was sent over to her

VIII

The reader of *Sir Gawain* will remember that the hero of the romance set off from Camelot in obedience to his solemn pledge to the terrible Green Knight that he would seek him out at the Green Chapel on New Year's day. This is his first and greatest obligation, to which all others must yield; failure to keep this promise would give to all men the right to call him "recreaunt."

The Green Knight had, one will remember, given him no road-map to the Green Chapel, and Gawain blundered over England and West Wales in search of it. Eventually he found a splendid castle and a most hospitable host within it. The lord and his wife, a very lovely young lady, enter-

husband for her support (Mrs. Green 3. 216, note 1). He did, however, defray the expenses for the maintenance and education of his elder daughter, Mary, whom he kept with him as his heiress, for payments for her support are not found in English documents. By provision of her father's will Isabella did receive 300 mks. per annum for her own support and that of her daughter Philippa from the estates of her prospective son-in-law, the Earl of Oxford, while he was her ward (Mrs. Green 3. 220). That income she doubtless received regularly, since the Earl did not attain his majority until 1382, several years after her death (H. Wallon, *Richard II*, Paris, 1864, 1. 252-3). 300 mks. from Oxford's estates plus the much larger sums paid out to her by the trustees appointed by Richard II was presumably her total annual income. It was evidently deemed sufficient for proper maintenance of herself and her daughter.

The final record of her that we have (April, 1379) is that of the delivery to her of Garter robes, probably in anticipation of the annual assembly of the Order at Windsor on St. George's Day, April 23 (see G. E. Cockayne, *Complete Peerage* 2, Append. B. Isabella seems to have received robes of the Garter continuously through 1376-79). Whether she went to the festival we know not; she might have been ill at the time. All that we do know is that before May 4, 1379 she was dead (Mrs. Green 3. 220-1). Speculation or surmise that is not based upon fact or trustworthy report is dangerous, and on the cause of Isabella's death we have neither fact nor report, but it does not seem to be stretching one's fancy too far to believe that separation from the only man she seems ever to have loved was the chief cause that brought her to—and through—death's door.

For a discussion of the situation of Philippa, Countess of Oxford, younger daughter of the Sire and Lady de Coucy, and heiress of their English lands, and the possibility of a connection between her and the writing of *Sir Gawain*, see Appendix F, "Philippa Countess of Oxford," below.

tained lavishly over Christmas, and in the society of this aristocratic pair and their guests, Gawain thoroughly enjoyed himself. His enjoyment was all the keener because he learned from his host that the Green Chapel was not two miles distant, and that a guide would bring him to it early on New Year's morn.

But the holidays were over, the guests were to depart, and the lord advised Gawain to sleep late into the mornings that remained before New Year's. He, for his part, would rise early and go hunting; and he made an agreement with his guest to give him what he gained in the hunting field in return for what Gawain could manage to pick up within the castle during his absence. The bargain was sealed by a draught of wine.

On December 29 the lord sallied out early to hunt, and Gawain found his early morning hours enlivened by a visit from his hostess, who appeared in négligée and was in a sportive mood. However, no harm resulted, and on her lord's return with the *curée* of venison, which was Gawain's by right, the hero duly delivered one kiss, which was all he had acquired during the day. Where he got it, he told his host, was none of his host's business. Next day's happenings repeat almost exactly those of the previous day. Gawain accepted his host's winnings and bestowed two kisses as his own. But on the third day matters ran very differently. Gawain found the lady most embarrassingly importunate, and had need to summon back to his memory all the obligations which he owed—to his formidable opponent of one year ago, to his host, and to his own good name and self-respect, in order to resist her solicitations. When she found that he was adamant, she sighed and said that since he had naught to give her, she would give something to him.

She offered him a costly ring, with a self-illuminated stone in the center of it. But he would have none of it. Re-

marking that he evidently held her at little worth, she proffered a less costly present. Loosing a bright green lace from
about her kirtle, she presented it to him, begging him to
accept it for her sake. He refused it, as he had refused the
ring she had first proffered to him. Then she added that he
must not despise it for its simplicity, for anyone who wore it
would be safe from any blow of any kind of weapon. He
hesitated, thinking how useful it would prove next day. Finally he allowed her to press it upon him, promising never
to reveal it to her lord.

At first, I believe, he was hardly aware of what he had
done. He had yielded, as politeness demanded, to a lady
and had promised secrecy on her behalf. In his position none
would or could have done otherwise. Still he had hardly
acted on unmixed motives: fear for his own life, as much as
politeness, had made him accept something that he knew
he should find useful. Yet the incident had been brief and
trivial, and was so far forgotten that, shortly afterward,
when he approached a priest for confession, he seems to have
forgotten all about it. When his host returned he paid duly
the three kisses the lady had given him, but did not hand
over the belt. His promise to the lady had been allowed to
cancel out his earlier one to her lord.

On New Year's morn, after having carefully bound the
green lace over his red garment, he and his guide were off to
the Green Chapel. There he had expected to lose his head;
instead, he came out safe and sound—save for a small wound
in the neck.

But that small wound bulked large in Gawain's mind.
He had received it because he had broken his plighted word.
He had sworn to keep faith with his host, and then, to pro-
tect a lady, had broken his promise. Yet his sin had its ex-
tenuating circumstances, one might almost say its reason.
One could not "tell" on a lady who had put herself in one's

confidence. The Green Knight did not and could not hold
Gawain to blame, for he had been all the while aware of the
embarrassing plight into which the actions of his wife had
placed his guest. The truly honorable and conscientious
blame themselves far more deeply than any critic can. Sir
Gawain was so distressed and shamed that on his return to
Arthur's Court, the lords and ladies therein instituted a new
order of chivalry, that of the green lace, to keep its unwilling founder from becoming too downcast over the outcome
of his adventure—or misadventure.

IX

At first glance there is a certain general similarity between
the cases of the lord of Coucy and the hero of the romance.
The one journeyed to another country to fulfill a feudal
obligation, his oath to remain a hostage to the English king;
the other did the same in order to keep his pledge to appear
in the Green Knight's territory. In each case a lady was the
cause (in Coucy's case possibly only an indirect cause) of the
violation of a second obligation—by Coucy in his acceptance
of English fiefs and the garter of the famous English order
of that name, at the very moment that he still professed his
French allegiance; by Sir Gawain in his refusal to hand to
his host the green lace given him by his hostess. Furthermore, an identical situation faced both the historical hero and
him of fiction: their return to their native place was celebrated by the foundation of an order of chivalry, of which
matter, in the case of Coucy, more anon. Yet this general
similarity we have been speaking about remains only a general one. When the circumstances of each case are examined
in their details, differences and discrepancies between them
are not long in making their presence felt. Whether the
case in fact ever underlay the case in fiction is a matter still
unsure. What is certain is that only an approximate parallelism can be drawn between them. If the poet drew any

analogy between the two cases, he drew it in lines that are only remotely suggestive. And it is upon this basis of remote suggestion that we shall have to treat each case.

But the very fact that the brush-strokes that render the portrait of a very perfect, yet very human knight, remotely suggest the figure of a famous contemporary, makes it all the more imperative that we give them full and minute examination. After such an examination, I think we shall come to the conclusion that the chances are rather more than less that the poet intended to represent an actual sitter: and of all known sitters the likeliest is the seventh Sire de Coucy, particularly when we note in his career three coincidences that find their counterparts in the story the poet relates. One might call the first coincidence between the romance and the reality "the rejection of the lady"; the second, "the infraction of the oath"; and the third, "the foundation of a new order of chivalry." In the poet's romance they occur near the end of the story, and they mark also the finale of the Sire de Coucy's alliance with an English suzerain.

As to the first coincidence, we should note that certainly Gawain, and in all probability Enguerrand de Coucy, were compelled to reject the affectionate pleadings of a lady,[105] and to adopt the attitude, however unwillingly, of refusal; then to go firmly and finally from the loving female who bade stay. True, in the one case the lady in question was a would-be paramour, and in the other a wife; and there is, if one may say so at the risk of incurring the charge of lack of humor, a vast difference between the two! And it is just here that the parallel breaks down. One cannot push it further, because the evidence that would tie the incident in the story to the incident in life is wanting, if indeed it ever

105. Cf. the lady's words in 1794-95.
  Kysse me now comly, and I schal cach heþen;
  I may bot mourne vpon molde, as may þat much louyes.

existed. Yet it can safely be said that in the complex creative
process as it goes on in the mind or imagination of the poet,
exact symmetry, architectonic equation, is seldom observed.
One has but to read Kittredge's account of how the poet of
Gawain melted away the rigidities of the original *donnée*
of many stories to make his one, to see how easily he could
have effected the sea-change that altered the wifely functions
into those of a paramour. For this poet, or for any maker of
a medieval romance, nothing would have been easier. Let
us ask of him, or them, something really difficult! But of
this matter more later, in our résumé.

Concerning the seemed coincidence, in *Gawain* "the infraction of the oath" resulted from the hero's acceptance of
the green lace. A belt, a band that one ties about some part of
his body, made Gawain break his promise to his host, who, in
his turn, had accepted all that his guest had given him with
full belief in the donor's good faith.

Now the matter that particularly and specifically complicated Coucy's relations with the monarchs of both England and France was his membership in the Order of the
Garter. The best authorities are agreed that the Garter on
a knight's left leg symbolized the band which united him
with his fellow-members in support of the royal claim to the
throne of France. "Who took the king of England's garter
became the king of England's man." Enguerrand could have
freed himself with no great difficulty from his obligations as
an English landholder;[106] he could have resigned his English title when occasion seemed to demand that he do so.
But the Garter oath was a more difficult matter to dispense
with. It enrolled him within the comitatus of the English
King, and *ipso facto* made him the sworn foe of the King

106. Some such intention may have been in his mind, for, as previously
noted, in 1367 he had made over the reversion of his ancestral lands to
the King. His letter of resignation of Aug. 26, 1377, served notice upon
Richard II that he might take over all lands that he, the grantee, had
held before that date.

of France, his own natural lord. Frenchmen could ask him, with perfect justice, why he wore it; Englishmen, with equal justice, why he failed to perform what he had already promised. Like Gawain's green lace, it was seal and sign of his own false and impossible position. His situation exactly paralleled that of the "almost perfect" Sir Gawain. He had become a faithless man.

But though the two situations be parallel, in each there are details that are discordant. In the romance the hero accepts a green lace, a lady's belt worn about the body—*not a garter*. Whether Polydore Virgil's story that the Order of the Garter was founded because of Edward III's rescue of the Countess of Salisbury's garter be true or not (and it is now widely doubted), the best authorities seem agreed that its members wore upon the *left leg* the *blue* garter which gave its name to their brotherhood.[107] There seems no evidence that a green lace (or a lace of any other color) formed an essential part of the Garter costume.[108] The modern Garter "riband" (which is not worn around waist) appeared long after the close of the fourteenth century. The parallelism between the cases of Sir Gawain and the Sire de Coucy certainly breaks down when one remarks that what caused embarrassment to the one was a ribbon, and to the other a garter. Any poet (the *Gawain*-poet most of all) who knew his business would never have allowed such a discrepancy to vitiate the equation he was seeking to establish. Either he was not seeking to establish such an equation, or else some reason or preference of his own kept him from making his parallelism exact in all its parts.

If we take into account, however, *all* the evidence that

107. Froissart, ed. Kervyn, 4. 205; "Chevaliers du Bleu Gertier."
108. The Knights of the Order seem to have worn around their waist the military sword-belt, but the poet's words (2032-36) imply, if I am not mistaken, that Gawain, though he wrapped the lace twice over his surcoat, did not use it to support the sword.

the poem provides, I think we shall see that the last possibility of the preceding paragraph may be an explanation of whatever discrepancies exist between the case in fiction and that in fact. For, as the poem stands today in its unique manuscript, it seems most probable that either its author or some subsequent copyist was bent on establishing a connection between it and the famous order of Edward III's foundation. *Hony Soyt Qui Mal Pence* is written down after its concluding lines, though in a somewhat later hand than that which wrote out the story.[109] Lines 1928-31, which certainly appear to contain a description of the Garter costume, strengthen this possibility and indicate that it was not a scribe, but the author himself, who sought to establish that connection.[110] If I know him rightly, his "Garter poem" would not be, as Lydgate's were, a eulogistic tribute to the Order as an institution, but verse that celebrated (and revealed as well) some one outstanding personality among its members. Whether that personality is Enguerrand de Coucy or not, *Sir Gawain and the Green Knight* is just such a poem. Its author seems more interested in some one member of the Order of the Garter than in the privileges and glories of that honorable fraternity.

But if such a connection there be—and I do not press it upon the reader—one can wonder why the poet seemed to remain content with a remote rather than a close resemblance between poem and person. Here, indeed, one may wonder far in the realm of surmise. Let us seek to keep within the paths of sensible surmise. It is possible that the author found that his sources, whichever they may have been of that mass of Celtic folk-tale, Breton *lai*, and French romance, bound him too straitly to allow of the transformation of a lace, a magic girdle, into a garter. Professor J. R. Hulbert tells us that in the earlier stories, many of which the *Gawain-*

109. Facsimile of MS Cotton Nero A. x., EETS 162, 1923, p. 8.
110. See Appendix D, below.

poet certainly knew about and may very well have used, a magic ring or belt that the hero acquires, either by gift of a faery or otherwise, was a well-known tool in the story-teller's working kit. Professor R. S. Loomis is convinced that the lace of our romance has just such a time-honored ancestry, and it would be difficult to disprove his conviction.[111] To have changed the lace into a garter might have hindered or offset some of the other adjustments necessary in the re-working of the poet's material, or disturbed the telling of his story. It is obvious that he wished it to be read as a ro-mance, and therefore to run true to the contemporary type of romance that had found and was finding such favor in his day. Too many liberties with the stock machinery expected in a romance might have made his own less popular. Minor alterations that we of today suppose could have been easily made, or made for the better, in medieval days might seem made for the worse.

But a more probable reason for such a discrepancy be-tween the romantic story and the very real situation, is, I be-lieve, to be found in the author's discretion and good taste. An exact equation between his hero and the son-in-law of his sovereign was precisely the thing he would not make. It might have been dangerous to do so. Spenser found it safer to veil his references to contemporary happenings and those who brought them about within the turnings and twistings of his story. Though Coucy had gone, the memory of his charm would not have faded so soon, and his wife and daughter lived on in the England he had left. But even if there had been no danger in pressing his parallel, the poet could never have forgotten that he was writing poetry, and not an alliterative poem on particular social or political events within the verge of the Court. Such goings on he might glance at, or finger briefly, but to him they would have

111. For Professor Hulbert's views, see *Mod. Phil.* 13. 689-730, espe-cially 707; for those of Professor Loomis, *JEGP* 42. 149-84.

been things to catch at and let go. The study of *Pearl* shows us something of the Protean quality of medieval symbolism and its author's skill in veiling with such good taste the bitter reality of what I believe to have been an actual incident. In his own day the poet's allusions to the Garter would have carried their implications to those whom they were supposed to reach. Today, having lost the clue, we are condemned to wander in the labyrinth of surmise. But being in that unfortunate position does not excuse us for failure or refusal to seek again the clue that can lead us out.

Coming now to the third coincidence, "the foundation of a new order of chivalry," we find that lines 2513-20 of our poem describe quite definitely the foundation of a chivalric order—instituted, the poet informs us, to commemorate the successful completion of Gawain's adventure. By this means Arthur and his court honor the knight whom they did not expect to see again. What to Gawain had been, and was still, a source of shame and contrition underwent the transformation into a mark of honor eagerly sought and highly prized by those who had won it:

> Vche burne of þe broþer-hede a bauderyk schulde haue,
> A bende a-belef hym aboute of a bryȝt grene.
>
> .   .   .   .
>
> And he honoured þat hit hade euer-more after.[112]

Quite evidently, as Professor Hulbert has shown,[113] the poet was not alluding to the Garter, which, as far as extant records go, never seems to have had as part of its insignia "a

112. 2616-17, 2520. One would naturally conclude that this "bende" would have been worn as Gawain himself wore it, over the right shoulder and bound under the left arm (2486-88), which the poet implies is a position of dishonor. But, as borne by the members of the new brotherhood, nothing is said of its being worn in that manner. We are left to wonder, therefore, whether what was sown in dishonor was not raised in honor; whether the members of the Order may not have worn it in the reverse sense *pro honoris causa.*

113. *Mod. Phil.* 13. 711-12.

bende a-belef hym aboute of a bryȝt grene,"—or if it ever did, certainly not as the principal or distinguishing part. It remains, therefore, to ascertain whether the Sire de Coucy can be connected with some other brotherhood of chivalry.

Fortunately we are here upon solid ground. We know that shortly after his return from England he founded, or there was founded in his honor, the Order of the Crown (*Ordre de la Couronne*). Its purpose, costume, and insignia are almost—but not quite—unknown to us, despite the efforts of many zealous writers of history, who have undertaken to supply information that was lacking—though I ought to add that they would not be unknown to a courtly poet of the fourteenth century. The one cognizance which we know it possessed, the one which must have given it its name—was the crown.[114] One wonders whether a green lace could have been a part, either permanent or for one year only, of the costume of the Order, but further history sayeth not. Though further information be lacking, the correspondencies that exist between the order of Gawain and the order of Enguerrand are close and suggestive enough to tantalize and vex us that we know no more.

We have followed the English career of the Sire de Coucy in some detail. We have sought to wring from the ancient records all the clues that might tell us where he was at any given time during the years 1363-77; why he was there, rather than elsewhere; and what it could have been that was occupying his time and attention in the place where the records allow us to find him.

We have pottered over his track through *Patent* and *Close Roll,* I fear to the point of tediousness, but we have pottered over it for a purpose. There is a connection that

114. Crowns appear, apparently for the first time, upon one of Coucy's wax seals attached to a document dated July 2, 1379. Thereafter his seals seem always to have borne them. See Appendix J, "The Order of the Crown," below.

can be established between the events of the years in which
(to use his own phrase) he "had alliance" with the English
King, and the episodes of that brilliantly written poem of the
fourteenth century, *Sir Gawain and the Green Knight*. Allusions that lurk in the lines of the poem recall in striking
fashion situations or facts which are (or were) true of the
seventh Sire de Coucy—or of the house whence he sprang.

Of course it remains still to be proved whether the connection that seems indicated is valid; whether the allusions
might not equally well apply in the life of another than
Coucy, to situations true of other contemporary men or
families.

All the present writer would do is, first, to bring out the
possible connection; next to muster the evidence that sup-
ports it, and that which tells against it; and, finally, to weigh
the one against the other—to determine whether the connection should still remain conjecture or surmise, or become a
possibility, or something stronger. He has no desire to push
a new theory about the composition of a famous romance,
or to advance views that rest on weak or inadequate evidence.
All students of medieval literature wish to know more about
this skillfully told alliterative poem whose author is still
anonymous, but they wish the new knowledge to be true,
not false.

Unfortunately, true and certain knowledge about the
origin of the poem is not something that has already been
attained. Towards its attainment we must, of necessity, move
forward by inference and circumstantial evidence. At such
procedure some careful students may feel alarmed, but in
this short span of human life what other method of attaining truth in any field do human beings have than the method
of putting two and two together? I shall, then, ask my
readers, however mistrustful they may become of some of my
arguments, to trust in the honesty of my intention, and to be-

lieve me when I say that I shall not consciously suppress any
evidence pro or con. We, author and reader alike, are interested not in advancing views, but in attaining certainty; and
if we are to attain to some greater measure of certainty, we
shall do so, first, by making the effort, and secondly, by the
wise use of those means men adopt in just such searches—inference and circumstantial evidence. Let us, then, in the com-
parisons that are to be developed, follow where the evidence
leads—or seems to lead.

We have weighed the pros and cons of the suggestion
that *Gawain and the Green Knight* is in some way to be connected with the sojourn of Enguerrand de Coucy at the
Court of his father-in-law. Let us now briefly recapitulate
the evidence, strike as clear a balance as we can, and state
the conclusion of the whole matter.

Against that suggestion is to be placed the fact that our
knowledge of the poet is still quite incomplete. We know
nothing of the events of his life, have no knowledge of what
he did, or exactly where he sojourned during his mature
years.[115] We know something of his genius as a writer, and,
1 think, will realize still more of its range and height. We
have begun to find out something about his interests, and can
begin to predicate something also, to use a bad modernism,
of his method of attack. Yet (again a modernism) his writing psychology is still largely unknown to us, and, more significant for this enquiry, the situations and impulses that im-
pelled him to write.

And if the poet be unknown to us, still more unknown
are the inner lives of those whom we assume that he was
writing about. Of their doings history records some facts,
but on those factual dry bones we ourselves must pack the
flesh and blood. His is indeed a hard task who attempts to

115. It can be quite safely stated, I think, that his early and youthful
years were passed in the West Midlands.

swing the writing of this romance into the scope and current
of two human lives that are now little more than names on
history's pages.[116]

Yet when the difficulties are admitted, there remains an
argument of a similar generalized nature on the other side.
Those who doubt that there exists any connection between
the poem and contemporary personages fall into this egre-
gious error. They suppose that if the entire series of events
within the poem cannot be fitted neatly into the known events
of the lives of those contemporary personages, then any connection between them and the poem is impossible and belief
in it fallacious. Those who so think, I am convinced, do not
know truly the *Gawain*-poet, nor, I may add, the practice
of many other medieval poets as well.

Once and for all, let it be said that this story, like some
others of medieval growth, cannot be forced into a pot-
pourri of personal relationships and political events dressed
up in fictional form. Such is not our author's method in
Pearl, where personal history on a factual foundation certainly does not determine the course of the story or the succession of its incidents. It is certain carefully selected aspects,
certain significant incidents of a human life, aspects and incidents that illustrate the warfare of a human soul, that interest this author. He is no three-decker Proust.

I have the feeling that he, like Spenser, was aware of the
danger, aesthetic as well as legal, of tying up his story to
people and events.[117] I am quite certain that he knew as
well as his sixteenth-century successor that art is betrayed
when actuality or "realism" is allowed to dictate to the imagination. His sense of narrative, his love of and success at

116. This last judgment is certainly true of Isabella, but a bit unfair,
perhaps, of her husband.

117. I amused myself some years ago by equating as closely as I could
situations and characters in the romance with events and personages at
the English Court in 1363-77. I saw that if I persisted in that fascinating
task, I should have to compose a "Memoir of the Edwardian Court" that
would have laid heavy demands upon the reader's imagination.

making it take on the smooth and steady throb of motion, would have forever prevented him from sitting and playing with similes, literary or factual. Not for him the labored comparison between real things and those of the spirit or imagination made by the theologians and philosophers of his era. If there were prototypes in actual life for the happenings of the story, and I think there were, the poet's allusion to them would have been brief. Their existence might have prompted and suggested, but did not dictate, the course of his story. His imagination was quick, and he expected the imaginations of his best readers to be equally so. His was not the direct "swashing blow" of his contemporary Langland, but, instead, a quick *touché*. He lived in the heyday of heraldry (which he knew well), an art (not a science) that, like poetry, conveys its meanings by the glancing touch of allusion. Like Dante, Langland, and others of his poetic brethren, he was practiced in the symbolic lore of the Middle Ages, the lore of allusion and of the secondary meaning, and, like them, used it, not as a philosopher or theologian, fully, extendedly, with close and minute application, but as a poet, briefly, allusively, tellingly.

Having seen something of the manner in which the *Gawain*-poet reacted to a stimulus or impression from the contemporary world of grandees and politicians, of chanceries and dynastic ambitions, and how this found subsequent expression in the poetry he wrote, let us now list and evaluate the facts which suggest a connection between the writing of the romance and the doings of the Sire de Coucy.

1. *Gawain and the Green Knight* was almost certainly written in the English Northwest Midlands: quite probably in the northern or eastern portions of Lancashire, to the west of and above the course of the Ribble, *or* the westerly portions of the Yorkshire West Riding; less probably in South Lancashire, Northeast Cheshire, or Northwest Derby. Within

the region first named, the houses of Coucy and of Coucy-Guines had long held in various localities lands of wide extent and considerable value, so wide and so important as to make their possessor second only to the Duke of Lancaster as a magnate of importance within the county of Lancashire and the western portion of the West Riding. At the time of their marriage these were granted to Enguerrand and Isabella de Coucy for direct holding by them and their heirs male. Thus *Gawain* would appear to have been written by an author whose origin and upbringing were in the region where the Earl of Bedford and his brother-in-law became the leading landed proprietors.[118]

2. Nearly all dates suggested for the writing of *Gawain* fall within a period of years ranging from 1350 to 1400, with the weight of scholarly opinion favoring a date in the sixties or seventies of the fourteenth century.[119] The composition of the poem could, therefore, have fallen within the years of Coucy's English alliance (1363-77). It could have been even later, for after his departure his daughter, the Countess of Oxford, inherited the ancestral lands that had once been his, and had her possession of them confirmed through the favor and regard of her first cousin, King Henry IV. The last mention we find of her is in 1401.[120]

3. As previously stated, some sort of connection between the poem and the Order of the Garter is plainly indicated. Enguerrand de Coucy and his brother-in-law, John of Gaunt, were the only two members of the Order whose holdings were at all extensive in the localities where the poem may

118. See Appendices A and B, below.

119. For discussion of the chronology of the works of the *Gawain*-poet, see Appendix C, below.

120. *Cal. Pat. Rolls* 1399-1401, p. 528, gives a compact dated July 2, 1401 West. between the Countess of Oxford and her older sister Mary de Bar, that the latter should be sole heiress of the French and the former of the English estates. Cf. Mrs. Green, *Princesses of England* 3. 223. See also Appendix F, below.

be supposed to have been written.[121] Lancaster, thirty-sixth knight, named in or shortly before April, 1361, occupied stall No. 13 (modern 14) on the north side of the Garter Chapel at Windsor, being transferred thence to stall No. 1 (modern 2) on the north side at the accession of his nephew, Richard II. His brother-in-law, named some time after May 28, 1365, the year of the death of Sir Thomas Ughtred, his predecessor, as forty-second knight, occupied stall No. 23 (modern enumeration 24) on the north side of St. George's Chapel at Windsor.[122]

4. Lines 863-70 of the poem may reasonably be construed as a possible description by the poet of the coat of arms of the Coucy family or that of the family of Guines. True, other interpretations of the lines are possible, and some readers may prefer one or another of them to the one here

121. During the founder's (Edward III) sovereignty two other members of the order were of Lancashire origin or held lands in that county. Thomas Holland, 1st Earl of Kent, younger son of that branch of the Lancs. family of Holland which held Upholland and other lands in the W. Derby Hundred of Lancs., was one of the founders of the order. Sir Thomas Banastre, 55th knight, named to the order between June 1375 and April 1376, possessed considerable holdings in Leyland and Amounderness Hunds. Kent, though he had some holdings in the N. and E. Ridings, left Lancs. to seek a younger son's portion elsewhere, and never seems to have acquired any holdings in his native county. (*Vict. Hist. Lancs.* 4.93, note 24). He would seem, therefore, an unlikely patron of a poem hailing from Craven or Lancs. Banastre was a tough hard-bitten soldier. who died Dec. 16, 1379. He owed his membership to his devotion to Gaunt and to his fighting qualities. He was no county magnifico and, therefore, also an unlikely patron of poetry.

Certain other members of the Order held lands in West Riding areas near the country of the poem's supposed origin during Coucy's lifetime. They are Edmund of Langley, Earl of Cambridge, son of the monarch, 37th knight, nom. in or shortly before April, 1361; Sir Edward le Despenser, 38th knight, nom. 1361; Thomas Mowbray, Duke of Norfolk, 72nd knight, nom. 1383. For further discussion on them and others, see Appendix D, below. But the bulk of their holdings, or those that produced the greater portion of their income, were in other counties. An alliterative poet in search of a patron, would more naturally address the Duke of Lancaster or the Earl of Bedford before turning to them.

122. See W. A. Shaw, *Knights of England* (London, 1906), p. 3; E. H. Fellowes, *The Knights of the Garter* (SPCK), London. n.d., pp. 58, 68, 75. See Appendix D, below.

adduced (and further explained in Appendix G), but there are fewer objections to this one than to any of the others, and eminent authorities on heraldry have stated that it is an interpretation which could not be driven out of court.

5. There is a strong possibility that lines 642-50 of the poem contain a possible allusion to the *cri de guerre* which we know that Enguerrand de Coucy VII used. The house of Coucy seems to have had several battle-cries, but these lines could allude only to that one which, from contemporary mention, we know the seventh Sire de Coucy preferred— "Nostre-Dame au seigneur de Coucy!"[123]

6. There is quite evidently an allusion in lines 2505-20 to the foundation of an order of chivalry which is certainly not that of the Garter. That foundation occurs after the return of Sir Gawain to his sovereign's Court. As we have seen above, shortly after his return to France, Enguerrand de Coucy either founded *L'Ordre de la Couronne,* or had it founded in his honor by those who were glad of his return.[124]

7. For an explanation of the poet's careful description of the Pentangle (lines 623-34) and his assignment of it as a device appropriate to Gawain, I can offer no explanation that seems to me completely satisfactory. Yet there are two explanations that swing the mystic sign of Solomon within the orbit of Coucy's activities between the years 1363 and 1377. I present them in Appendix G for what they are worth, without special pleading or any attempt to force them upon the reader. Those two attempts to learn that *aliquid novi,* reveal something of that milieu of historic event and social convention that lies behind the poem, and suggest to the reader that some of the "unknowns" in it are, after all, not incapable of reasoned explanation.

I have made a rather long preachment on the history of Coucy's English years, because what happened in their pas-

123. See Appendix H, below.
124. See Appendix J., below.

sage may throw a light upon the genesis of one of the finest of the Middle English romances. The evidence for a connection between the career of that attractive French nobleman and the romance of Gawain the Courteous depends upon a number of isolated facts such as those I have listed, and upon the possibilties and probabilities that ensue from the existence of each particular one of them. Of and by itself, each fact, with its implications, is merely an interesting observation and carries little meaning. United one with another, they present together a rather imposing body of evidence that cannot be, as yet, disproved. To render nugatory the possibilities they suggest, one would have to bring forth other facts that suggest more likely possibilities, and to date this has not been done.

And now let us hear the conclusion of the whole matter. It is possible that the author of *Gawain* wrote his story with the career of this Anglo-French nobleman in mind. How long it may have remained in his mind, or how closely he allowed his thought to follow it, we shall probably never know. Persuasion is no part of my plan, and the reader will be convinced or remain unconvinced by his own good judgment. I rest the case to await judicial decision, regretting, as I do so, that in order to fill up the story of Enguerrand de Coucy's English days (a necessary part of my task) it has also been necessary to interrupt narrative by exposition, and discuss at some length the genesis of a poem to which he probably gave little thought—if, indeed, he even knew of its existence. Enough has been said, however, to indicate that the writing of *Sir Gawain and the Green Knight* by some member of his English *familia* may well have been part of the story of those English days.

XI

With a wife and his younger daughter on the other side of the Channel, Coucy began life again in his native country.

He had not long to wait for employment, for Charles V saw to it that enterprises of great pith and moment were committed into his hands. The activities of his later life are a bewildering succession of campaigns, diplomatic negotiations, foreign embassies, confidential errands, and interviews, where powers of persuasion and adroit manoeuvre were at a premium. Several episodes of his later career, his years as a campaigner and negotiator in Italy, and his part in the Crusade of Mahadia (1390), deserve much more study than they have received. Elsewhere (*Speculum* 14.423 ff.) the writer has sought to appraise his soldiership in his last campaign—that of the fatal Crusade of Nicopolis. But busy and important as the later years undoubtedly were, they lack the glamor that illuminates those of his debut in England, when he had just won a wife, and enjoyed the affection and favor of the most chivalrous and powerful monarch in Europe. In February, 1386, seven years after Isabella's decease, he married again, his second wife being Isabella, daughter of the Duke of Lorraine. They appear to have been happy, for we know the Dame de Coucy to have been much distressed by the news of his death in captivity at Brusa (1397).[125]

Yet Enguerrand's affection for his daughter Philippa, and the zeal and persistence which he displayed in hunting out of France her worthless husband, Robert de Vere, show that his memories must have often strayed back to Philippa's mother.[126] What he remembered and what he forgot, we

125. Mas Latrie, *Commerce et expéditions militaires de la France et de Venise au Moyen Âge* (Paris, 1880), p. 168.

126. "So fondly did Earl Ingelram cling to the memory of his first wife that, eleven years after her death, when he erected the church of the Celestines, at Soissons ... which he destined for his burial-place, and placed therein his own monumental effigy, he erected by its side a companion statue, not of Isabella of Lorraine, but of the object of his first and lasting affection, Isabella of England" (Mrs. Green 3. 228). These statements are apparently based upon *Maurice, sur le Maison De Coucy, et sur la branche De Vervin encore existante,* a very vague and unsatisfactory reference. Isabella of England (d. 1379) was buried at the Church of the

shall never know, but his native country and that of his temporary adoption have not forgotten him. On the frieze of the Salle de Croisades in the Palace of Versailles are painted his arms *fascé de vair et de gueules de six pièces;* and the same arms adorn the ceiling of St. George's Hall at Windsor—the same Windsor where once he had wooed and won his bride.

Greyfriars, commonly called Christ Church, Aldgate. It would seem more likely that the "companion statue" beside Coucy's effigy was that of his second wife. In the absence of illustrations of the tomb (I have found none), which might enlighten us as to the armorial bearings of the spouse, Mrs. Green's words are at present impossible of either disproof or verification.

Appendices

The English Estates of the House of Coucy-Guines

I

As HAS BEEN stated before, the marriage of Enguerrand de Guines with Christina de Lindsay, daughter and heiress of William de Lindsay of Lamberton, County Berwick, in 1282-83[1] brought into the house of Guines a moiety of the inheritance of the barons of Kendal.[2] The following pedigree will make clear how that inheritance was transmitted to the descendants of that marriage so that Enguerrand VII, Sire de Coucy, came to be recognized as the heir to it, and eventually to be seised of the greater part of what his ancestors had once held.[3]

1. Christina was heiress of her father, who died before Nov. 12, 1282. She was married before May 28, 1283. Cf. *Cal. Documents relating to Scotland* 2. 69, 72.

2. The Lindsays were co-heirs of the great native house of the de Lancasters, barons of Kendal, who were descended from Elfred, a native thane.

3. I owe to the kindness of George Andrews Moriarty, F.S.A., the pedigree of the house of Coucy-Guines. From C. A. Kennedy, secretary to the Garter King at Arms, I received in 1935 two other pedigrees of the same persons, which he had found in "an old MS in Vincent's collection" (Library of the College of Arms). One corroborates Mr. Moriarty's by listing Eng. VII as the grandson of William de Coucy who married Isabel de Chatillon. The other makes Eng. VII nephew of that William. It should be added that Mr. Moriarty lists only those descendants of a particular marriage with whom our story is concerned.

Arnoul III Count of Guines   = Alice (or Alix) dau. of Ingram III Sire de Coucy

Ingelram (Fr. Enguerrand) de = Christina (or Christiana) Guines. Younger son. Summoned Dau. and heir of Wm. de Lindsay, 1295-1322, as Lord Guines (Gynes). Lamberton, Co. Berwick, by Ada, Lived mostly in England. d. June dau. of John de Balliol and De-6, 1323. Retained name and arms vorgille of Scotland (dau. David, of Guines. Earl of Huntington).

William de Guines, or = Isabel, dau. of Guy de   Enguerrand, Robert de Coucy, Sire de Chatillon, Count of St.   Vicomte de Meaux, Coucy, *de jure* Lord Pol. Alive 1357.   Seigneur de Condé-Gynes b. ca. 1279.   en-Brie, de la Lived in France, hav-   Ferté-sous-Jouarre, ing gone there in   de Tresmes. 1318. d. 1335.

Ingelram, Sire de = Catherine, dau. of   William de Coucy or Coucy, aged 26 in Leopold of Austria.   de Gynes. Rec'd the 1343. Claimed Eng-   English lands before lish fees on death of   July 4, 1334. Died his brother William   1343. in 1343. Did not re-ceive them on account of being a French-man, and they were granted to others. Did receive, however, right of herbage and pas-turage in his brother's parks in Westmore-land and Lancs. Died 1344.

Enguerrand VII Sire de Coucy.   = Isabel, eldest dau. of Ed. III. Came to England as hostage after Died Oct. 5, 1382 (or 1379?) Poitiers. Granted estates of his great grandmother. Created Earl of Bedford 1366.

Marie.   = Henry,   Philippa.   = Robt. de Inherited French   Duke of Bar   Inherited   Vere, Earl of estates.   English fees.   Oxford,   Duke of   Ireland.

The inheritance that the ancestors of this seventh Sire de Coucy had once held was scattered over three English counties. His uncle William (d. 1343) at his death held in Westmoreland, Kirby in Kendal, Winandermere, Grasmere, and St. Mary Holm (St. Mary's isle in Winandermere), and the advowsons of the chapels in the last three places; in Yorkshire, Middleton by Multon (M. Tyas) in the North Riding, and Thornton-in-Lonsdale in the West Riding;[4] in Lancashire, Ulvereston, Mourholm, including lands in Carnforth and Lyndeheved, a moiety of the manor of Wyresdale, the Wardship of Whittington, the moiety of the manor of Ashton, and a third part of the manor of Scotford.[5] A look at a fairly large-scale atlas or map of the northwestern counties of England will reveal to the reader the wide extent of these ancestral fees. That they were also valuable is certain; for their whole history from times that long antedate those with which we are concerned is marked by lawsuits between those who happened, rightly or wrongly, to hold them and those who sought to do so. It should be emphasized that they actually were "ancestral" fees, manors, lands and rights which Coucy's forebears had held, and which he, as their heir, seemed entitled to hold. But extensive and valuable as they were, they formed only a portion of all the manors, *terrae et tenementa,* advowsons and knight's fees which had been from time to time granted to him or

4. Some official documents state that Coucy held in Yks. the manor of Coghill, but that manor may have been a part of the larger holding of Thornton-in-Lonsdale; see *Cal. IPM* 11. 427.

5. *Cal. IPM* 8. 306 (No. 462). Wyresdale is Nether Wyresdale in the parish of Garstang. That name and Garstang "were used indifferently to denote the fee of the barons of Kendal in this part of Lancashire, including the whole or large parts of the parishes of Cockerham, Garstang, and St. Michael's, and some part of Lancaster also" (*Vict. Hist. of Lancs.,* 7. 300). These holdings in Lancs. seem identical with those of William de Coucy's grandmother, Christina de Gynes, in the same country; see *Cal. IMP* 7. 394-96 (No. 561).

to his countess alone by the monarch who delighted to honor them both.[6]

The question naturally arises whether Coucy ever visited his ancestral domains. If we knew that he had ever been in residence at his country seat (or seats), the possibility of a nexus between the new lord and the alliterative poets of the Northwest Midlands would lead to a good deal of quite legitimate speculation as to the effect of aristocratic patronage on the poetry of the alliterative school. Unfortunately, I have found no evidence that Enguerrand ever sojourned upon his ancestral acres in Lancashire and Yorkshire. So far as we can learn, nearly all the time he passed in England seems to have been passed in the vicinity of London. But since we cannot account for all the time he passed in England, a visit or visits to Lancashire or the West Riding is by no means improbable. It is certain that he was once at his manor of Corsham in Wiltshire (see *Cal. Pat. Rolls* 1374-77, p. 396). Since the document that attests his presence there is one giving a slight increase in pay to one of his park-keepers, and parts of the modern parish of Corsham were probably within ancient forest land (*Place-Names of Wiltshire, EPNS* 16. 95-99 *passim*), it is no hazardous guess to say that Coucy must have gone there to hunt. Now, since many parts of Lancashire were forest land, and game plentiful therein, it would be dangerous to state that Coucy never visited his domains in that county.

6. Coucy's non-ancestral holdings and all those of Isabella are enumerated in a patent roll of 1 Rich. II which is printed *in toto* by Mrs. Green (*Princesses of England,* 3. 443-44, Append. VII). In 1367 Coucy had given back to the crown the reversion of these manors in Lancs. which Joan de Coupland then held. See *Arch. Jrnl.* 35. 168; *Abbrev. Rot. Originalium* (Rec. Com.). 2. 300; *Cal. Pat. Rolls* 1367-70, p. 295. Edward III, however, seemed determined not to allow his son-in-law to have the last word, for hardly had Coucy executed the deed mentioned in preceding sentence, when the monarch regranted the same holdings back to him and his wife in tail male (*Cal. Pat. Rolls* 1367-70, p. 46, West. Jan. 12, 1368).

The question posed at the beginning of the last paragraph inevitably raises a further question: Could the Sire de Coucy, who presumably spoke only French, have concerned himself with, or made anything out of, a poem of whose language he may have been quite ignorant—even though it was written in the speech current in his ancestral domains?

This query is but a more specialized case of the many raised by the fact that fourteenth-century England was to some extent a bilingual country. However, scholarship has been slowly establishing the additional fact that English was spoken far more widely in courtly and aristocratic circles than earlier writers believed possible (cf. O. F. Emerson, "English or French in the time of Edward III," *Chaucer Essays and Studies*, Cleveland, 1929, pp. 271-97, and A. C. Baugh, *Hist. of the Engl. Lang.*, N. Y., 1935, pp. 178-79: "We may be sure that the court that Chaucer knew talked English even if its members commonly wrote and often read French.") Since Chaucer in *The Book of the Duchess* addressed John of Gaunt in the speech of the Southeast, there would have been nothing improbable or strange in his anonymous contemporary's addressing John of Gaunt's sister (or niece) in the speech of the Northwest Midlands: for it is more likely that the poet would have written rather to impress the Countess (probably much more proficient in the speech of her native land) than the Earl of Bedford.

Yet I am chary of believing that Coucy knew no English, or had spent little time or effort in acquiring the language his wife and father-in-law spoke. We know that the messenger, who presented his letter of renunciation to Richard II is described as *"quendam Pagettum, se Johannem Pieres nominantem, qui, ydioma Anglicanum loquens"* (Rymer, *Foedera*, 1709, 7. 173), and while the quotation is no evidence that Coucy himself spoke English, it does show that he was aware of the importance of having someone to represent him who could, and is evidence of his recognition that the *ydioma Anglicanum* was a tongue to be used rather than eschewed.

Of one thing we can be certain. Had Enguerrand de Coucy heard the poem read, or received a manuscript of it as a gift, whether he understood it or not, he would have rewarded the author handsomely. He seems to have held men of letters in high esteem. Both Froissart and Deschamps praise his generosity; he is known to have owned the incomplete but fine Boxmer MS of the former now in Bibliothèque Royale at Brussels (cf. J. Bastin, *Jean Froissart*, Brussels, 1942, p. 13); and Mazas (*Capitaines Français* 3.28) informs us that during his first campaign "il avait fréquenté, en Italie, Pétrarque et Boccace." I am dubious about the accuracy of the last statement, since Mazas cites no evidence. I can only say that it is chronologically not impossible, since Coucy left Italy some time after January, 1374, and Petrarch died some months later (July 18) in the same year.

APPENDIX B

Linguistic Evidence as to Place of Origin of the Author of *Sir Gawain and the Green Knight*

THE POET'S LOCALE

IN MY STUDY, "A French Knight of the Garter," Chapter III, above, reasons were advanced for believing that the Middle English alliterative poem *Sir Gawain and the Green Knight* was in some ways connected with the events of Enguerrand de Coucy's sojourn in England. Let us see whether this belief is weakened or strengthened by the evidence gleaned from a linguistic study of the poem. Is it possible that *Sir Gawain* could have been written within a district whose speech could have been spoken also within some one of the numerous Coucy lordships?

The unique manuscript of the poem, almost certainly a copied manuscript, is written in the dialect of the Northwest Midlands, and there is a preponderance of evidence to show that the author wrote his original copy in the same dialect. Speaking very generally, one may say that *Gawain* (and the three other poems contained with it in the same manuscript and supposedly by the same author) shows the verbal endings and plural forms that one would expect to find in North Cheshire, North Derby, Lancashire, the West Riding of Yorkshire, South Westmoreland and South Cumberland; and a treatment of vowels and consonants (from whatever source, OE, OF, or ON) that one would be apt to find uniform in those same localities, South Westmoreland and South Cumberland excluded. However, Professor Oakden and Miss M. Serjeantson, who have made quite recently the most detailed studies of the dialect of this poem, are inclined to assign it, on dialectal evidence alone, to Southern Lancashire,[1] rather than to a more northerly region. They do so because in *Sir Gawain* there are two linguistic facts that would have to be taken into account, if the poem is to be assigned to any portion of the area of the Northwest Midlands.

1. J. P. Oakden (*Allit. Poetry in ME*, 1. 86), the greatest authority on the linguistic background of the four poems, believes the dialect to have been that of Rossendale (S. of modern Burnley) rather than that of the Peak dist. (Derby). Philological evidence within the MS excludes Derbyshire as its home, and distinctly favors S. Lancs.; see Oakden, pp. 82-87. Miss M. Serjeantson (*RES* 3. 327-28) believes "Derbyshire seems the least improbable area to which the Nero MS may be assigned, whatever the original dialects of the poems may have been." One can only say that the place of the poem's provenience ought not to be determined by linguistic evidence alone.

The first fact is that the poet made ME *wh* (=OE *hw*) alliterate with original *w*, and not with *qu* (=OE *cw*). This practice is rather in contrast to that of the author of the Middle English *Destruction of Troy*, probably written also in the dialect of the Northwest Midlands. He regularly makes *wh* alliterate with *qu*, the representative of OE *cw*. Now Professors Tolkien and Gordon inform us that the *wh-w* alliteration indicates that *Sir Gawain* was written farther south than the *Destruction of Troy:* "The line between the different developments of OE *hw* which made possible these different types of alliteration seems to have been roughly the valley of the Ribble. Thus local names originally beginning with *hw-* written down at Cockersand or Furness are spelt *qu-*, whereas such local names written at Lancaster, Whalley, and elsewhere south of the Ribble are spelt *wh-*, *w-*."[2]

Thus the poet of *Gawain* could have written his poem at a place slightly to the north or anywhere south of the valleys of the Ribble and the Aire.[3] Though the second

2. *Sir Gawain and the Green Knight*, p. xxiii. Oakden (pp. 78-79) gives the following list of *wh* and *qu* spellings in the poems of the MS:

> *Pat.* 48 *wh*, 1 *w*, 5 *qu* spellings
> *Pur.* 97 *wh*, 5 *w*, 14 *qu* spellings
> *Pearl* 44 *wh*, 4 *w*, 36 *qu* spellings
> *Gaw.* 82 *wh*, 3 *w*, 82 *qu* spellings

Gawain, it will be noted, contains many more *qu* spellings than do the three other poems of the Cotton Nero MS. But Professor Harold Whitehall (*Phil. Quart* 9. 1) produced evidence to indicate that *qu* was a mere scribal spelling, used in S. Lancs. as well as in more northerly areas, and therefore no evidence of dialectal provenience; see also Oakden, p. 79.

I am a little puzzled by the inclusion of the name "Lancaster" in the quotation above. Does it refer to the city or to the whole parish which includes the modern townships of Myerscough and Fulwood, the latter being just north of the Ribble? In medieval days both places were apparently part of the Forest of Lancaster.

3. Oakden (1. 28) warns us that "the approximate line which divides the two developments is the Ribble-Aire valleys." The word "approximate" gives clear warning that we may expect to find at time *qu* spellings in documents written in places south of the Ribble, and *wh* spellings in those written to the north of it. Did the poet write south of the river valleys or slightly to the north? All that our evidence tells us is that he

possibility may seem the more likely, Oakden tells us the *qu* spellings are merely scribal. The first cannot be quite excluded because the presence of many *qu* spellings in the poem may be a faint indication that it was written down at a place not far above the course of the Ribble-Aire river lines, the approximate boundary between the *wh* and *qu* spellings, and that its journey from the abode of its maker to that of its first copyist might have been in a general southerly direction, i.e., from a *qu* into a *wh* region; in other words, that some of the *qu* spellings may go back to the original draft of the poem, and that its copyist(s) may have diminished the original *qu* in favor of *wh* spellings.[4]

The second important linguistic fact about *Sir Gawain* is the unusually high proportion of ON words to be found

did not write far north of those valleys. The possibility that the poem was written by a poet living north of the river valleys, and copied by a scribe living south of them, is of definite interest to us, because that poet may have been resident in regions where the house of Coucy held lands. The reverse possibility—a scribe who dwelt above and an author who dwelt below the river valleys—is less germane to the present discussion; see following section of this Appendix, also note 22.

In explanation of the above let me quote Professor Marckwardt (personal letter of October 11, 1954):

". . . let us grant for the sake of argument that at some time there was a definite *wh-w* isogloss along the Ribble-Aire line. In the first place, we cannot assume that such a boundary necessarily will remain fixed; it can shift either northward or southward. In the second place, we must know whether such a boundary represents the farthest extension southward of the *wh* forms or the farthest extension northward of the *w* forms. I doubt that anyone knows the situation well enough to take a strong stand on this point. It would be possible, however, to contend that since [hw] was becoming [w] generally throughout southern England, that such a boundary would imply that you would not be able to find [hw] forms south of it, but that [w] forms might well occur north of it. Certainly as one moved northward from the Ribble, it would not be surprising to find [w] spelled with the *qu* form or some variant thereof."

4. For the number of copies between the original MS of the author and the Cotton Nero MS, see Oakden, 1. 261-63 (Appendix 3). For W. W. Greg's objections to Oakden's views, see the *Library* (*Trans. Bibliog. Soc.*, 2nd Ser.) 13. 188-91. For Oakden's reply, see 14. 353-58 of the same periodical.

in it.[5] Their number, as Oakden suggests, may indicate "an area of composition in a dialectal region in which the Scandinavian element was very marked," though he also adds, "owing to the wide circulation in the west of typical Norwegian test-words such as *caple*, it is impossible to say whether the author was in touch with the West-Scandinavian settlements in the northwest of England."[6]

In the light of the two linguistic facts just mentioned, one can be safe only in cautious affirmation. The poet, then, may have been reared either in Lancashire, or in the Yorkshire West Riding that adjoins Lancashire; possibly near the Ribble-Aire valleys, possibly not; but probably not very far north of that line, and certainly within an area of former Scandinavian settlement where ON words and locutions were thick. If he were a native of Lancashire—and, as we shall see below, there are some reasons for supposing that he was —and not a Yorkshireman, he is much more likely to have grown up within the northern portion of West Derby Hundred, or in that part of Leyland Hundred that abuts on the Ribble estuary, or anywhere in Amounderness Hundred, except that portion that borders the hundred of Blackburn (i.e., the eastern and southeastern portions), all districts where Scandinavian settlement had been thick. Of the four other hundreds of the county, Salford has few Old Norse or Danish place-names, and the two Lonsdales (North of the Sands and South of the Sands) are too far north of the Ribble valley to bring them within an area where *wh* alliterated with *w*, while Blackburn, except in the Parish of Whalley (colonized by Old Norse immigrants from the West Riding of Yorkshire) where the Old Norse element is more marked,

---

5. Oakden (1. 86) gives the following percentages:

Pat.	9.4 per cent
Pur.	7.6 per cent
Pearl	9.2 per cent
Gaw.	10.3 per cent

6. 2. 190-91.

but still not abundant, has few Scandinavian names.[7] Were one to seek an area in which the *Gawain*-poet might have lived and written, upon the basis of linguistic evidence alone, some locality within the hundreds of West Derby, or Leyland, or Amounderness, seems "warmer" than elsewhere in the county.[8]

COUCY'S HOLDINGS WITHIN THE POET'S POSSIBLE LOCALE

Andre Duchesne, the indefatigable historian of the Coucys, informs us that Edward III granted to Enguerrand de Coucy in 1365 "diuerses Terres et Seigneuries, à sçavoir *Morhollm*, la moitié de *Wirisdale*, d'*Ashtton*, & d'*Uluerston*, le tiers de *Whittington* en la Comté de Lancastre, & autres: avec plusieurs grands reuenus sur ses coffres,"[9] and the *Inquisitions post Mortem* confirm the correctness of his statement and inform us more precisely than does Duchesne's word *autres*, that Enguerrand's uncle, William de Coucy, held not only those territories, but lands in Westmoreland and Yorkshire as well.[10] Were one to seek, upon the basis of linguistic evidence alone, a locale in which the poet might have written, one would see that the Westmoreland lands are too far to the north of the Ribble-Aire boundary for any poet who employed the *wh-w* alliteration to have hailed from that county. The same reason would hold for the Yorkshire manors of the Coucy family. One tract which

7. For detailed discussion of the Norse influence on Lancashire place-names see the section entitled "Norsemen in Lancashire" (pp. 248-56) in Eilert Ekwall's *Place-Names of Lancashire*, Manchester, 1922. See also an important chapter by the same author on "Norwegian Settlements in the West" in H. C. Darby's *Historical Geography of England before 1800*, Cambridge, 1936.

8. All three hundreds lie near the Ribble. West Derby and Leyland lie south (and near its mouth), and Amounderness to the north of its course.

9. *Histoire Généalogique*, p. 266. The manor of Carnforth (Lancs.) was held in demesne with Warton, and since it adjoins Moureholm and both are in the parish of Warton, Duchesne has probably included it with Moureholm because his source did so.

10. *Cal. IPM.* 8. 306 (no. 462) dated Feb. 24, 17E3.

comprised Middleton Tyas and Moulton in the parish of Middleton Tyas, and adjacent Kneeton in the parish of Barton (all in the West Riding) is much too far north for *wh-w* alliteration. The other manor, Thornton-in-Lonsdale in the West Riding, but just over the Lancashire border and not far from Enguerrand's Lancashire manor of Carnforth, lay out of the *wh-w* and well within the *wh-qu* area.[11] One of the Lancashire manors mentioned above would seem a more probable place for the poet's upbringing or residence, and the question before us to decide is which one of the several mentioned seems the likeliest.

Examination of the maps in the several volumes of the *Victoria History of Lancashire* shows us that the manor of Ulverston lies in country too far north of the Ribble valley to be a very likely place in which the poet might have written. Moureholm in Warton parish, Lonsdale (S.), which is not far from Cartmel (well within *wh-qu* area), is out of the question also. Any poet who was reared on its manor lands would alliterate *wh* with *qu*. Whittington (Whittington parish, Lonsdale [S.]), a manor which lies on a wedge-shaped strip of the county that is bordered on the north by Westmoreland and on the east by Yorkshire is probably, like the others, too far north.[12] Ashton with Stodday in Lancaster parish, Lonsdale (S.), is a possible home for the poet. It is today a suburb of Lancaster (a place of *wh* and *w* spellings, according to Tolkien and Gordon), but it is still very near Cockersand Abbey, whose *Chartulary* contains *qu* spellings, and roughly twenty miles as the crow flies from the Ribble, quite a distance in a country as small as England.[13]

The most probable locality in Lancashire (linguistic evi-

11. See note 9, above.

12. Ekwall (*Place-names*, p. 184), gives three spellings of this name with *wh* and one (from Cockersand Abbey *Chartulary*) with *qu*.

13. For the manors of Moureholm and Carnforth, see *Vict. Hist.* 8. 162-70; for Whittington, pp. 241-48 of same volume; for Ashton, pp. 51-55 of same volume.

dence alone considered) in which *Sir Gawain* could have
been composed is somewhere on the lands of Nether Wyresdale in Amounderness Hundred. The *Victoria History* informs us that Nether Wyresdale and Garstang (both in what
is now Garstang parish) "were used indifferently to denote
the fee of the barons of Kendal in this part of Lancashire,
including the whole or large parts of the parishes of Cockerham, Garstang, and St. Michael's, and some part of Lancaster also. Members of the fee [i.e., lands] were granted
out to free tenants or to religious houses, but Nether Wyresdale, Holleth and Cabus in Garstang seem to have been retained in demesne."[14] Half of those demesne lands had
escheated to the crown (*circa* 1342) through the forfeiture
of their holder, an Ingram de Gynes, who had espoused the
French cause, and the crown had entered into possession and
made various grants. At the time of Coucy's marriage the
situation seems to have been that Joan de Coupland held
them of John of Gaunt by knight's service, with reversion to
the Earl and Countess of Bedford. But some sort of change
in their tenancy seems to have been brought about before
July 24, 1369, for a letter patent of that date informs us that
Joan had done fealty for them to the Earl of Bedford.[15]By
1369, then, Enguerrand had been brought into some sort of
close and direct relationship with those demesne territories
which his forbears had held. It was somewhere on those lands
that I believe the *Gawain*-poet might have lived. The reader
will remember that the Coucys seemed ever to have retained
them in demesne: on other portions of their inheritance the

14. *Vict. Hist. of Lancs.*, 7. 300. Sir G. Duckett (*Original Documents
relating to the Hostages of John, King of France*, etc. London, 1890, p.
19, footnote), tells us that Coucy "had large possessions in the Barony
of Kendal, and his name is of frequent occurrence in deeds pertaining to
the north." *Vict. Hist. of Lancs.* (7. 302-3 and footnotes) gives many
details of the administration and legal position of the Coucy estates in
Lancashire.

15. See note 45 in "A French Knight of the Garter" (Chap. III,
above).

tillers of the soil probably knew little about or of them, because of the host of sub-feudatories and/or sub-holders between the lord and his lowest vassals. Here, however, those who lived on the land would have known and remembered the family to whom they and theirs had ever been so closely attached. Fealty was firmer, loyalty to the associations of the past closer, in the north and northwest of England.

For us the situation of these Wyresdale lands, a large lordship including several manors, is interesting because they lie within that portion of Amounderness, a hundred bordering on and north of the Ribble, in which Old Norse names abound, Garstang itself being one;[16] and because they were granted to Enguerrand de Coucy in 1365.[17]

Within the lordship, however, there are two manors adjoining one another whose situation might seem of particular interest to those who would give the poet a local habitation, if not a name. They are those of Little Eccleston (in the modern township of Little Eccleston with Larbreck, Kirkham parish) and Great Eccleston (in the modern township of that name, St. Michael's-on-Wyre parish).[18] The modern villages that bear those names are a little less than eight miles distant from the Ribble (as the crow flies). Within the parish of Kirkham, Ekwall gives some 56 place-names; of this number 21 are either wholly or partially of Scandinavian origin. Within the neighboring parish of St. Michael's-on-Wyre the proportion is 5 out of a total of 17 place-names. Furthermore, within Kirkham parish there are two place-names that most probably began in ancient times

16. See Ekwall's analysis of place-name situation in Amounderness Hundred, *Place-Names of Lancs.*, pp. 251-53.

17. *Vict. Hist. of Lancs.*, 7. 303.

18. Both parts of the lordship of Nether Wyresdale and both held by the de Coucy family in 1324. The Coucys seem not to have held any manors nearer to the Ribble than these. That family in 1346 also held two oxgangs of land in the neighboring manor of Greenhalgh, which is even closer to the Ribble than the two Ecclestons.

with initial *Hw*. They are Whittingham (OE. Hwītinga hām) and Wharles (probably began with initial *Hw*, Ekwall, p. 152). It is worthy of note that both have retained the *Wh*-spelling.[19] Could one of these manors have been the home of the poet?[20] We may ask the question, but we lack the evidence to answer it.

CONCLUSION

So much, then, for the phonological and linguistic evidence. Where it leads, or seems to lead, we are bound to follow, but no further. It has led us, thus far, to see that the supposition that the *Gawain*-poet may have written his romance on Coucy's Wyresdale lands in Amounderness Hundred is an entirely possible one. But as a faithful guide I must warn the reader that here the road has ended, and that beyond lies the morass through which he can proceed only by surmise and conjecture. For after the most precise and careful efforts to localize the poet's speech, there remains the baffling problem of transcription. The Cotton Nero MS, if one may trust Professor Oakden, is full of scribal errors, and there may have been two copies, or more, between it and the author's original.[21] If such be the case, then Gollancz's belief that the romance has had a different manuscript history from the other three poems may well be true,[22] and the

19. All place-name spellings that Ekwall lists for Whittingham have initial *W* or *Wh*. Wharles has one *Qu* spelling from the *Cal. IPM* (Rolls Ser.) 1904, No. 153, and three other spellings with *W* and *Wh*.

I shall conclude this note with a comment on an interesting old place-name found by Ekwall within the Cockersand *Chart.*, and referring to a place in Kirkham parish, Amounderness Hundred. It is *Gaseflosland*, apparently derived from ON *gás*, "goose," and perhaps ME *flosh*, "pool," an infrequent word in ME writings. *Flosh* has been found in the *EE Psalt.*, in the *Wars of Alex.*, and in *Sir Gawain and the Green Knight*, and almost nowhere else.

20. Whether Wharles (or more properly Roseacre and Wharles) was ever considered to be a manor is dubious; see *Vict. His. of Lancs.*, 7. 178.

21. See note 4, above.

22. Miss Mabel Day writes me in a letter of 7/5/'37 that Sir I. Gollancz believed that *Gawain* had a different manuscript history from the

possibility that it was written by the author in a more northerly locality than Amounderness Hundred—conceivably within the Coucy manors of Ulverston, or Moureholm, Carnforth or Whittington—remains an open one. Indeed, Dr. R. Kaiser, the latest scholar to examine the linguistic evidence, would emphasize the word "North" in the compound adjective "Northwest" Midland, and assign *Gawain* and its companion poems "nach dem aüssersten Norden von Lancashire, besser nach Westmoreland oder Süd-Cumberland."[23]

But I must keep my promise to the reader, not to lead him farther than the evidence will go. Dr. Kaiser's ascription, not to speak of my own more conservative one, are only suggestions, capable of affording clues for further research, but supported by evidence that is, as yet, scanty.

APPENDIX C

The Date of *Sir Gawain*

THE PREVIOUS appendix, by the very nature of the matters it discussed, was detailed and lengthy. This one, fortunately, can be more brief.

If there be indeed a connection between the writing of *Sir Gawain and the Green Knight* and the career of Enguerrand de Coucy in England as an English nobleman, what conclusions are we justified in drawing about the date at

---

other three poems: "that someone had collected the poems from different sources."

23. R. Kaiser, *Zur Geographie des mittelenglischen Wortschatzes* (*Palaestra* 205. 168). Kaiser would ascribe a particular poem to a particular locality almost entirely on the basis of its vocabulary. His conclusions as to the locality of the poems of the Cotton MS are interesting, but ascription of a poem to a particular locality on the basis of vocabulary alone, without reference to phonological or morphological characteristics, is a foolhardy business.

which the present romance was written? Downright prediction that it was composed at a particular time or written in a particular year is, in the nature of the case, but desperate guessing. It will be safer to content ourselves with conclusions that are, on the whole, possible rather than precise and certain; to move within that pale, beloved of scholars, that lies between the *terminus a quo* and the *terminus ad quem.*

A *terminus a quo,* even though it be not an exact one, is easy to name. The romance could not have been written before May 26, 1363, the date of Coucy's arrival in England.[1] A *terminus ad quem* is more difficult to predicate; yet conclusions about it may be reached without too much bepuzzlement.

But before we reach them, we must glance at two certain events that stand out as milestones in the Earl of Bedford's English career, and of those two, either one might have been made a more memorable milestone by the composition of *Sir Gawain and the Green Knight.* The romance might have been written to celebrate the wedding of the Sire de Coucy with the Princess Isabella (July 27, 1365), though one need not necessarily conclude that it was composed during the week of the marriage festivities. It might also have been composed to celebrate Coucy's installation as a companion of the Garter (1365), *or* at some Christmas celebration after he had been admitted into that chivalric brotherhood.[2]

1. See Chapter III, above, "A French Knight of the Garter," note 11.
2. It is impossible to ascertain whether his installation took place on St. George's Day (April 23) or not. Under ordinary circumstances the presumption would be that it did take place on that day. Hulbert (*Mod. Phil.* 13. 142-44) suggests the possibility "that *GGK.* was written not for an order but for a Christmas-New Year's celebration." He calls attention to the special insistence placed throughout the poem on that season of the year and the sports and pastimes peculiar to it. This connection with Christmas was apparently of the poet's own making, for Hulbert points out that it does not occur in *Fled Bricrend* and some of the French sources or analogues. His conclusion is that in any case it seems certain that the poem was written for a Christmas celebration. It

Should this latter possibility prove to be a fact, it would explain alike the allusions to Edward's order and the poet's emphasis upon the holiday festivities of Christmas and New Year's.

Yet one who has followed in the preceding study the tale of the Sire de Coucy's English years, and read through this and other appendices which dissect and analyze, weigh and evaluate the problems raised by the text of the poem, must in the end come to only one conclusion: that *Sir Gawain and the Green Knight* was written after the Sire de Coucy's final severance of all the ties that bound him to his adopted country. For *Gawain* is the story of an action that was begun and carried through to an **end**. It tells the story of a man who left his own land, journeyed to a far country, solved the dilemma in which he found himself as best he might or could, though not with satisfaction to himself or to some others, and then, refusing all invitation to tarry, departed on his homeward way. If the romance does in very truth carry any reference or allusion to King Edward III's distinguished son-in-law, it seems almost certain that the poet would have written it only after his tale had been told—at least as far as English auditors were concerned. The cruel quandary in which Gawain finds himself by virtue of his double and antithetical promises, and his final, and slightly unsatisfac-

---

should be remarked, however, that it may also be connected with an order which held celebrations at Christmas time. In support of Hulbert's surmise it should be noted that G. Beltz (*Mem. of the Order of the Garter*, London, 1841, p. xxxviii) quotes a passage indicating that a Garter celebration was held at Christmas, 1343. The court was at Windsor for Christmas in 1364-65-66, the years of Coucy's admission (*Chronica Johannis de Reading*, ed. J. Tait, Manchester, 1914, pp. 160, 163, 168). Coucy's whereabouts at Christmas, 1365, is uncertain. He was granted permission to go to France by a letter patent of Nov. 26 of that year, but he might have been back for the holidays. He would appear to have spent the Christmas of 1366 in England. If Beltz's allusion be true, some sort of Garter celebration might have been held at Yuletide season of 1365 or 1366, and Coucy initiated into the Order in either one of those years.

tory, resolution of them, parallels the case of Enguerrand de Coucy, only after the year 1377.

Therefore, at any time from 1377 on, into the early years of the reign of King Henry IV, the poem might have been written. It would have a *raison d'être* as long as there survived in the England that the Seigneur de Coucy left anyone who bore his name (and the reader will remember that his daughter Philippa, Duchess of Ireland, lived on into the reign of her first cousin). The year of his wife's death (1379), or a year shortly after it, would, therefore, be a safe, if somewhat over-cautious, *terminus ad quem.*

But if I may gloss upon the text, and express a purely personal opinion, I will say that it would seem far more likely that the *Gawain*-poet wrote in the years that followed immediately after Coucy's departure than in the later eighties or nineties of the fourteenth century. For in 1378 and the early months of 1379, Isabella, to whom his departure meant most, was still alive, and our poet would probably have seized the occasion and written while the tide of popular interest in and the gossip about this startling and unusual separation within the royal family were running at the full. I should prefer to place the composition of *Gawain* within a period between the final months of 1376 and the early months of 1380 rather than later. This, however, is only my private opinion.

I may say, however, that a date in the late seventies or early eighties of the century is supported by the conclusions of scholars who have studied the poem. The consensus has been, and still is, that the literary activity of the *Gawain*-poet covered the forty years between 1360 and 1400. Scholarship of the last thirty years would place *Gawain* as the last of the poems of the Cotton Nero MS[3] written within that

3. In my ed. of *St. Erkenwald* (New Haven, 1926) I have advanced conclusions, which have met with general acceptance, namely, that that saint's legend was written by the *Gawain*-poet, and that it was the last to

limit of forty years, a belief justified by the careful balance of its structure and the finish and maturity of its style. Thus it would come after the homilies *Patience* and *Purity*, and after the elegy *Pearl*, which would bring it into the later decades of the fourteenth century.[4]

APPENDIX D

Enguerrand de Coucy and the Order of the Garter

THE READER has seen that even before the rediscovery of the poem, in the nineteenth century, a connection between it and the Order of the Garter had been postulated, by the inscription of the *Mot* of the Order after its concluding lines. The possibility of such a connection is, therefore, no modern notion.[1] That possibility is, indeed, slightly strengthened by the deliberate statement in the *Ballad of the Green Knight*, a

---

issue from his pen. I shall not at this time raise the question of the common authorship of *Erkenwald* and the poems of the Cotton Nero MS. For the composition of *Erkenwald*, 1386 seems a safe date.

4. For discussion of the chronology of the works of the poet, see my ed. of *St. Erkenwald*, p. lxxvii. Gollancz (*Pearl*, Oxford, 1921, p. xxxvi) believed that *Gawain* was the last of the four poems of the Cotton Nero MS to issue from the poet's pen. Osgood (*Pearl*, Boston, 1906, p. xlix and Menner (*Purity*, New Haven, 1920, p. xxxviii) agree. Tolkien-Gordon (*Sir Gawain*, pp. xxi-ii) would not place it earlier than the last quarter of the 14th century. The late Miss M. C. Thomas (*Gaw. and the Green Knt.*, Zürich, 1883, p. 33) would place the poems in the following order: "*Pearl* before *Gawain; Gawain* c. 1375-7;—*Cleanness* 1378-80, and *Patience* after *Cleanness*." Brandl (*Grund.* 1st ed. 2, 661-63) agrees. Ten Brink (*Hist.* 1. 348) would change this order by transposition of *Gawain* and *Pearl*. The consensus of scholarly opinion during the past twenty years would place *Gawain* as a late work of its author.

---

1. Since it is impossible to be sure that the inscription was not added as a later marginal notation by some reader of the poem, the supposition that it was the work of a copyist who transcribed from the original MS is consequently a mere guess.

"broken-down" and telescoped retelling of the romance,[2] to the effect that Gawain's acceptance of the lace led to the foundation of the Order of the Bath. Since the so-called "foundation" of the Order of the Bath in 1399 by Henry IV is fanciful, the term "Knight of the Bath" being found for the first time in an inventory of the effects of Henry V (ob. 1422),[3] the ballad must be much later than the romance. But, on the other hand, what is significant about both poems is that each, despite their many discrepancies and their separation in time, seems tied in some way to an English order of chivalry. What one tells implicitly and inferentially about the Order of the Garter, the other tells explicitly about the Order of the Bath. It would seem that in the later *rifacimento* expansive loquacity might have been at work, that inference might have been changed to downright statement. Two anonymous poems tied by tradition to two chivalric orders: tradition thus bids fair to intertwine two single cords into one of double strands. One is at a loss whether to postulate imitation of the earlier poem by the later, or the association, real or attempted, of each poem with an order of chivalry.

The most convincing evidence, however, for the connection between the romance and Edward III's famous Order, is that discovered by Professors Schlauch and Cargill in the very lines of the poem.[4]

When Gawain first appeared in the hall of Sir Bercilak de Hautdesert he wore a set of robes that (I believe) bore a heraldic blazon. We are not told whether he doffed this and donned another on the days that followed Christmas, but we are told that by the night of the 31st of December he had changed his apparel.

2. See J. E. Wells, *Manual of the Writings in ME* (New Haven, 1916), p. 58; G. L. Kittredge, *A Study of Gaw. and the Green Knight* (Cambridge, Mass., 1916), pp. 125 ff., 296.
3. N. H. Nicolas, *Orders of Knighthood* (London, 1842), 3. 16.
4. *PMLA* 43. 119-20.

The poet describes Gawain's garb on that evening in the following lines (1928-1931):

> He were a bleaunt of blwe þat bradde to þe erþe,
> His surkot semed hym wel, þat softe watȝ forred,
> And his hode of þat ilke henged on his schulder,
> Blande al of blaunner were boþe al aboute.

The blue bleaunt or mantle, the surcoat apparently of the same color, and the hood of blue furred within—why such care to specify cut and color? A study of Norris, *Costume and Fashion*,[5] shows us that Miss Schlauch and Mr. Cargill were correct in their belief that the poet was describing the habit of the Knights of the Garter. The blue woolen mantle of the knight was originally lined with white damask, his surcoat of the same material and, at first, of the same color, was lined with miniver. The hood of the Order was of the same material and color as the surcoat, and had also the miniver lining.[6] It is to be noted that, for some reason or other, Gawain did not wear the sword-belt of the Order;

5. 2. 237-41.
6. See G. Beltz, *Memorials of the Order of the Garter* (London, 1841), pp. li-liii. In later times different colors were used for the surcoat: in annual rotation blue, scarlet, sanguine in grain, white. Green is not mentioned, though Sir Hugh Wrottesley and his fellow-knights "kept the solemn feast of the garter, clad in coats of russet powdered with green garters" (*The Ancestor* 7. 173). Froissart (ed. Kervyn, 4. 205) tells us that the members were called "Chevaliers du Bleu Gertier," and the *Gawain*-poet certainly corroborates him, and would have us understand that the color of the mantle and surcoat was blue. The word *blaunner* (1931) evidently refers to a white-colored material of some sort. My late colleague, Professor E. C. Armstrong, informed me that as etymons *blanc-noir* ("black-white," i.e. ermine, see Kaluza's note on *Libeaus Desconus* 129; it should also be stated that the statutes of the Order prescribe for the surcoat and hood of the knights not ermine, but miniver), and *blanc de mer* (suggested by Tolkien with a query) are unsatisfactory, the latter being particularly dubious. He calls my attention to Wallon *blanmoir*, "pale, livide," a deriv. of *blanc-mort; see* Wartburg, *Etymolog. Wörterbuch* 1, s.v. *blank*. Pale would fit miniver which, according to Planché (s.v. *Cent. Dict.*), represents the white portions of the patchwork design of the different furs used in the middle ages.

possibly because he was not on that evening wearing the sword.

Why the poet was intent to inform us that Gawain had changed his dress to that of the Garter, I cannot say. I firmly believe that the change was intentional. I venture the surmise (it is no more) that the change from one garb to the other is to be explained by Gawain's acceptance of the green lace. Before he had accepted that lace, he did not don (possibly could not have donned) the insignia of the Order. Was the lace part of the apparel of the Order for a particular year, a Garter riband?[7]

Some of the claims of Isaac Jackson (*Angl.* 37.395), who first broached the idea that *Gawain* had a connection with Edward's Order, were quite fantastic, and at times may merit Kittredge's characterization of "eccentric," but those who scornfully dismissed the possibility of his claims were themselves writing in days when little was known of the poem or of the social conditions which fed its growth. After all, the poet's description of what is apparently the costume of the Garter is not proof of a connection, but only evidence for it. Yet it is evidence at first hand, and not of a secondary nature. It is what we find before us, not the result of conjecture or surmise.

If *Gawain* has a connection with the oldest and most honorable of all the orders of chivalry, it ought, perhaps, to be possible to find out about the poem more than we now know. The dialect localizes, even though somewhat indefinitely, the region in which it was written, and within that region one may hope to find out with accuracy members of the Order who had extensive holdings of land. And now some preliminary words on its membership of the fourteenth century.

Since 1348 is generally taken as the year of the foundation of the Order, any effort to discover among its com-

7. Needless to say, it is not the present Garter riband.

panions members whose incomes were derived from, or largely supplemented by, West Midland manors, must cover the original companions, their immediate successors of Edward's day, and the recipients of Richard II's conferring. Those who composed the Order in the days of its first three sovereigns achieved the honor because they were men whom the king loved and trusted, by whom he preferred to work, and with whom he preferred to relax. Yet the Order seemed always to have had a military cast; we find in it no *gens de robe*, save the clergymen who kept its records and said its collective prayers. In theory its individual companions were to regard one another as equals, because of their common membership in a nobler brotherhood of arms.

Actually, however, they were far from equal in wealth or social position. Members like Sir John Chandos or Sir Thomas Banastre were hard-bitten old campaigners who owed their selection to Edward's admiration of their fighting qualities rather than to any influence they could exert as wealthy landed proprietors who could bring big contingents of fighting men to the royal hosting. As I have remarked in a preceding essay, it is far more likely that the *Gawain*-poet served in the household of some great landed proprietor of the West Midlands, than that he followed the fortunes of some knight whose lands were of meagre extent, whose income was won by his sword, and whose ability to maintain or reward protégés was quite limited, if not nil. His *semblaunt sade*, "his concerned expression," would indeed be "for doc oþer erle," rather than for the simple and intrepid soldier whose renown was high and whose purse was light.

In the fall of the year 1937 I began an examination of the territorial holdings of those knights who were members of the Order under the sovereignty of Edward III and Richard II. My purpose, as the reader may well imagine, was to ascertain what knights of the Order were conspicuous holders of territory—manors, honors, knight's fees, messuages, etc.—in the West Midlands. Three months' search of the *Inquisitions post Mortem*, the *Charter, Close, Fine* and *Pat. Rolls* enabled me to eliminate from consideration companions whose holdings in the Northwest Midlands were nil or sporadic, or overshadowed in importance by those they possessed in other districts or counties. The residue of companions included members of the Order whose possessions, antecedents, or family position marked them out definitely as Northwest Yorkshire, Cravenshire, or Lancashire men. This residue included members of both the categories I have distinguished: (1) those who owed their selection to their fighting qualities, and (2) those whose territorial importance and influence, whatever their own merits or deserts may have been, made them natural candidates for such an honor.[8]

In the first category one would find Sir Thomas Ughtrede (No. 31),[9] who owed his Garter honors to the fact that

8. I shall have to ask the readers' indulgence for a good deal of condensation in this discussion of potential patrons of the *Gawain*-poet. Space and time forbid detailed arguments for the inclusion or rejection of many names because those arguments would have to be based on long lists of a man's holdings or the piecing together of isolated bits of evidence drawn from a search of public records. As I have explained above, I examined the written records at my disposal to ascertain magnates of the N.W. Midlands who "had possibilities" of turning into patrons of the alliterative poetry of their native region. But I concluded that the only way one could meet this tough problem of research was to take each and every Garter member and pass him through the corpus of rolls published by the PRO. This laborious task is still proceeding. To date, out of a membership of 92 to be considered, the holdings of 31 knights have been examined without my finding that any of them, except No. 31, Sir Thomas Ughtrede, was possessed of any considerable territory in the "warm" region. Possession of one or two manors, or of several knight's fees, within that region, when the bulk of a man's holdings lay in other districts or counties, hardly constitutes ground for considering him an influential figure therein. Cf. F. M. Stenton, "Changing Feudalism of the Middle Ages," *History* 19. 290: "A gentleman's influence in his own country or in the state depended far less on his own pedigree than on the connections which his ancestors had been able to establish with families of equal or higher rank." If influential he were to be, in a particular area, that influence had to be built up, by one means or another, within that area.

9. Numbers that follow the names of Garter knights indicate order of their election.

he had been "a first-class fighting man" in France. He appears to have been an important man in his native Yorkshire. He was frequently named as a member of commissions of enquiry into cases of disturbance or trespass in his county, and frequently given by his royal master such plums as licences to unpark wood, or grants of free warren. But his manor of Monkton on the Moor in the West Riding[10] was situated in Ainsty Wapentake, some distance from *Gawain*-country, and his other holdings, in the North and East Ridings, were still further removed.[11]

A Garter knight who arrests attention, because he had considerable holdings in Leyland and Amounderness Hundreds, Lancashire, is Sir Thomas Banastre (No. 55.)[12] Those hundreds contain a part of the county where we might expect to find the author of *Gawain*, but the facts of Sir Thomas' life, though few, stamp him as a tough soldier, more at home in the field than elsewhere.[13] The little that we know of him rather tells against his having sat for his portrait to the poet of *The Pearl*, as one who *alle þe los walt* among all ladies *ayquere aboute*.

A member of the Order who is a distinct possibility is Edward, Lord Despenser (No. 38). The bulk of his holdings were in counties other than Yorkshire, but in the West Riding he did have the manors of Kimberworth and Maltby,

10. *Cal. Pat. Rolls* 1334-38, p. 36.

11. M. E. Richardson (*Notes and Queries* 180. 96-97) suggests that Ughtrede may have had some connection with our poem and others of its school, but his evidence is of a generalized nature, and he presents none that links Ughtrede with those areas of Yks. or Lancs. that seem more likely to have bred the *Gawain*-poet.

12. Abstracts *IPM* (Lancs., Chetham Soc. XVC) 1. 14-15. See also inquisition on his grandfather, *Cal. IPM* 6. No. 488.

13. *Pat. Rolls* of 1350 record a pardon granted him by his royal master for a homicide [murder?], because of his good services done in a late sea-fight with the Spaniards. He died (*John of Gaunt's Reg. 1379-83* Camden Soc. 3rd Ser. 56, London, 1937, 1.153), as one would expect, with his boots on, when his ship was lost at sea (1379) on the return from a plundering expedition into Brittany.

and *terrae et tenementa* in Bawtry and Austerfield, all in the wapentakes of Strafforth and Tickhill.[14] Maltby and Austerfield are in the southern West Riding, sufficiently distant even from the Northwest tip of the county of Derby whence the poet might conceivably have come, but Strafforth Wap. is one of the "warm" spots, so that we dare not dismiss the possibility that Despenser's stake in the West Riding might have prompted a native of one of his manors to sing his praises— particularly when we survey the evidence that follows.

Froissart describes Despenser as the most handsome, courteous, and honorable knight of his time in England, and adds a welcome bit of information, namely, that ladies considered no social function perfect if Despenser were not present.[15] Clearly a possible candidate. Against him the most valid argument is the fact that the bulk of his holdings lay without Yorkshire, and that he seems to have had none in Lancashire.

We cannot pass over one Knight of the Garter who does not seem to have held any stake whatever in the northwest counties, but whose forebears and brother did—Sir Lewis Clifford (No. 64), Chaucer's friend, and the friend and favorite of many others, too. It is probable that he was a younger brother of the famous soldier, Roger Clifford, fifth lord of Skipton. Skipton Castle in Craven was the seat of the Cliffords. Sir Lewis was, therefore, a member of a distinguished family of Cravenshire.

Of his career we must speak only briefly. In 1352 he had been captured by the French, and ransomed by his own side. In 1389 he was one of the Englishmen who met the French challengers at the tournament of St. Inglevert. In 1390 he had crusaded with the Duke of Bourbon to Barbary. Thus

14. *IPM* (Rec. Com.). 49E3, No. 46.
15. Ed. Kervyn, 2. 106-7. For a further account of Despenser, see Sister M. A. Devlin, "An English Knight of the Garter in the Spanish Chapel at Florence," *Speculum* 4. 270 ff.

he had had opportunity to meet and know many French lords and ladies. We shall not, therefore, be surprised to find him mentioned by Deschamps in the *ballade* he addressed to Chaucer. Again, it is Clifford to whom Deschamps refers in a poem addressed to the Seneschal d'Eu. In it Deschamps avers he wishes to marry and ventures to ask the Seneschal to answer certain queries. If in doubt, he is to consult the "amorous Clifford."[16] Apparently Clifford was an authority on love and the proper way of making it, an expert in the art which the Green Knight's wife declares to be the crowning glory of chivalry. Sir Lewis thus satisfied one of the requirements of a prototype of Sir Gawain—he was a favorite with the ladies.

Nor was he a favorite with the fair sex alone. He held the confidence and favor of Richard II and of his powerful uncle of Lancaster also—something of a feat, for nephew and uncle did not always hold one another's confidence and favor. Time forbids our recital of the numerous positions of trust and importance that Clifford filled. His ability, despatch, diplomatic tact, and general popularity had made him a personage to whom the royal family often turned. It is quite possible that a poet who might have hailed from the vicinity of Craven wrote his romance with his eye on this accomplished gentleman as his model. If the poet lived or wrote near Skipton Castle, or was a dependent of Lord Clifford, a poem celebrating the renown of a conspicuous scion of the family might have been welcomed by the Cliffords, a family whose power and prestige in the northwest of England was growing. If he lived and worked in London, the poem, a tribute from one native of Cravenshire to another, may have procured him some reward from the rising luminary at the English Court.[17]

16. G. L. Kittredge, "Chaucer and Some of His Friends," *Mod. Phil.* 1. 6 ff.

17. *Vict. Hist. of Lancs.*, 4. 349 informs us that Sir Lewis, in right

In the second category five noblemen at once attract attention. We list them according to the year of their nomination to the Order, though in subsequent discussion we shall follow, not the order of time, but that of the probability of their having had to do with that anonymous master of the poetic school which flourished within their domains. They are (1) John of Gaunt, Duke of Lancaster (1361); (2) Edmund of Langley, later Duke of York, his brother (1361); (3) Enguerrand de Coucy, Earl of Bedford (1366); (4) Thomas Mowbray, Earl of Nottingham, later Duke of Norfolk (1383); (5) Robert de Vere, Earl of Oxford, later Duke of Ireland (1385, probably degraded in 1388). It is certainly noteworthy, and perhaps significant, that all five are related, closely or remotely, to the royal family, are kinsmen of the king.[18]

Let us take the last first, and begin with Thomas Mowbray (No. 72), a colorful figure in that turbulent period; it is he who takes our eye in the opening scenes of Shakespeare's *Richard II*. There are a few happenings in his scheming and tortuous career that make it not at all unlikely that *Gawain* might have been connected with him. Besides manors in the North Riding, he held Dinnington, Kirby Malesart (Claro Wap.), and Burton-in-Lonsdale, the last named being *extra* Ribble (*i.e.*, on the far side to a Cravenshire man). Besides manors, he was seized of an immense number of knight's fees in Yorkshire, some of them in West Riding[19] and on that count alone would have been a magnate well worth cultivating by a West Midland poet. Possessed of great wealth and, more important still, of the favor of

of his de la Warre wife, was in 1372 patron of the church at Ashton-under-Lyne, Salford Hund., Lancs.

18. Two are sons, one a son-in-law of Edward III; Robert de Vere married a granddaughter of that monarch. Thomas de Mowbray was a great-grandson of Thomas of Brotherton, 5th son of Edward I. Richard II recognized him as a kinsman; cf. *Cal. Pat. Rolls* 1381-85, p. 176.

19. *IPM* (Rec. Com.) 3.268, 1 Henry 4, No. 71.

the young monarch, his equal in age, there seemed no limit
to the power and influence he might achieve. His first marriage (May 6, 1382?), entered into while he was a minor
and his wife but ten years old, lasted but a year, and seemed
but a prelude to a more splendid one two years later (July,
1384).[20] In the year preceding, the Garter had been conferred upon this young nobleman *læta fronte*. Its possession
must have added éclat to those second nuptials.

It is just such an event happening to just such a young
nobleman that is likely to have inspired the writing of a
poem like *Sir Gawain*. If, indeed, it were inspired by aught
that its writer hoped for or had received from Thomas Mowbray, it would seem more likely to have been written at or
about the time of his second marriage than some years after
that event. For Mowbray did not improve with age, and it
is more reasonable to imagine the poet celebrating the rise of
a hopeful young nobleman than praising the callous and
faithless politician of later years. But whatever his conduct
became, or however we regard him, we cannot, as yet, rule
out the Earl of Nottingham as a possible patron of the *Gawain*-poet.

The four other potential patrons might almost be considered and dilated upon en masse, for they all fall into a
fraternal-avuncular-nepotal relationship. Perhaps, and it is
a big "perhaps," the least likely "patron" of the four is Edmund of Langley (No. 37), Earl of Cambridge and Duke
of York (in or before 1361). If he be a "less likely patron,"
it is only because we do not find that he held lands in Lancashire. By far the greater portion of his territorial appanages
were in other counties than Yorkshire, but in the West Riding he did hold "castra, maneria, villæ et dominia."[21] Some

20. Higden's description of the second marriage (*Polychronicon* 9.44)
indicates that it was an event of unusual brilliance.
21. Coningsburgh (Straff. Wap.), Sandhale (prob. Long Sandall,
Kirk Sandall in Straff. Wap., rather than Sandall Magna in Agbrigg

of these "castra et maneria" may have been quite removed from the speech area in which *Gawain* was written, but they are in West Riding wapentakes that border Lancashire, and thus possible "warm" localities. Furthermore they were held by a prince of the blood who could have rewarded or provided for a *protégé* or dependent who was born on them. Moreover, Edmund of Langley was of a lenient and generous nature, "who had no care to be a lord of great worldly riches." A versified characterization of this good, easy man recalls to our minds the interest our own author took in hunting:

> When all the lords to councell and parlyament
> Went, he wolde to hunte and also to hawekyng.[22]

Apparently the sort of person who might have patronized poets who were also huntsmen par-excellence. We cannot dismiss him as a possible patron, though his brother John is a more likely one.

Three candidates for the honor of having paid or protected the master of all the alliterative poets remain for our consideration, and he would be bold indeed who undertook to say which one of them was likely to have been the very man. Indeed, the poet might well have received favor from any two, or from all three of them. As suggested in a previous appendix, he may have been a West Midland man attached to the household of Philippa, Countess of Oxford and Duchess of Ireland (last creation dated October 13, 1386), who had received the lands of which her father was seized in Yorkshire, Lancashire, and Westmoreland. Having eaten the bread which the father and mother had provided, he

---

Wap.), Haitefeld (probably Great or Little Hatfield, Straff. Wap.), Wakefield (Morley Wap., though in the eastern end of the Wap.), Thorn (probably Thorne near Coningsburgh), Fishlake (Straff. Wap.), Holmefrith (?) and Sourby (probably Sowerby near Wakefield, see *Vict. Hist. of Yks.*, 2. 302[n]); see also *IPM* (Rec. Com.) 3. 282, 3 Henry IV, no. 36.

22. *Dict. of Natl. Biog.* 32. 110, "Edmund of Langley."

may have tarried on in the *familia* of their daughter, and filed his pen to compliment her husband when he had won (or was granted) the Garter.

Indeed, where three such powerful noblemen as Vere, Earl of Oxford (No. 73), Coucy, Earl of Bedford (No. 42), and John of Gaunt, Duke of Lancaster (No. 36) were all so closely related, one pays his money and takes his choice. As far as discussion has hitherto gone, what speaks for a connection with the house of Coucy-Guines speaks as much and as well for the house of Lancaster. A glance at the map of the "Lancashire Estates" in S. Armitage-Smith's life of the Duke[23] will show that he was feudal lord of nearly the whole county of Lancashire. A cursory perusal of the introduction to the invaluable *Register* published by the Camden Society will show how large was his household and how great its need for a trained clerical personnel and administrative officers of real ability. Deeper study will reveal that a very large part of the business which employed the pens of the ducal secretariate had to do with the county palatine, and that among the writers and those to whom they wrote there were not a few Lancashire men. It is quite possible, as Oakden has said, that the author "was connected with John of Gaunt's household."[24]

Whose the household that harbored the poet we cannot now know. We have, I believe, limited the number of possible patrons, but unless the author himself and something of his career as well were to be suddenly discovered, I know not how one could undertake to say that he was a dependent of the Countess of Bedford rather than one of the Duke of Lancaster. Even if such a happy discovery were made, one might find out that he had been a dependent of both. The most that we can say is this: that whoever he was and wher-

23. *John of Gaunt*, N. Y., 1905.
24. *Allit. Poetry in ME*, 1. 261.

ever he wrote, it is altogether likely that he wrote under the ægis of some Garter lord.

But there is one obligation binding upon the conscience of a member of the Order to which we shall have to give our particular consideration. When we have done so, we shall, I believe, be led to entertain as a good possibility the belief that the poet may have shaped his story with the case of Enguerrand de Coucy in mind.

At the time that he wrote, the "tres noble Compaignie et Ordre du Jartier," as Coucy himself called it, was in its "first age." Tradition had not gathered about it and the obligations which it imposed upon its membership were well known.

Few scholars today believe the romantic story of the loss of the Countess of Salisbury's garter as the cause of the foundation of the order. That story appeared first in Polydore Virgil (1470?-1555?). Froissart does not mention it; contemporary historians know it not. G. Beltz, historian and official of the Order, believes that the Garter "may have been intended as emblem of the *tie* or *union* of warlike qualities to be employed in assertion of the Founder's claim to the French crown; and the motto as a retort of shame upon him who should think ill of the enterprise, or of those whom the king had chosen to be the instruments of its accomplishment."[25] He adds, "The taste of that age for allegorical conceits, impresses, and devices, may reasonably warrant such a conclusion."

Instances from history confirm most strongly this opinion. French kings and diplomats were certainly under no illusions as to what the Order meant. One of the regulations of the French Order of the Star (founded after the Garter) forbade a member to accept membership in any foreign military order without the sovereign's consent, a provision probably aimed at the prestige of Edward's order.

25. *Mem. of the Order of the Garter*, p. xlvii.

In 1390 when the first cousin of the French King, the Count of Ostrevant (son-in-law of Philippe le Hardi, Duke of Burgundy), rather tactlessly accepted an election to the Garter from King Richard II, he found himself upon his return in very hot water indeed. Froissart informs us that Charles VI reproached him,[26] and Barante gives the reason for that reproach and for all the criticism that followed his thoughtless action:

On ajoutait que celui qui recevait le ruban de la Jarretière prêtait serment au roi d'Angleterre de ne jamais faire la guerre contre lui, que c'était se faire son homme, et beaucoup d'autres propos qui n'avaient pas grande vérité. Toutfois, lorsque le roi le sut, il en pensa de même et fut très-courroucé.[27]

Now by his acceptance of the Garter, Enguerrand de Coucy had taken oath to support the claim of the English King to the French crown. He may have been politely deceived about the purposes of the Order, its true purposes concealed from him; he may, like the Count of Ostrevant, have accepted it for "amour et compagnie"; in fact the indications are that he did, but if that acceptance seemed a trivial thing at first, a favor to a generous father-in-law whom he seems always to have loved and admired, its implications must have become increasingly evident with the passage of time. "Who takes the King of England's Garter becomes the King of

26. Ed. Kervyn, I. 208 (the quotation below is taken from Kervyn's *Life of Froissart* in the first volume of the set):
Le comte d'Ostrevant, à qui le roi de France reproche "de ne pas avoir refusé l'ordonnance de cet ordre," répond "que toutes gens doivent savoir que oncques n'y eut parole qui pust porter préjudice au royaume de France, fors amour et compagnie."

The historian Gilles La Roque (*Traité de la Noblesse*, p. 299) tells the story of a Breton nobleman who was put to death on April 4, 1450, by order of his brother the Duke of Brittany, because he had accepted the Order of St. George of England (which I take to be the Garter). The story sounds improbable (though I have not had opportunity to verify it), but offers some evidence for the resentment which the French bore to the Garter.

27. *Histoire des Ducs de Bourgogne* II. 97.

England's man." The truth of those words must have often distressed and perplexed him in the night watches.

Once a member, what could Coucy have done? To have resigned shortly after election, his best course after all, would have been ungrateful and discourteous. It is significant that in 1367 he gave the king the reversion of all his Lancashire manors.[28] To have taken up arms on the French side, when the war broke out afresh, would have been the act of a boor and an ingrate; to have fought in the English armies, as his Garter oath required, treasonable. He had been placed in an impossible position from both the French and the English point of view. He had gone to England as a French hostage. From the obligations of hostageship he was not legally free until his wedding day. He tarried thereafter in England to receive the Garter. His countrymen might well have considered such conduct equivocal, to say the least. On the other hand, when finally he did return and had accepted service under the French King in 1376, he could rightly and fairly have been criticized (and probably was) by his wife's countrymen. There he was assisting French policy, which was opposed to that of his father-in-law, yet all the while wearing his father-in-law's Garter around his knee![29] Is there not a parallel between his situation and that of the perplexed and embarrassed Sir Gawain?

28. These were the manors and holdings which Joan de Coupland had been occupying. Coucy's grant (Nov. 26, 1367) in reversion is printed *in extenso* in *Arch. Jrnl.* 35. 166. In it he declares that he has made it *pro certis et evidentibus causis.* See also *Vict. Hist. Lancs.,* 7. 303, note 48; *Cal. Close Rolls* 1364-68, p. 403.

29. Robes were issued to (or prepared for) Coucy against the Garter celebration of 1376; see Beltz, p. 10. Footnote 80 of "A French Knight of the Garter" (Chap. III, above) shows that he was still in England before May 12, 1376.

APPENDIX E

The Pentangle

I

ONE OF THE MOST mystifying puzzles of the poem is the import and significance of the Pentangle, or Endless Knot as the English call it.[1] Why should the poet have spent so much time describing the figure, and assuring us that it was particularly appropriate to Gawain's character and personality? For myself, I may say frankly that I can see no reason for his having done so, if he were not designating a particular person whose device actually was the "endless knot."

The origin of the Pentangle, Pentagram, or Pentalpha, i.e., the Five-Pointed Star, lies buried in the mists of history. It is said to have been used by the philosopher Pythagoras, and to have become associated with the secret rites and practices of his followers. The Greek Christians were said to have employed it, and possibly through them the Jews adopted it. It became associated with the name of the most powerful and sagacious of the Jewish monarchs, King Solomon, as the *Gawain*-poet himself tells us.[2] Neoplatonist and Alexandrian

1. The word "Knot" is used here in the sense that heralds employ it; cf. "Bourchier Knot."
2.   For hit is a figure þat haldeʒ fyue poynteʒ,
        And vche lyne vmbe-lappeʒ and loukeʒ in oþer,
        And ay-quere hit is endeleʒ, and Englych hit callen
        Ouer-al, as I here, þe endeles knot.
Tolkien and Gordon (620 n.) suggest that the poet found an account of the Pentangle "in some treatise or commentary of the Alexandrian school." The poet himself tells us that
        Hit is a syngne þat Salamon set sum-quyle.

schools used it in astrological calculations and magical formulae. Either through Byzantium, or Moorish Spain, or the wanderings of the Jews—possibly from all three sources—it reached western Europe, there to be employed again in mystic enumeration, magical incantation, and medical research. In Freemasonry today its benevolent symbolism is known and revered.

An extended search into its powers and properties for good or evil would drive one to a sanitarium. I have sometimes felt in the course of my labor that I have tarried with it too long. The poet mentions some of its mystic implications and allows others to be revealed by the course of the story.[3] Within the five points of the Pentangle we find sometimes written the five letters *SALUS*, one at each point. These, of course, spell out the Latin word for "Health, Completeness or Soundness" (of body and mind).[4] Gawain is then sound in his five wits and in his five fingers.[5] When delineated on the body of a man in the crucified position, the apices of its angles point out the five places where the Saviour was wounded, and then *SALUS* carries the meaning "salvation." Association with the Five Wounds of Christ leads to association with the Five Joys of His Blessed Mother. This mystic sign can ward off the attacks of wild beasts, as lines 720-22 of the poem show, and because it signifies the Five Wounds of the Saviour of Mankind, it is particularly effica-

---

I suggest that he need not have gone much further for the source of his description than the ecclesiastical writers of the Roman Church. William of Auvergne in his *De Legibus*, caps. 23, 27, refers to it as being connected with King Solomon.

3. The import of its endless lines is explained in *Encycl. of Occultism*, pp. 261-62.

4. F. E. Hulme, *Symbolism in Christian Art* (London, 1891), p. 218.

5. Since Five is composed of both odd and even numbers, it had good and bad properties. Thus the fingers do good and evil works. The complete number Five, however, binds all into a unity of Soundness. See E. Beschoff, *Geheime Wissenschaften, Die Mystik und Magie der Zahlen* (Berlin, 1920), pp. 203-7.

cious against evil spirits, who dread any sign that has associations with Him. One can readily see why Gawain bears it
on his shield when he goes to seek the Green Knight. It is
noteworthy that he was tempted when he wore it not.[6]

As the symbol of Christ, the Pentangle is, therefore, the
Star of the Magi, was so recognized in medieval symbolism,
and is so recognized in Freemasonry today.[7] As the Pythago-
rean sign of COMPLETION and UNITY, "Zeichen der
Vollkommenheit," it would naturally under Christian auspices denote Christ; and thus in a manner which we might
deem irreverent, but which was perfectly understood in the
symbolism of medieval days, The Perfect Man, Sir Gawain,
who is on earth in some sort an image or type, imperfect
though it be, of Christ's perfection in Heaven. So much,
then, for the endless knot, and now for an attempt to untie it.

II

There are some little-known facts in the contemporary
history of France that may furnish an explanation of why the
poet used a golden Pentangle on a field gules as the device on
Gawain's shield. I am inclined to doubt whether the explanation that one arrives at when one has ingeniously pieced them

6. As to its efficacy in repelling evil spirits, F. Friedensburg (*Die
Symbolik der Mittelaltermünzen*, Berlin, 1913, p. 26), says:
"Als 'Siegel Salamonis' oder 'Drudenfuss' ist dieses Zeichen dem Mitte-
lalter überliefert worden, ein Zauberbild, das hauptsächlich das Eindringen
böser Geister und ihr Entweichen, wenn sie gefangen sind, verhütet."
It is a tribute to the poet's sense of dramatic verisimilitude (as well as
to his sense of humor) that Gawain is tempted in bed, where he naturally
has no shield blazoned with the Pentangle to protect him. Any medieval
auditor or reader would know that though Gawain sallies forth to meet
a pretty powerful opponent when he departs from Camelot, the Pentangle
on his shield would do something to equalize the odds. Yet for artistic
reasons the poet allows the lords and ladies of Camelot to forget this fact
as Gawain departs; see lines 674-85.
7. See L. Spence, *Encycl. of Occultism*, p. 261; A. E. Waite, *The
Hist. of Magic of Éliphas Lévi* (London, 1913), pp. 1-2; and *A New
Encycl. of Free-Masonry* (London, 1921), 2. 108-9, by the last named.
For a suggestive description of the Star of the Magi, see Chrysostom in
Matt. Hom. VI (*Opera*, ed. Montfaucon (Paris, 1836), 7. 101-3).

together cross-word-puzzle wise is necessarily a true one. It rests too much upon possibilities rather than likelihoods— and, as it seems to me, upon "outside possibilities, possibilities that have to be thought up," not those inherent in the historic situation. Yet the reader and I have bound ourselves to follow out *all* paths that might lead to certainty—or, if that is unobtainable, to conclusions that seem to have some likelihood of being true. There is one chance that the explanation that follows might be correct. I offer, therefore, no apology for bringing it forward.

In 1351 the chivalrous and bellicose Jean le Bon of France instituted what many believe was intended as a rival order to the English Garter, the Order of the Star (*Ordre de l'Étoile*). Since Edward's Order claimed to be a revival of Arthur's Round Table, Jean dedicated his own to the same ideal, and as the English King had placed his under the patronage of the national protector, St. George, he invoked for his the favor of the Blessed Virgin, the Lady of the Fleur-de-lis.

The King's circular letter of November, 1351, to prospective members is the only contemporary record of the Order.[8] It mentions several of the rules ordained by Jean for its governance, among them, one to the effect that no member shall accept membership in a foreign order without royal permission,[9] appoints a day of assemblage, and requests that a representation of the recipient's arms be forwarded so that the decorators may be enabled to do their duty before the initial feast-day of the Order. The Star appears to have had only one feast (January 6, 1352, day of the Three

8. Printed in E. de Laurière, *Ordonnances des roys de France* 2. 465-66; L. d'Achery, *Spicilegium* 3. 730-31; L. Pannier, *La Noble Maison de Saint-Ouen* (Paris, 1872), pp. 88-90.

9. Should he be a member of another order at the time of his nomination he must swear to prefer the Star, and consider its interests of prior importance (Pannier, p. 89).

Kings). For us the most important regulation is that which defines the costume of the members.

The knights of the Order were to wear "un cote blanche, un sercot et un chaperon vermeil, quant ils seront sans mantel."[10] When they wore the long mantle, such as Gawain wears, it was to be red in color and furred with vair, not with ermine, and the surcoat or cote-hardie (if no surcoat were worn) was to be white. In other words, there was to be a red robe over a white undergarment in every case of public appearance on the part of a member: "vestus de vermeil dessus et de blanc dessoubz."[11] The ring worn by the members was of rather intricate design, and does not directly concern us, but on the shoulder of the mantle there was to be clasped a white star (which might also be worn in the "chaperon"). When the mantle was doffed, the knight might wear the star-shaped jewel in any coat he pleased, or on his cote-armure; only it must at all times be plainly visible. In order to save himself the trouble of unclasping his jewelled star too often, the knights came to wear the five-pointed star sewn or embroidered on the shoulder of the mantle.[12]

We have spoken of the star worn by the knights as being white (argent). That borne by the king and members of the

10. *I.e.* "Over a white jacket or cote-hardie is to be worn the red surcoat and the hat or head-covering is also to be red."

11. *Grandes Chroniques de France (Chron. des Quatre Premiers Valois,* ed. S. Luce, Paris, 1862), pp. 23-24.

12. It is generally or usually true that the heraldic painters in France or England render a star (or mullet unpierced) with five points, in Germany and Italy with six. See C. Menestrier, *La Nouvelle Méthode Raisonnée du Blason* (Lyon, 1761), p. 40.

In *Chron. de Jean II et Charles V,* 4. 14-16, there is an illustration (from a contemporary manuscript) of the Knights of the Star. The stars on their mantles are out of all proportion, have eight or more points, and have taken on a black coloration because of the oxidation of the illuminator's paint. The illustration is conventionalized, and any discrepancies with the information given above can be so explained. Strange to say, in a lower portion of the same illustration the stars on the knightly mantles are five-pointed!

blood royal was of gold.[13] We know this to be true, because we have the French Exchequer Accounts to prove it, and we also know that the star worn by the king and princes of the blood did not have to have the elaborate design of the finger-ring.[14] *L'Étoile Royale* was then the Golden Five-Pointed Star, the Pentangle. Gradually the golden star on the red ground, the colors associated with the Order, came to be a device of the French kings. It remains to add that the motto of the Order was *Monstrant regibus astra viam,* a plain reference to the Star of the Magi.[15]

After the capture of Jean le Bon at Poitiers, his policies and ideas were completely reversed by his canny son Charles. Among the first of them to be discarded was the Order of the Star. Charles summoned no meetings, and, after leaving its seat, La Noble Maison de Saint-Ouen, in disrepair for some years, deeded it away to the canons of the Sainte Chapelle in Paris. Long ceremonies tired him, and the first and only session of the Order that he attended as Dauphin, probably was for him a horrible memory. But, and this fact is im-

13. There is some evidence to show that the star worn by the knights came to be made of gold or was thickly gilded. See a description of a surviving specimen of "l' ancienne décor. de l'étoile," *Bull. monumental,* 1868, pp. 254-55; also Grandmaison, *Dict. Hérald,* p. 564: "ils devaient porter une étoile d'or brodée sur le mantelet."

14. See Pannier, *La Noble Maison, Pièces Justificatives,* pp. 71-72, where the accounts of the French Exchequer are printed:

> *Pour le Roy:* pour faire et forgier une estoille
> et un anel tout d'or à XXII caraz.
> *Pour . . . le Dauphin:* pour faire et forgier une
> estoille d'or toute plaine, sans perrerie.
> *Pour monseigneur d'Orliens:* pour faire et forgier une
> estoille d'or sans perrerie.

15. Pannier (p. 116 n.) denies that there is any record of this motto in ancient documents. Dacier, one of the most trustworthy historians of the Order, asserts the existence of the motto, though he notes that it is not mentioned in the King's circular letter. Other historians corroborate Dacier, though many are simply repeating him. It will be remembered that the first feast was held on the day of the Three Kings. I am quite willing to accept Dacier's statement in toto; see "Recherches Hist. sur L'établissement et l'extinct. de l'Ordre de l'Étoile," *Mem. de Lit., de l'Acad. Royale des Inscrip.* 39. 679, note.

portant, he was accustomed sometimes at audiences or by letter patent to grant to the deserving to bear as a device *L'Étoile Royale.* Two records attest this practice.[16] One should note that the distinction he granted as regent or as king was not a "badge," which could not be borne on a shield, for joustings or tournaments, but a "device."[17]

The final step to which our discussion of the Order of the Star leads is this. In 1358 the young Enguerrand de Coucy distinguished himself in putting down the *Jacquerie.* He was called to Paris, as the historian Mazas informs us, to receive the thanks of the regent Charles. There in March, 1360, the regent conferred upon him "L'Ordre de la Chivalerie."[18] The phrase *conférer l'ordre de la chivalerie* is vague. One would naturally understand it to mean that Coucy received from the regent the accolade of knighthood; yet I have found one instance where it refers to a man's being received into a military or chivalric order after he had already received the accolade that dubbed him knight.[19] The question confronts us, "did the regent confer upon Enguerrand merely the accolade of knighthood, or was it the right to bear the royal device of the Star?"

Any answer to it is dependent upon two other questions: (1) At what age would the honor of knighthood have been bestowed upon the young lord of Coucy? (2) How reliable and accurate a historian is Alexandre Mazas?

To the first question there is no definite answer. If born

16. Dacier (677) informs us that "l'Ordre subsista, non plus comme Ordre de Chivalerie, mais comme marque de distinction, en forme de devise honorifique, que les Rois accordèrent quelquefois pour récompense des services, sans aucune formalité." As an instance of such a grant he cites that to Armand Courbon by royal letters patent of Feb. 20, 1371. A. Favine (*Theater of Honour and Knighthood*, London, 1623, p. 347), records in 1376 a similar grant to John de Roche-Chouard and John de Beaumont.

17. For the distinction between the words, see J. R. Planché, *Cycl. of Costume* 1. 525-26.

18. *Capitaines Français* 3. 5.

19. Cf. *Hist. des Ordres Militaires* (Amsterdam, 1721) 3. 402-4.

in 1339, Enguerrand would have been in his majority in
1360. Knighthood was conferred quite early; the knight was
a fighter, and youth and strength were necessary to his success. Chaucer's squire—twenty years old—was not a knight,
but it is more likely that the heir of the Coucys would have
been in a more favourable situation for receiving the honor
during or after his first campaign than the son of a simple
banneret like Chaucer's knight. It is possible that the Sire de
Coucy was knighted in the field by some older and more
approved warrior—an especial honor. On the other hand, it
would have been an honor to receive the accolade from royal
hands, an honor worth waiting for. There the question
stands.[20]

To the second question there can now be no final answer.
To ask about a historian's accuracy is a good deal like asking
about a Christian's possession of grace; sometimes he has more
of it, sometimes less. The case of Mazas seems a chequered
one. I have detected him in several minor inaccuracies.[21] Yet,
as I have said elsewhere, he seems to have had access to documents that others did not. At times he relates events and
makes allusions in a manner so precise and definite that one
wonders whether he had not combed the *Bibliothèque Nationale* more assiduously than other biographers of Coucy;

20. I took opportunity to place this question before authorities upon
English medievalism in the summer of 1937: S. M. Collins, Esq. F.S.A.,
the Rev. E. E. Dorling, F.S.A., and Oswald Barron, F.S.A. The first
remarked that Mazas' statement did not sound as if the accolade of
knighthood was the honor conferred. The second was strongly of the
opinion that Coucy would have received the accolade before his appearance
at the Hotel St. Pol. He based his belief upon the general custom of the
times. With this belief Mr. Barron was in entire agreement.

21. Mazas gives (pp. 65-76) quite a thrilling and vivid account of
Coucy's presence in Scotland in 1385 as a member of a French expedi-
tionary force, and of his subsequent invasion of Cumberland. Terrier de
Loray (*Jean de Vienne*, Paris, 1878, p. 204 note 2) shows that at the
time he was supposed to be in Scotland, he was all the while at L'Ecluse
(Sluys) preparing for an invasion of England which never came off.

whether his relation may not be quite solidly based upon *fonds historiques,* even though the exuberance of his fancy and the gay eulogizing of his hero makes us suspicious of him. Obviously there is no available answer to the question now, and until there is, the statements of this French historian who wrote in the Age of Romanticism must be received with caution.

So of solution, right or wrong, there is none. Gawain does bear the golden Star on the red shield. It may be the *Étoile* of the French kings Jean and Charles. It is possible that in England Jean conferred the Star upon the young hostage who had arrived as one of his substitutes. It is possible that the future Charles V suggested that he bear it when jousting at Windsor—as a reminder of his French origin and allegiance. Yet these suppositions are only possible ones; their correctness depends also upon other "ifs" and upon the accuracy of a somewhat shaky historian. No chancellery of the Star ever existed. It is doubtful whether it had records, and if it did, they are hopelessly gone. If Coucy were ever granted its privileges and honors, we shall probably never know it as fact. Indeed, fact it is not—and even as possibility it seems highly unlikely.

III

And now I may be permitted to say what I think is the most likely reason for the appearance of the mystic Pentangle in our romance.

The late Max Prinet, one of the most distinguished students of medieval heraldry and sigillography in the world, wrote in 1916 a paper entitled "Les Usages Héraldiques au XIVᵉ Siècle."[22] It is based upon the heraldic information to be gleaned from a search through the *Chronicles* of Froissart, who, it will be remembered, was a protégé of Coucy and a contemporary of the *Gawain*-poet. Prinet's words, which

22. *Ann. Bull. de la Soc. de l'Hist. de France* (1916) 53. 141-55.

I quote below, therefore apply to the heraldic practice of our author's own day.

> Froissart signale un petit nombre d'écus armoriés: les uns sont des écus de tournoi; les autres, dont la destination n'est pas spécifiée, sont généralement mentionnés de telle manière qu'il semble bien que ce sont des objets de parade ou de simples figures emblématiques.

> Les récits du chroniqueur permettent de constater la concurrence que les symboles du fantaisie, les "devises" galantes, faisaient aux armoiries, tant à la guerre qu'aux tournois.

Prinet's words, to my mind, furnish the best explanation for the appearance of the five-pointed Star of the Magi in our poem. The author describes the Pentangle, or "Endless Knot,"[23] so minutely because it was the "device" of some nobleman or banneret whom he had known, or known of, or wished to bring to the minds of the readers of his day. That gentleman had borne it upon shield or coat at some jousting at Windsor or at Sheen. Possibly it had been the cognizance of a "team" of knights who had challenged all comers "all a summer's day," and the poet was complimenting some member of the victorious combination. Or he may have been glancing at some one particular person whom all lords and ladies alike united in praising, and to whom the Pentangle, the symbol of completeness or perfection, had been unanimously assigned, as a cognizance "to bear on shield and coat." No mention of Sir Gawain's bearing of the Pentangle is to be found in any of the Arthurian stories in which he appeared. The poet himself must have introduced it into the romance that he wrote. And if he did, it was because it had an association that was current in his time amid courtly

23. The poet informs us (630) that the Pentangle was so called by the English. His use of the phrase, the only use recorded in *NED* (s. v. *knot*, sb.[1], 6), would seem to associate it with the use (*NED* sense 2b) in such phrases as the Bourchier, Bowen, Heneage, Ormond, Stafford, and Wake knots; see Woodward and Burnett, *Heraldry, British and Foreign* (1892) 2. 585.

circles, an association with a particular knight. Who he could have been we know not, but one's mind turns quite naturally, and with perfect right, towards one whom all noblemen, knights, dames, and demoiselles of the poet's day praised as the nonpareil—Enguerrand de Coucy.[24]

APPENDIX F

Philippa Countess of Oxford

PHILIPPA, daughter of Enguerrand and Isabella, was twelve years old when her mother died. Her future had been, however, somewhat anticipated. At an early age she had become affianced to Robert de Vere, second earl of Oxford, who, as a young boy, had been placed under the wardship of her father and mother. The lad would have, at his majority, great possessions, and a large rental from them. So far as wealth and prestige were concerned, he was indeed a catch, and Edward III and his daughter quite evidently felt that they would be lacking in parental providence, if they failed to bring such a windfall in for their daughter's possessing.

The wishes of the young gentleman, or of Philippa herself, in accordance with medieval practice in the matter of marrying and giving in marriage, seem never to have been consulted or ascertained. However horrible such procedure may seem to us of today, it was the usual custom in the Middle Ages (as it is today on the continent of Europe), where the perpetuation of a family, its honors and posses-

24. "Le Sire de Coucy étoit fort aimable près de dames, qu'il en avoit la réputation, & qu'il étoit très bien-vu des seigneurs & des dames partout" (quoted from Zurlauben, *Bibliothèque Militaire*, etc., 2. 401, note e). To Baron Zurlauben's paraphrase of Froissart, one can add the chronicler's own words (Kervyn, 7. 321): "le gentils sires de Couci . . . qui bien afféroit en un feste, et mieuls le savoit faire que nuls aultres."

sions,, was deemed of greater importance than prepossessions or whims of callow youth.

But whether the practice in its general application is sound or not, in this particular instance it proved unfortunate. With all that seemed propitious and favorable to the mutual happiness of husband and wife, the marriage was a failure. Possibly the fact that the young couple had no children had something to do with its unhappy outcome; but this is only a guess, and in gauging the causes and reasons for marital disagreement in past, as in the present, centuries, we are always on ground where scandal and whispering grow rife, and truth but sparse and poorly.

The exact date of the marriage between Philippa and Robert de Vere has not been stated by chroniclers of her own day or historians of the present.[1] She was married at eleven years, and the bridegroom could not have been much older, but such early unions, reprehensible as they appear to us of today, when the newspapers record their occurrence among the mountaineers of the southern Appalachians, were by no means unknown amid high society of the medieval centuries. Perhaps—it is a guess and nothing more—their early union may have been the cause of their later unhappiness.

The young couple must have been often at Court, for Robert de Vere soon became a prime favorite with the youthful monarch, Richard II. We can see on the *Patent Rolls* evidence of the young Earl's favor with his royal master. On October 25, 1382, the Coupland lands, which Philippa's father had held before he surrendered them, and whose income her mother had enjoyed, were granted to her

1. A. Mazas (*Capitaines Français* 3. 28) says that Philippa married Vere four years after the return of her mother to England, which would make 1381 the year of their union. *Complete Peerage* 2. 591-92, however, shows that they were already married before April 23, 1378, and therefore in Isabella's lifetime (she died in 1379). The reader hardly needs any reminding that the bride's father was not present at the wedding.

husband and herself, "especially for the support of the said Philippa."[2] About a year later (October 7, 1383), those same lands were granted to Vere in fee simple in the event that his wife should predecease him.[3] What is important for us to notice, however, is that whatever may have been the reasons that prompted Richard to make these grants to his cousins, the result of them was that Philippa and Robert held what her father's family had held. Her tenants and sub-feudatories still owed allegiance to the lineal descendant of the lords to whom their parents or predecessors had paid it; or in the event of their liege lady's death, to the nearest relative she possessed.

Meanwhile all had not been going well with the youthful pair. Robert de Vere had progressed so far into the affections of his King, that Richard seemed wholly swayed by his wishes and advice in matters great and small, momentous or trivial. He had created him Marquis of Dublin on December 1, 1385, an unprecedented title, with unprecedented powers and privileges joined to it. When the magnates of the realm objected, the patent was cancelled, and another creating him Duke of Ireland, issued in the next year (October 13, 1386), with even wider powers. Philippa had become a duchess, but the higher honor probably brought her little satisfaction, for she must have seen that her husband, if a king's favorite, was no general favorite, particularly with some of those whose opinions she must have been taught to respect. If at that time she could not altogether share in the general opinion about him, she was soon to be thoroughly

2. *Cal. Pat. Rolls* 1381-85, p. 177. The grant was made on the complaint of the Earl and Countess that they had not sufficient to maintain their estate. A grant to his first cousin of what her parents had held was a perfectly natural and defensible act on Richard's part, but the record of his subsequent actions towards Robert de Vere gives ample ground for the suspicion that concern for Philippa's needs was not the only motive that prompted him in this case.

3. *Cal. Pat. Rolls* 1381-85, p. 314.

disillusioned. In his comings and goings at Court, the Earl had found the charms of a certain Bohemian attendant on the Queen so seducing, that he sought to repudiate his wife and marry his inamorata. Strangely enough, far from calling a halt to such a mad idea, Richard actually seems to have supported and abetted it. His infatuation with his favorite had become so great, Froissart tells us, that had the Duke said that black was white, the King would not have contradicted him.[4]

In 1387, so the chronicler Malverne informs us, Vere's emissary, through the stories of false witnesses, pushed through the Roman Curia a decree of divorce. This he could hardly have done without royal support. He was then free to marry his lady-love and put away his wife.[5]

Public opinion was pretty well aroused against the King's protégé as the man whose unwise counsel was responsible for a number of Richard's political blunders and errors. This outrageous act made him still more unpopular. The Duke's mother condemned her son's act, and made a point of showing her sympathy with her daughter-in-law. Philippa's uncles, the Duke of Gloucester, York, and Lancaster, were gravely offended. Of Vere's action, Talleyrand's famous criticism of Napoleon's execution of d'Enghien is fully as applicable as it was to Napoleon: "It was worse than a crime, it was a blunder." He had in the most open and nonchalant manner insulted and injured a lady generally respected and admired and made three of the most powerful noblemen in the realm, already his enemies, even more im-

---

4. *Dict. of Natl. Biog.* 58. 245, and authorities therein cited.

5. Malverne's account of Philippa's rejection is found in the Rolls Series ed. of *Higden's Polychronicon* 9.95. Froissart's (12. 238-39) account of the affair is interesting because he seems to blame the Roman (as against the Avignonese) pontiff for permitting the scandal: "et (Vere) fist tant par devers pape Urbain VIe qui lors se tenoit à Romme et qui se nommoit pape, que il se desmaria de la fille au seigneur de Coucy sans nul tiltre de raison."

placably so; while the monarch who was his friend had become, through his deed, more unpopular that he was before, and hence less able to protect him. He was soon to find that the daughter of Enguerrand and Isabella de Coucy had a good deal of influence, and kinsmen whom it was not wise to offend. "L'affaire de Philippe" only added one more to the mounting total of ineptitudes and scandals that finally convinced Englishmen, high and low, that Richard's ministers were better out of office than in it; and Richard himself better off the throne than on it.

We have no call to animadvert upon the resulting fall of the Duke of Ireland which followed (1388) hard upon the repudiation of his wife. After his defeat at Radcot Bridge in the same year, he fled overseas.[6] But even in foreign parts the enmity of his wife's kindred gave him no peace. Her relative, Albert of Bavaria, who held Holland, Zeeland, and Hainault, found ways of ousting him from Dordrecht,[7] and when he entered French territory, he did so with the knowledge that the Sire de Coucy would spare no effort to get Charles VI and his ministers to eject him from that kingdom.[8] The wretched exile died in Louvain in 1392.

After this unfortunate affair, Philippa appears to have been treated with much more consideration by her royal relative—or the new councillors whom the events of 1388 brought forth. The income of the ancestral lands, which by

6. Miss Maude Clarke in her study, "Forfeitures and Treason in 1388" (*Fourteenth Century Studies*, Oxford, 1937, 115 ff.), has thrown a good deal of light upon the household ménage and the personal possessions of Robert de Vere at the time of his attainder.

7. Froissart, ed. Kervyn, 12. 287.

8. Froissart (14. 33) tells us that Coucy "le haioit de tout son coeur." Despite Coucy's feeling about Vere, Charles VI and his advisers found it politically inconvenient to oust him immediately, and plans to do so were held in abeyance (Froissart, 13. 98). But though balked at first by reasons of state which he quite understood, Coucy never forgot Vere's presence in the kingdom, and the knowledge of his former father-in-law's inveterate enmity so worked upon the fears of the banished favorite that he left France and sought a more healthful asylum in Brabant.

her husband's attainder had lapsed into the King's hands, was now regranted to her, and, what is also important to note, the officers who held the lands for the King were directed to honor her nominations to benefices falling vacant within their extent.[9] At the accession to the English throne of another first cousin, Henry IV, this grant was confirmed.[10] The same monarch, by an act of belated justice, also restored her dower lands as Countess of Oxford.[11]

It is pleasant and reassuring to find that Philippa and her father were on terms of affection, if not of intimacy. Rymer prints a safe-conduct (dated July 24, 1389, West.) for a messenger, the chevalier Jean de Chateaumorand, sent into England by the Sire de Coucy "to see and speak with our said cousin on certain matters *depar le dit Sire de Coucy.*"[12] It seems almost a certain guess that Enguerrand

9. *Cal. Pat. Rolls* 1385-89, pp. 423-24. The grant, dated Mar. 25, 1388, is vacated, because the King later granted them to her by a writ dated May 18, 22 R.II. In 1392 by a writ dated West. Feb. 27, Richard II took the ancestral lands out of the hands of the royal agents and granted them to Philippa to hold in her own name, with the further provision that they were to be so held for a year after her decease for the payments of her debts and remuneration of her servants (*Cal. Pat. Rolls* 1391-96, p. 34). For other information about the state of her finances, see *Cal. Pat. Rolls* 1388-92, pp. 117, 151.

10. *Cal. Pat. Rolls* 1399-1401, p. 273, dated West. Nov. 22, 1399. For further information about the status of these English lands, see also p. 528. This letter patent (dated West. July 2, 1401) in which confirmation is again made recites an agreement between Philippa and her elder sister Mary, that the former shall hold the English lands which had once belonged to their father, and the latter the French territories of which he died possessed.

11. *Rot. Parl.* 3. 460. See Mrs. Green, 3. 223. See also *Fourteenth Century Studies,* p. 144.

12. *Fœdera* 7. 636. The safe-conduct states that Coucy, desirous of hearing and knowing with certainty good news as Nature requires, of his daughter, and the king's cousin, Philippa, wife of Robert de Vere, lately Duke of Ireland, has arranged and purposed to send to England one of his knights, Jean de Chateaumorand, to see and speak with Philippa of certain matters on the Sire de Coucy's behalf. This messenger Richard takes into his protection and grants him a safe-conduct. It is probable that *Cat. des Rolles François* 2. 160 refers to this very document. It contains the following entry "salvus conductus pro le Sire de Coucy de Francia in regnum Anglie veniendo and colloquendam cum filia sua uxore Roberti

wished to learn from his daughter what her plans and financial position might be after the distressing business of her divorce.

This parental solicitude must have touched Philippa, for a few years later when they did meet for the first time since 1377, Froissart in touching words describes her eagerness for the reunion.[13] The occasion was the conference between the French and English *seigneurs* held in March, 1392, at Amiens, "sur fourme de paix ou de trièves," as Froissart succinctly puts it. Philippa landed at Calais with her uncles, the Dukes of York and Lancaster, and was met by her father.[14] The change of scene and that of mind which it and

de Veer nuper Ducis Hiberniae." Its date is identical with the safe-conduct in Rymer. I regret that the Princeton Library does not possess a set of the *Cat. des Rolles Fran.* I transcribed the information about the safe-conduct to Coucy from the copy at PRO, and forgot to ascertain whether the author printed *in extenso* the writ that Rymer had previously printed with the Latin heading quoted above, or whether that Latin heading refers to another safe-conduct issued to Coucy and *not* to his messenger. It is interesting to note that Coucy had been named Captain-general of Guyenne, and proceeded to that province in 1389, to supervise enforcement of the provisions of the truce with England (Lacaille, *Étude*, 89). The grant of a safe-conduct to his emissary may have been an adroit attempt to secure his good will. One wonders why he himself did not go to England on the safe-conduct which he could have used, if the Latin phrases printed in *Rolles François* are authentic. He may have been too busy to do so. Or he may have felt somewhat shame-faced before his former friends and associates because of his repudiation of ties that he had entered into voluntarily—his acceptance of the Garter for instance. It is to be noted that when in 1395 Froissart asked him (among others) for letters of introduction to influential Englishmen, he excused himself, and would give him only one to his daughter (15. 141): "réservé le Sire de Coucy; car, pour ce que il estoit françois, il n'y osa escripre fors tant seulement à sa fille." However, Froissart's words may mean no more that that Coucy did not wish to ask favors from the magnates of a country with which his own was at war.

13. 14. 378: "car je suppose qu'en devant ce elle l'avoit petit veu. Si avoit trés-ardant désir de le veoir."

14. *Froissart*, ed. Kervyn, 14. 376 ff., especially 378, 381. S. Armitage-Smith, *John of Gaunt*, 346, informs us that Lancaster landed on March 11. The permission to leave England which authorized her departure is found in *Cal. Pat. Rolls* 1391-96, p. 34, dated Feb. 27, West. It gave her permission to go to France, sojourn there with her father and return. Baron Kervyn de Lettenhove in the historical index of his ed. of

the occasion provoked must have done her great good, and given her other and different thoughts than those sad ones which had been her companions for several years past. Froissart tells us that she came prepared to enjoy herself.[15] While the conference continued she sojourned at her father's.[16] Her experience there was doubtless enjoyable, for Enguerrand made a point of being well served and attended, and his wide popularity, high prestige, and influential position in all probability drew much company to his doors. Perhaps the presence of an unmarried daughter in his household helped to swell its numbers.

This brief picture of a very brief reunion is almost the last glimpse that we have of the Duchess of Ireland. The death of her father in 1397 as a prisoner of the Turkish sultan, after the fatal battle of Nicopolis, must have been a bitter sorrow. Froissart tells us that she was in attendance upon the unfortunate Isabella of France at Havering-at-the-Bower, after the deposition of Richard II.[17] We know also another fact about her well worth the noting, namely, that she was one of those few ladies associated with the Order of the Garter.[18] Since the last recorded delivery of Garter robes to her is in 1409, she was living in the early months of that year, if not later. And here we must leave her. We may do so with the conviction that in her existence the law of compensation was at work, as it is now in ours. Life took from her much, a happy marriage, a beloved father; it

the *Chroniques* (see Oxford, Philippe de) implies that Philippa visited her father at the Chateau de Coucy, but Froissart's language does not warrant such a conclusion.

15. 14. 378: "Si venoit en bon arroy aussi comme une dame vesve qui petit de joye avoit eu durant son mariage."

16. *Froissart*, ed. Kervyn, 14. 381.

17. 16. 220. One cannot but wonder whether Froissart may not have confused her with her step-mother Isabella, Coucy's second wife, who had come to England with the Queen, and departed with her.

18. In 1378 Garter robes were first delivered to her as Countess of Oxford; see *Complete Peerage* 2. 591-92. for record of subsequent deliveries.

gave her much again, the ability to reward those who had given her devotion or paid her honor, and the possession of those lands that her father had long held. In their confines she would be recognized by the folk as the lineal descendant of their ancient lords, and

> heȝly honowred with haþeleȝ aboute.

She would have still held the devotion of these born on the lands or employed in the households of her father and mother—among whom may have been the *Gawain*-poet.

APPENDIX G

The Meaning of *Sir Gawain*, Lines 862-71

LINES 862-871 of *Sir Gawain and the Green Knight* present one of the knottiest cruces among the number that vex the reader or translator of that romance. Just before these lines the poet has been describing the prompt and ready courtesy with which Bercilak's menials received the newly arrived Gawain. Bercilak himself had ushered Sir Gawain into a room off the main hall, and there had straightway summoned an attendant to whose care he commended his guest. The tired knight had been therewith taken off to the bower (bed-chamber), where his armor and the jewelled surcoat that covered it were at long last removed for the "softer weeds of peace." And it is just at this point that the lines (862 ff.) occur that have puzzled all who have studied the poem, and for which no solution that has been proposed has as yet proved satisfactory. We must let the poet speak in his own person and in his own tongue, as he describes the "look" and "fit" of the rich apparel that his hero had just donned:

Ryche robes ful rad renkkeȝ hym broȝten,
For to charge and to chaunge and chose of þe best.
Sone as he on hent, and happed þerinne,
Þat sete on hym semly, wyth saylande skyrteȝ,
Þe ver by his uisage verayly hit semed
Wel neȝ to vche haþel, alle on hwes,
Lowande and lufly, alle his lymmeȝ vnder.
Þat a comloker knyȝt neuer Kryst made,
                    hem þoȝt.

Previous to the more detailed discussion of the meaning of
the passage, it is to be noted (1) that in these lines the poet
is describing what we have called above the "look" and
"fit" of clothing, the impression that it makes on those who
observe how its wearer wears it. And it is to be further
noted (2) that there are in this passage, where much depends
on how it is to be translated, several words whose exact meaning is uncertain. For *his* and *uisage* (line 866) either one
of two meanings is possible, and the author has not enlightened us as to which he used. In the case of *his*, the genitive
singular of the pronoun of the third person, the gender may
be either masculine or neuter. If the first meaning be
adopted, the reference is to Gawain; if the second, the reference is to the preceding noun *ver*. As to *uisage*, it may mean
"face" (*NED*. s.v. *visage*, sb. 1, 2), or "appearance, aspect"
(*NED*. 7), or may indeed have some possible suggestion of
the now obsolete meaning, "outward show, semblance"
(*NED*. 8). We shall see later that one explanation that has
been suggested stands or falls by whichever meaning of
uisage one adopts, and that in general the poet's meaning
is affected by the interpretation we give to these two words.

Let us now examine the explanations that have been advanced by the several scholars who have commented upon
the passage. The first was Richard Morris, who edited the
poem. He glossed *ver*, "man, knight," citing ON *ver. verr*,

"man, husband," as a related word, but failed to note, as
the late O. F. Emerson points out, that the *v* of the ON word
is phonetic *w*, and, therefore, incapable of alliterating with
uisage and *verayly*.[1] Furthermore, as Professor Menner
points out, the translation of *ver* as "man" makes the syntax
of 866-67 difficult, "since one would expect 'he semed' rather
than 'hit semed'; and one has either to supply that he was,
or assume an anacoluthon of some sort."[2] Consequently
"man, knight, hero," are unacceptable renditions of *ver*.

Emerson's interpretation of the passage is more ingenious. It "has the advantage of simplicity, preserves the alliteration, and follows more closely the poet's syntax." "Gawain's
borrowed finery," according to Emerson, "is probably of the
host's favorite color"—green, and with such a hypothesis in
mind his reading of the lines runs as follows:

> Soon as he took one and decked himself therein,
> One that sat on him seemly with its sailing skirts,
> The spring (*ver*), compared with his appearance (*uisage*),
>   verily seemed
> Well nigh to each hero all one in hue;
> Glowing (*lowande*) in looks and lovely in all his limbs,
> A comelier knight Christ never made, they thought.

Emerson takes *ver* as the Latin word for "spring," which
is quite possible as a rendition, and *uisage* as "appearance,"
rather than "countenance." But his rendition has against it
the minor objection that Latin *ver* ("spring") is not to be
found in any other works of this poet,[3] and the major ob-

---

1. As Emerson remarks, "the translators have followed Morris in using
one word or another suggested by his gloss" (*MLN* 36. 213). **During**
the past twenty years critical comment on the vocabulary of *Gawain* has
changed materially our understanding of the poem; yet, with very few
exceptions, translators have shown little appreciation of the change that
time and scholarship have wrought, and in some cases versions which
are now quite out of date are still being reprinted and sold.

2. *MLR* 19. 205.

3. To argue that because the poet did not use *ver* ("spring") elsewhere
it is unlikely that he used it in the present passage, has a certain validity.

jection that it is based upon the quite fanciful assumption, nowhere supported by the text, that Sir Gawain's robe was green. Moreover, Emerson's translation of the second half of line 867, "all one in hue," is a bad rendition of the poet's *alle on hwes*. Yet, despite its defects, the translation has been adopted by Tolkien and Gordon in their edition of 1925 (and subsequent reprints),[4] and by Miss Day in hers of 1940,[5] with such changes of phrasing as those editors deem fitting.

Much nearer to the poet's thought, or at least more germane to his discussion of apparel and attire, is the translation of Professor R. J. Menner.[6] Menner would interpret *ver* as a mere spelling-variant of ME *vair* (OF *vair, veir, ver*), "spotted or variously coloured fur, used for lining or trimming." He would place a comma after *uisage*, thus making the first half of line 866 an additional descriptive detail similar to "wyth saylande skyrteȝ." His translation then runs: "As soon as he took one and wrapped himself in it, which fitted him fairly, with flowing skirts, the fur-trimming (i.e., a collar of fur) by his face, truly it (the robe) seemed well nigh to every man there wholly of glowing and lovely colours, . . ."

Menner's interpretation has a number of advantages over others that have been offered. It satisfies not only the re-

---

One can believe that other meanings for *ver* than "spring," a word with which the poet certainly shows no acquaintance, are more likely to hit off what seems to be the sense of the passage. But one cannot argue that the word is an impossible one, in view of what has been said in a previous essay about the poet's willingness to use—or coin—new words, and of the fact of its use by two of his contemporaries, Chaucer (*Troil.* 1. 157) and Gower (*Conf. Amant.* 7. 1014).

4. Tolkien-Gordon (p. 96): "As soon as he took one and was clothed therein, (one) that fitted him well with flowing skirts, the spring-time verily it seemed to each man in his appearance, well-nigh, all his limbs under it glowing and delightful all in colours."

5. Miss Day (p. 108): "verily by his appearance the spring it seemed well night to everyone, colours all over him, glowing and lovely, his limbs all covered."

6. *MLR* 19. 205-6.

quirements of syntax and phonology, but directs our attention where that of the poet seems also to have been centered, to the texture and coloration of Gawain's garb. The only objection to it comes not from syntax, spelling or etymology, but from the fact that it takes no account of the fashion of dress in the fourteenth century. In lines 875-81, we are told that after Gawain had been attired in the manner just described, he moved to the fireplace where a cushioned chair awaited him, and then a splendid mantle of a brown fabric *lined with ermine fur* was thrown over him. Miss Day remarks, quite rightly I think, that "it does not seem likely that a robe to be worn under a fur-lined mantle and hood would have a fur collar."[7]

Menner's suggestion that *ver* refers to the fur collar of the surcoat, seems, therefore, unlikely, if Miss Day's point be well taken. Yet his identification of the word may very well be correct. *Ver* may refer, not to the squirrel fur stitched onto a collar, but to the heraldic "fur," that arrangement of small shields or bells alternately argent and azure (white and blue). In other words, the poet may be alluding not to peltry at all but to some form of heraldic pattern displayed upon Gawain's robe.[8]

7. In 1937 the late Rev. E. E. Dorling, F.S.A., expressed, in an informal conversation, the same doubt to the writer. If, as Tolkien-Gordon believe, Gawain's robe (of line 864) was the *bliaut*, and the mention of "sailing skirts" makes that belief quite possible, it is unlikely that it would have had a fur collar or trimmings; see H. Norris, *Costume and Fashion* (N. Y., 1927), 2. 32-33, figs. 22, 23, 33 (incidentally *NED*, s.v. *bleaunt*, obs. which defines the word as "a kind of tunic or upper garment," fails to note that it had a skirt part; see Norris, p. 32, and *Gaw.* 1928). But it is quite possible that Gawain's robe was not the *bliaut*, but the long surcoat, which also seems to have lacked the fur collar and fur at the sleeves; see N. Truman, *Historic Costuming* (London, 1936), pp. 20, 21, 25, 30. The surcoats, worn in the days of the three Edwards, would have been more familiar to our poet than the *bliaut* which was out of date in the Edwardian era. Since the poet does use (in line 1928) *bleaunt* to denote a long gown, the word had probably become generalized to include any long gown (not a mantle) "þat bradde to þe erþe."

8. It seems hardly necessary to remind the reader that heraldic *vair*, though classed in heraldic language as a fur rather than as a metal or

When one thinks of medieval coats of arms, one is accustomed to think of them as appearing only when embroidered on the military surcoat (jupon) or on flags, or painted on the shield. But in the days of the *Gawain*-poet, and even before his days, arms identified their bearers in peace as in war. The years of our anonymous author were those of the armorial robe, when ladies and gentlemen wore robes with their own personal heraldic blazon upon them. Such armorial devices were not only borne on the mantle but also on the surcoat worn beneath it, so that they might be visible with the mantle doffed.

For further information upon this point, any good history of costume or of medieval social life may be consulted,[9] but since the evidence of medieval documents may be more reassuring to the reader, let me pick two examples from the great number that could be quoted, both of them dating from the later years of the fourteenth century. The first is a clause from the will of John of Gaunt, who apportions all his armorial robes and hangings.[10] The second example comprises certain of the illustrations that are to be found in the sumptuous *Coronation Book of Charles V* (Brit. Mus. Cott. Tib. B VIII),[11] in which many of the ecclesiastics and noble-

---

color (because patterned after a usual design made of fur), is in reality of like material as anything else—of paint on a shield, and of fabric in vestments and flags.

9. Cf. M. Mercier, *Portraits des Rois de France* (Neuchâtel, 1783) 2. 327: "La mode d'armorier les habits commença sous ce règne [that of Charles] Les femmes portoient sur leur robe, à droite, l'écu de leurs maris; à gauche, le leur"; P. L. de Grafferri, *Hist. of French Masculine Costume* (Paris), 18, " 'parement' indicated a garment embroidered with armorial ensigns . . . the fashion developed under Charles V, and increased in favour, until the reign of Louis XI."

10. *Collection of Royal Wills* . . . (printed by John Nichols, London, 1780), p. 152: "Jeo devise [to the monastery of St. Edmund at Bury, Suffolk] . . . trestoutes mes draps d'armes texes d'or pur parcelles q'sont fais de Dieu & de n're dame."

11. Ed. E. S. Dewick, vol. 16 of Henry Bradshaw Society, London, 1899. See particularly plates III, IV, V, VII. The long gowns (armorial) of the lay peers who take part in the Coronation ceremony are not

men depicted are to be identified by the arms borne on their pontificals or surcoats, and by the arms alone. That the poet's eye was quick to notice just such distinctions of dress and what they revealed about the status of their wearers is quite evident from lines 1928-31, which contain a description of the robes of the Order of the Garter.[12] It would not, then, be strange or unusual to find him pointing out that it was an armorial robe that Gawain was wearing. Furthermore, let it here be noted that he is careful to point out also that it was Gawain himself who had chosen from among several other robes the one now described. If the chosen robe were armorial, the arms upon it must have been in some way connected with the chooser.

But if it be an armorial robe that our hero wears, it is certainly described in a very curt fashion, so briefly that identification with any known coat of the time may seem impossible. Be it remembered, however, that the *Gawain*-poet does not speak as a professional herald of the eighteenth or nineteenth century, but as one for whom heraldry is a living reality. To him and to his audience a heraldic description could be of the briefest. The mere mention of one element of a coat, such as the color of the field, the principal fur, or one of the charges, would almost automatically evoke the usual image of the whole achievement. To a brain that thought "heraldically," and to eyes that had seen it often, the picture of a particular coat would be brought up from memory by a touch-and-go allusion. An exact verbal blazon is not, therefore, to be expected from a poet who has excelled most of his brethren of later eras in packing so much meaning, so many nuances, into so few words.

"mantles," as Dewick calls them, but surcoats. See Truman, *Hist. Cost.*, pp.17, 21, 25; Norris, 2. 155-56, 165-66, 209-10, 245, for description of both garments.

12. Professors O. Cargill and M. Schlauch were first to call attention to this point (*PMLA* 43. 119). Norris (2. 239) gives an illustration of the Garter costume in the days of the founder of the Order.

The upshot of our discussion is that Sir Gawain seems to be wearing a surcoat or long gown which has, beside whatever other colors are woven into it or embroidered upon it, a design in heraldic vair.[13] If so much be admitted for the purpose of argument, what further information is possible?

Only an etymological caveat now stands between us and the complete immersion into heraldic deeps. I utter it with what brevity and concision I can. The reader can see at once that the interpretation of *ver* as "heraldic fur" necessitates our reading *uisage* not as "countenance, face," but as "appearance," and *his* as "its." If there is no fur by Gawain's visage, i.e., on the collar of his robe, *uisage* can hardly have the meaning "face," nor can *his* refer to a person.

Up to the present moment we have established the possibility that Sir Gawain's robe had upon it a design in heraldic vair. But for the identification of an heraldic coat of arms more information is necessary. One should know, for instance, whether the vair be on the field or on an ordinary, whether other metals or colors adorn the shield that displays it, etc. On such matters, this writer's writ no longer runs. He and his colleagues in literary studies at this point of our inquiry step down from the cathedra, in which the heralds now seat themselves. The question whether the words of our passage can or do carry an heraldic sense, is rightly one for phonologists and etymologists. If it be decided that they do or may, then *la parole est aux héraldistes*. Let us, then, sit at the feet of the heralds for instruction.[14]

13. It is interesting to note that the poet of our romance shows no knowledge of any of the fabulous coats of arms made up for Gawain that are to be found in some of the rolls of arms composed in the fifteenth and later centuries.

14. A footnote is hardly the place to enlighten a reader about the authority of heraldic instruction, but he should, and can, be informed where to look for guidance in the art of blazonry. Sound conclusions in matters armorial are based on the study of heraldic practice in medieval rolls, seals, sculpture, and brasses. Few of the so-called guides or dictionaries of the 18th or 19th centuries are of much value in teaching us about

One will remember that Sir Gawain's vair, by its appearance, verily seemed to well nigh everyone all on (or "of"?) hues or colors. What colors or hues are those which may be (1) combined with vair; or (2) can vair be composed of other hues than the white and blue which customarily beautify its well-shaped figures?

1. *What colors or hues are those which may be combined with vair?* In medieval days heraldic practice rarely strayed far from good taste. Primary colors and simple designs, those colors and designs easily discernible from a distance, were a *sine qua non.* Clarity was the ideal of medieval shield-painters. It was obtained by the use of bold colors that did not merge. One can see, therefore, that black (*sable*) or green (*vert*) would blend badly in close proximity with the blue panes of vair. Yellow (*or*) and red (*gules*) are almost the only tinctures that would produce a harmonious composition with a vair design, and of those two colors red is to be found much more frequently than yellow. Of this fact medieval heralds were well aware. P. J. Spener, whose book preserves much of the best medieval practice, informs us that

that practice when the art was at its colorful zenith. J. R. Planché's *Pursuivant cf. Arms* (London, 1852, and subsequent editions), is valuable because of the emphasis it lays on ancient usage, but it does not touch many of the problems that have puzzled us in the past and remain unsolved today. The *Treatise on Heraldry, British and Foreign* (London, 1892) of Woodward and Burnett is good, but not particularly illustrative of medieval practice, and contains a deal of unchecked material. Valuable material exists in periodical publications, but a general history of blazonry has not yet been written, and three who might have written it, Messrs. Prinet, Barron, and la Rose, are no longer living to do so. In writing the present appendix I have gone for five years to those who are admittedly the best authorities, all of them students of the medieval records, to M. Jacques Meurgey in France, the late D. L. Galbreath in Switzerland, the late Oswald Barron (Maltravers Herald) F.S.A., the late S. M. Collins, F.S.A., the late E. E. Dorling, F.S.A., M. H. Stanford London, and A. R. Wagner (Richmond Herald) of England, and Dr. H. Bowditch, G. A. Moriarty, F.S.A., and the late P. la Rose in this country, and been guided by what they told me. For a brief account of the present state of heraldic studies, cf. the writer's review of Mr. Wagner's book, *Heralds and Heraldry*, in *Amer. Hist. Rev.* 46. 618.

"it is to be noted that this fur vair, and ermine as well, cannot generally be used in an escutcheon with any other color than red."[15] Far more important than quotations from books, however, is the authority of heraldic practice. The late S. M. Collins, who had long studied what he calls "the third tincture" in coats of vair, told me that though gold is often found with vair of blue and white, it is not nearly so frequent as is red;[16] and a search made by Mr. Stanford London through the Zürich *Wappen-rolls*, the *Wappenbuch von den Ersten*, the *Armorial de la Toison d'Or*, the *Parliament Roll* of 1312, and *The Siege of Caerlaverock*, "goes a long way," he tells me, "towards supporting Spener's dictum, but at the same time it is clear that, at least in earlier days, and especially in the territory of the Zürich *Wappen-rolls*, there was no objection to the use of vair with gold. On the other hand, I have found no single example of the juxtaposition of vair with any other tincture than gold or gules."[17] It seems, then, probable that vair and gules are combined in some sort of heraldic pattern upon Gawain's robe. Does the poet tell us what that pattern is?

Not specifically or precisely, like a seventeenth-century blazoner of arms. His words are that "the vair by his (its) appearance truly seemed to almost everyone 'all (*i.e.*, entirely, completely, throughout) on hues' (*i.e.*, in colors)." To quote S. M. Collins, "the whole garment was 'in color,' as it would have been if made up of varied strips of blue, white and red. If it had been only of 'ver,' as would normally be the case where that fur was used not as an armorial bearing (as you contend) but as a fashionable lining, 'in colours' would have been an overstatement. White is hardly a

15. *Insignium Theoria* (Frankfort A/M, 1717), p. 117, "Haec vellera, ut & hermionica, in scutis plerumque rubeo colori, non alii, jungi."
16. Personal letter 4/4/'38.
17. Personal letter 8/22/'38.

color to warrant the plural, but the addition of red justifies the phrase."[18]

In the *Gawain*-poet's day there was one coat—one of the oldest and most famous of Europe—that bore an arrangement of vair and gules—that of the Coucy's *barré (or fessé) de vair et de gueules de six pièces.* We have seen above that there is very good reason for associating this coat with the time and locality in which the poet wrote. Our poem is almost certainly connected with the Order of the Garter, and Enguerrand de Coucy was once a member of that Order, and among all the members who were made such within the reigns of Edward III and Richard II, his coat of arms was the only one which bore any vair upon it. The poet's blazon, as I have said before, is a poetic blazon, not a formal one. Yet it does identify, if one remembers that the argent of vair was thought of as being the tincture white, and not the metal silver, and that vair is much more frequently of horizontal or barry rather than of diagonal or bendy blazoning. It seems, then, quite possible that Sir Gawain was wearing a robe of alternate bands of vair and gules, and that there were six of these bands.[19] If his robe was so blazoned, then

18. S. M. Collins, Esq., personal letter 3/10/'38.

19. The poet would be under no necessity of specifying the number of the bands for two reasons: (1) Coucy, a famous coat, so invariably bore six pieces, that there was no need of reassuring readers that such was the case; (2) In a barry field barry of six is the normal number. If four or eight divisions be found the number of pieces must be named, whereas with no number named, a division of six pieces is to be assumed. See Oswald Barron, *"Heraldry"* in *Encyc. Brit.* 11th ed., p. 319.

The phrase *ver . . . on hwes* is indeed capable of being read as an almost exact description of the Coucy arms, if one lays emphasis on the word "on." It is possible to maintain the syntax of the passage by rendering (freely) "each stripe of the vair (fur) seemed (was) on hues (*gules*), when, as a matter of fact, each vair stripe has a red stripe beneath it." But such a translation would imply a French original *Barré de vair et de gueules* shortened down to *Barré de vair sur gueules,* with the French *sur* translated by the English "on" or "above." The late Mr. la Rose thought *vair sur gueules* a possible heraldic locution, and believed the rendition possible, *if one remembered that it was a layman writing verse who was blazoning.* But Messrs. Collins and Dorling believe that

only one conclusion is possible: he is the allegorization of the seventh Sire de Coucy.

The poet's phrase, *wel neʒ to vche haþel,* "to almost every man," at first reading seems strange. It implies that there were some who did not recognize the blazoning on Sir Gawain's armorial surcoat, some to whom it was unfamiliar, because it was incompletely viewed. Such indeed may have been the case. When a medieval lady or gentleman wore the armorial surcoat, it often happened that one half of the blazon was invisible unless its bearer stood full-face or with back completely turned to the gazer. Figures on brasses and the paintings in manuscripts illustrate the point perfectly, but if a particular instance of failure to recognize a blazon be needed to confirm what has been said, Froissart's story (*Chroniques.* ed. Kervyn de Lettenhove, Brussells, 1869, 8. 291) of how the English mistook the pennon of the Sire de Chin (*vair three bars gules*) for that of the Sire de Coucy provides an exact illustration.[20] Those who saw the pennon recognized indeed that it was barry of *vair and gules.* Its movement in the wind, however, probably made them uncertain whether it had five or six bars. But perhaps it is simpler to explain the poet's words as merely a case of understatement to which medieval, as modern, poets not infrequently have to resort, in which "well nigh each man=all men."[21]

---

the locution cannot be found in the corpus of French and English heraldry. If their belief be true, then it is very improbable that the poet intended to lay any particular or special stress upon the preposition *"on."*

20. S. M. Collins (personal letter 11/2/'37) shows how easily such confusion could arise. The Sire de Chin's *vair three bars gules* differs by only one bar from the Coucy *barry of six.* "On anything but an escutcheon the difference might vanish. On a mantle it might be impossible to differentiate between the five stripes of the two bars, the seven stripes of the three bars, and the six stripes of the barry."

21. I am indebted to Dr. Harold Bowditch for pointing out three examples of understatement (one of which I cite) in the heraldic poem of *The Siege of Caerlaverock* (ed. N. H. Nicolas, 1828):

I give in the note below a brief résumé of heraldic opinion upon the question we have just been discussing.[22]

2. *Can vair be composed of other hues than the white and blue . . . ?* In a personal conversation, afterwards amplified by a letter of August 20, 1937, the Rev. E. E. Dorling, F.S.A., suggested that the passage might contain a reference, not to the arms of Coucy, but to those of Guines *vairy or and azure*.[23] Elsewhere the reader has learned that Enguerrand

> Si ne faisoit pas malement
> Kant ses propres armes vestoit [Rauf de Monthermer].
> "He made no bad appearance
> When attired in his own arms."

22. The late Pierre de C. la Rose (personal interview and letter 4/3/'37) believed the view that the poet was describing a robe emblazoned with the arms of Coucy a very likely possibility. Anthony R. Wagner (personal letter 8/3/'37) believed that if the poet were referring to an armorial robe, it would be likely that the arms upon it were those of Coucy: "On thinking the matter over carefully, it seems to me that the point on which the proof of (the) theory must turn is on whether the possibility of a non-heraldic interpretation of the passage describing the surcoat can be excluded. If the probability of a heraldic interpretation could be established, I personally should think it fairly clear that the Arms of Coucy and no others must be meant." The late Oswald Barron (personal interview) was inclined to suspect that the text was corrupt (the unique manuscript presents no difficulties of reading: the handwriting is clear and there are no erasures or corrections). To him the armorial explanation and all others were unconvincing. The Rev. E. E. Dorling (see paragraph 2 and its footnote 23, below) believed that it might be an armorial robe that the poet was describing, but did not believe that the arms upon it could be identified with those of Coucy. S. M. Collins (personal interview, letter 3/10/'38) believed that the possibility that the poet was alluding to the Coucy arms was incapable of proof or of refutation; the suggestion he regarded as ingenious, one that would always have to be considered in any attempt to explain the meaning of the passage. Dr. Bowditch (personal letters 2/8/'41, 3/8/'41, 4/1/'41) makes the suggestion that "on hwes" may be equivalent to such expressions as modern "on fire," so that "on hwes" might mean brightly colored, ablaze with color, all a-color—the "a" being synonymous with "on," as in "afire" and "on fire." In 4/1/'41 he writes that "although I do not see in it [the passage] the description of an heraldic robe, I cannot deny the possibility of its being there. . . . Your letter shows me that my stand is exactly that of Dorling, Collins, and Wagner."

23. Dr. Bowditch says "the Rev. E. E. Dorling's interpretation, or more accurately, suggestion, is of great interest; from such a source, a suggestion worthy of great respect."

GVINES

vairy or and azure

VII, Sire de Coucy, was in reality a Guines, his great-grand-father Enguerrand de Guines (fifth Sire de Coucy) having inherited the title and lands of Coucy through the death of his maternal uncle Enguerrand IV, Sire de Coucy. Through his marriage with Christina de Lindsay, he and his children inherited the Balliol lands in Kendal, Lancashire, and York-shire. Enguerrand de Guines retained the name and arms of Guines all his life, and was summoned to Parliament temp. Ed. II as Lord Gynes. To those who in the later fourteenth century were reared or dwelt upon the Lancashire or Yorkshire manors that he had once held, the arms they would have known best would have been *vairy or and azure,* and not the *barré de vair et de gueules* of his Coucy great-grandson Enguerrand VII (in reality, be it remembered, a veritable Guines.)[24]

Mr. Dorling calls attention to the fact that the *Ancestor* (3. 210) gives from a fifteenth-century Roll of Arms (Harl. MS 2169) the arms of the Lord of Coucy as *vairy or and azure;* see also *Complete Peerage* VI. 224, in a note to title Guines or Gynes, where this statement is quoted; and a roll of arms circa 1280 (Harl. MS 6589) which gives to "Le Conte de Guines" the same blazon. "These notes," I quote from his letter, "point clearly to the fact that the early members of the Coucy house bore VAIR—not indeed the ordinary vair of white and blue panes but vair of gold and blue." To the writer *ver . . . on hwes* seems a more likely descrip-

24. This belief of mine is strongly supported by the following statement of G. A. Moriarty, Esq., F.S.A. (personal letter 9/7/'41) who has made a long and valuable study of the medieval land-holders in the counties of Cumberland, Westmoreland, and Lancashire:

"Henceforth he (William de Coucy, or de Guines, d. 1343) and his issue only came occasionally to England and the Earl of Bedford (Enguerrand VII Sire de Coucy) would be mostly at court and not in the north. With William now Sire de Coucy they would naturally use the de Coucy arms, but I doubt if these were much seen in and around Kendal which they probably visited only occasionally, and the coat that men in the north would be most likely to remember and associate with them would be of Guisnes or Gynes, as the na₁ e was written in England."

tion of *verre d'or et d'azur* than it is of *Barré de vair et de gueules.*[25] If Mr. Dorling's belief that Gawain is wearing a robe blazoned with the arms of Guines be correct, the conclusion reached above is in no way weakened: Sir Gawain still stands as the allegorized figure of Enguerrand de Coucy.

I have given at some length two possible explanations of the poet's meaning in the passage, and have striven to do so with complete impartiality. The explanations ought, I think, to be advanced, but ought not to be pressed too far. In advancing them it would be easy to resort to special pleading or to the pushing forward of scanty evidence; and in rejecting them it would be no less easy to close our eyes to the fact that the poet and his audience were more gifted with imagination that we are ourselves. Proof and rejection seem, for the present at least, alike impossible. One ought, however, to point out that rejection in no way invalidates the possibility that the writing of our romance was in some way connected with a member of the house of Coucy-Guines.

APPENDIX H

The *Cri de Guerre* of the House of Coucy

Lines 642-50 of the poem have often puzzled me:

And alle his afyaunce vpon folde watʒ in þe fyue woundeʒ
Þat Cryst kaʒt on þe croys, as þe crede telleʒ;
And quere-so-euer þys mon in melly watʒ stad,
His þro þoʒt watʒ in þat, þurʒ alle oþer þyngeʒ,

25. It would be impossible to distinguish clearly between the meanings "vair" and "vairy" if one depended on medieval spellings. The spellings *vair, veir, verre, vere, ver* could represent either meaning. The poet's *ver*, then, may perfectly well stand for "vairy."

Þat alle his forsnes he fong at þe fyue joyeȝ
Þat þe hende heuen quene had of hir chylde;
At þis cause þe knyȝt comlyche hade
In þe more half of his schelde hir ymage depaynted,
Þat quen he blusched þerto, his belde neuer payred.

The phrasing "all his fierceness he took from the Five Joys that the fair Queen of Heaven felt in her child" seems to offer an unreasonable, nay a contradictory, conjunction of ideas. The Five Joys of the Virgin Mother seem emotions far removed from that of "fierceness in battle (*melly*)."

The discrepancy between the emotional associations of the two phrases can be explained adequately by a *cri de guerre* or rallying shout of the Coucy, "Notre Dame au Sire de Coucy!" Whether this be the correct explanation, we cannot now say. All that we can say is that it is an adequate one, and that up to the present time no others which have been attempted are as satisfactory. Let us seek further confirmation and justification from medieval history for the explanation just advanced. Historians inform us that three *cris* were at various times used by the house of Coucy, and presumably the frequency of the use of any one of them depended upon the preference of him who happened at the time to be head of the house. Possibly the first in point of time was *"Place à la bannière!"* an allusion to the famous coat of arms of the Coucys.[1] Another was *"Coucy à la merveille!"* evidently an allusion to the great round donjon of the Château

---

1. One of the early Sires de Coucy took part in the first crusade. In this expedition, according to the legend, he and his were once surprised by the unbelievers. Missing his banner, and being unable to rally his troops to it, he cut off a piece of his mantle, which was scarlet with *pannes* of vair, and waving it about, gathered his scattered men, who eventually routed the enemy. Hence the famous coat of the family, *Fascé de vair et de gueules de six pièces.* The Sire de Coucy who executed this quick action has been variously identified as Enguerrand I, his son Thos. de Marle, or Enguerrand III; See *Versailles, Salle de Croisades*, ed. Ch. Gavard (Paris, n.d.), p. 7. Whether apocryphal or not, the story goes to prove that the family coat was one of the oldest in Europe.

de Coucy, the largest and highest donjon tower in Western Europe. This *cri* was certainly well known in the fourteenth century for the poet Deschamps speaks of it as being so at the time in which he enjoyed the patronage of the seventh lord of that race.[2] A third was the one alluded to above, *Notre Dame au Sire de Coucy!* and it is this *cri de guerre* that I would briefly call to the reader's attention.

We know that it is one that the seventh Sire de Coucy used, for we find it being shouted by his men in a skirmish with the Turks some days before the fatal battle of Nicopolis.[3] It might be objected that "Notre Dame" prefixed to the name of a particular house or family must have been a rather common form of *cri*, and that there were probably many families who used an invocation to the Virgin as a war-cry. Yet Ducange informs us that not every gentleman and nobleman had the right to use a *cri de guerre*, which was a privilege belonging only to those who were "chefs ou conducteurs de troupes, et qui avoient bannière dans l'armée." So the number of those who could have used a war-cry would have been limited. And, as the footnote below indicates, of that limited number only a few shouted an invocation to the Queen of Heaven.[4] Among those few Enguerrand de Coucy was conspicuous.

2. See his *ballade* on the *Domaines du sire de Coucy, Oeuvres inédites* (Paris, 1849), p. 134, n. 105.

3. Froissart, ed. Kervyn, 15. 267. The actuality of this skirmish has been doubted, see my study "Eng. de Coucy and the Campaign of Nicopolis," *Speculum* 14. 423 ff. But whether the skirmish be apocryphal or not, the fact that the chronicler, or the source of his story, used the *cri Notre-Dame au seigneur de Coucy!* for the creation of verisimilitude, is evidence that Enguerrand did use that particular war-cry.

4. A search through J. Dielitz *Die Wahl-und Denksprüche, Feldgeschreie, Losungen, Schlacht-und Volksrufe besonders des Mittelalters und der Neuzeit* (Frankfort A/M, 1884) shows that the number of such cries is not great. Dielitz cites (p. 222) the following: (1) "Nôtre Dame, Bourgoigne!," a cry of Philip the Good, Duke of Burgundy; (2) "Nôtre Dame, Guesclin!"; (3) "Nôtre Dame, Nôtre Dame, Bourbon, Bourbon!," Louis II, Duke of Bourbon; (4) "Nôtre Dame, Sancerre!," Louis de Sancerre; (5) "Nôtre Dame au seigneur de Coucy!" A checkup of

The last lines of the quotation at the head of this appendix tell us that the image of the Virgin was depicted on Sir Gawain's shield, and this detail of which the poet has been so careful to inform us impresses upon us still more deeply the fervor and singularity of that knight's devotion to the "hende heuen Quene." At first reading one might suppose that the image was blazoned on the chief of the shield "more half of his schelde," and Isaac Jackson actually so blazoned the shield in an illustration,[5] but line 650 shows us that the image was painted on the *inside* of the shield at the portion where its breadth was greatest, for Gawain was evidently in the habit of holding it in such a way that he might refresh his courage by gazing upon the image. A man with a shield on the left arm could not easily turn it over to gaze on its external side.[6]

Evidence gleaned from a study of the records of Coucy's life shows us that his family's devotion to the Blessed Virgin was manifested by him, their last descendant, upon every occasion. The phrases contained in two letters written to him

---

Dielitz's conclusions made only recently by means of A. C. de Vinckenhoef's *Cris de Guerre et Devises des États de l'Europe* (Paris, 1832), reveals only one other instance of such a *cri* among the nobility of Europe —"Vergy-Notre Dame!" (p. 145).

One ought to add that Louis II, the "Good" Duke of Bourbon, had been in England as a hostage for Jean II ("il demeura huit ans," C. Menestrier, *Nouvelle Méthode Raisonnée du Blason*, Lyon. 1780, 518). The circumstances of his life, however, do not indicate any reason for supposing that *Gawain* carries any reference to him.

5. *Anglia* 37. 412.

6. The inside of the shield was sometimes so decorated at the time when the author wrote. Planché (*Cycl. of Cost.* 1. 456) describes the decoration of the inside of the shield of King Henry V. Many chroniclers, from Nennius down, inform us that King Arthur had the image of the Virgin depicted *in interiori parte scuti*. To the examples cited by Miss Day in her comment on line 649 of the poem, can be added one to be found in *Gesta Edwardi Tertii* (Chron. Ed. I and Ed. II, Rolls Ser. 2.95): "in scuto depictam gessit ymaginem Virginis gloriosæ." The poet cleverly uses the detail of the internally painted shield to enhance the Arthurian background of his story. One wonders whether the tilting or war-shields of Coucy were so adorned.

by the famous Philippe de Mézières may have carried an implication now lost to us, which he would have been quick to catch and understand. The first exhorts him "à mériter, par sa dévotion envers la Sainte Vierge, de triompher de l'ennemi de l'Église"; the second assures him of the writer's prayers, and says that Augustine, his patron, and the Blessed Virgin will protect him.[7]

Once, indeed, Enguerrand de Coucy was certain that she had protected him. J. Delaville le Roulx found and printed a document which tells us of his gratitude for her grace manifested to him as a prisoner of the Turks.[8] After the outcome of the Battle of Nicopolis had made him a captive of the Sultan Bayazid, he was trudging one day in a prisoners' convoy, over the desolate and wind-swept landscape of Asia Minor, on towards the city of Brusa. Tired and bitterly cold, he invoked in his misery the Virgin of Chartres. Suddenly a Bulgarian appeared where no one seemed to have been visible a short time before, and gave him a robe and a "chaperon de gros drap." For this grace he left in his will a legacy of 600 florins to her church at Chartres.[9]

7. The date of the first is uncertain, though it was evidently written before his first departure for Italy. That of the other is probably sometime in 1394. See Abbe Lebeuf, *Mém. sur la Vie de Phil. de Maizières, Mém. de l'Acad. des Inscrip.* 17. 497; N. Iorga, *Philippe de Mézières, Bibl. de l'École des Hautes Études* (1896) 110. 481, note 1. It is to be noted that the crusade of Nicopolis was launched under the auspices and protection of the Queen of Heaven. The Admiral Jean de Vienne bore her banner as the ensign under which the French marched; see Terrier de Loray, *Jean de Vienne* pp. 271 ff. Coucy joined the crusade at the request of the Duke and Duchess of Burgundy, but he may have been influenced to yield to that request (which at first he seemed reluctant to comply with) by the thought of showing honor and devotion to his celestial patroness.

8. *Le legs d'Enguerrand VII sire de Coucy à la Cathédrale de Chartres, Mém. Soc. Archéol. Eure-et-Loir.* (1889) 9. 463-70. See p. 469: "dont il le loua et regracia moult devotement nostre sire et sa benoite mère aourée en son eglise de Chartres de la grace que en ce lui (avoit) faite."

9. The will is printed in A. Tuetey, *Testaments enregistrés au Parl. de Paris, Mélanges Hist.* 3. 1880 (*Doc. Inédits sur l'Hist. de France*), p. 281: The particular codecil with which we are concerned reads: "Item,

But I must bring this appendix to an end, for of evidence I have found no more. Possibly a study of documents in the Bibliothèque Nationale that cover Coucy's career as a diplomat and soldier in the service of his native country might prove more revealing. But up to the present writing I have found for those nine lines quoted above no other explanation that is as satisfactory as this I advance.

APPENDIX J

The Order of the Crown

THE READER will remember that Sir Gawain, when he came to relate the "chaunce of the chapel," was overcome with shame and contrition (lines 2505-12):

> "Lo! lorde," quoþ þe leude, and þe lace hondeled,
> "Þis is þe bende of þis blame I bere in my nek,
> Þis is þe laþe and þe losse þat I laȝt haue
> Of couardise and couetyse þat I haf caȝt þare;
> Þis is þe token of vn-trawþe þat I am tan inne,
> And I mot nedeȝ hit were wyle I may last;
> For non may hyden his harme bot vnhap ne may hit,
> For þer hit oneȝ is tachched, twynne will hit neuer."

The poet goes on to tell us that Arthur and his court made haste to bring the returned hero out of his "doleful dump" and into a more cheerful state of mind. The device they adopted to secure that very laudable end was the institution of an entirely new Order of Chivalry. Their action, so characteristic of the poet's age, for the later fourteenth century was the *Blütezeit*, the very hey-day, of chivalric orders, would have been approved by a modern psychiatrist

---

Fabrice Beate Marie Carnotensis, que, ut firmiter credimus, fecit pro nobis miraculum apertum, sexcentos florenos ad scutum."

as therapeutically sound. Gawain's remorse and shame had to be assuaged, and the lingering feeling of inferiority, which those emotions generate in a sensitive mind, removed. The best way to achieve that end was, as the King and Court correctly diagnosed, to convert the green lace, that reproach to the shining ornament of the Round Table, into a cause of honor. A cynical critic, disposed to remove some of the gilding which covers the (almost) flawless Gawain, might even suspect that the joy of King, Queen, lords and ladies, over the Jewel whom they had supposed gone forever from them, was so great that they were disposed to gloss over the fact that he had been taken "in tech of a faute." Whether or not there be aught of truth in so ungenerous a surmise, certain it was that what had been sown in dishonor was to be raised in honor; what had been reproach in the old life was to be glory in the new.

The description of the membership and insignia of the new order deserves attention. The King and Court amiably accord (lines 2515-20):

> Þat lordes and ladis þat longed to þe Table,
> Vche burne of þe broþer-hede a bauderyk schulde haue,
> A bende a-belef hym aboute, of a bryȝt grene,
> And þat, for sake of þat segge, in swete to were.
> For þat watȝ acorded þe renoun of þe Rounde Table,
> And he honoured þat hit hade euer-more after.

One will notice that apparently both gentlemen and ladies could be members of the Order;[1] that its members were to

1. Ladies were in our author's day admitted to what might be called associate membership in the Order of the Garter. The Garter was, of course, an honour granted to men, for it was men who were to subserve the aims of the Order. Ladies were not supposed to exhibit warlike qualities, though, as a matter of fact, some of them did so in the campaigns of the era. Consequently no provision was made for their occupancy of stalls in the Garter Chapel, and no stall-plates or banners recorded their armorial achievements. But robes of the Order were issued to them in preparation for the ceremonies of St. George's Day, and they were allowed to wear the Garter on the left arm. See E. H. Fellowes, *The Knights of*

wear a green baldric, or riband transversely across the body;[2]
that the Order was instituted to memorialize Gawain's adventure; that his personality, therefore, was to overshadow
it; that from him it was to receive its spirit and its tone.

It seems almost indisputable that the poet was alluding
or referring to an actual order of chivalry. Several com-
mentators have supposed that that order was the Garter.[3]
But Professor J. R. Hulbert has, I think, pretty conclusively
shown that it is certainly not to the Garter that the author

---

the Garter, SPCK. n.d. Appendix 1, who informs us that Isabella, Countess
of Bedford, received an issue of robes for the Feast of St. George in
1376. When the poet speaks of "ladis þat longed to þe Table," it seems
probable that he means no more than that ladies were united with the
order in just such an "honorary association."

2. Lines 2484-87

> Þe hurt watȝ hole þat he hade hent in his nek,
> And þe blykkande belt he bere þeraboute,
> A-belef as a bauderyk, bounden bi his syde,
> Loken vnder his lyfte arme, þe lace, with a knot...

seem to imply that the baldric worn by the members of the newly instituted Order was worn as Gawain wore it upon his return to Camelot: over
the right shoulder, across the body, and secured under the left arm.
But it is important to note that the poet nowhere says the knights of the
new brotherhood wore the baldric in that manner. One is left with quite
a definite impression that, since Gawain wore the "bende" thus openly
(and not concealed as previously) as a mark of his dishonor, the companions of the new Order wore it exactly as he did—to make honor out
of dishonor, the very purpose of the Order.

There is a possible explanation for the green "bende" given in a footnote to A. Mazas' *Vie de Bertrand Duguesclin* (*Capitaines Français* 2.
153. n.). According to Mazas, "l'écharpe verte annonçait un voeu con-
tracté; le chevalier ne la quittait qu' après avoir accompli son serment, ou
après en avoir été relevé. Les Français tenaient cet usage de celui qui
était pratiqué chez les anciens Francs, lesquels se chargeaient le bras
gauche d'une chaîne quand ils faisaient une promesse solennelle, ne la
quittant pareillement qu'après avoir rempli leurs engagements . . . il arriva
que les preux du moyen âge remplacèrent la chaîne par une écharpe de la
couleur la plus agréable à l'oeil." This practice might seem to offer some
explanation for Gawain's action in donning a green scarf as the token of
a solemn vow, but Mazas, as so often, gives no authority for his statements,
and I have found no allusion in treatises on chivalry or any of the ME
romances to the practice he cites.

3. Notably W. H. Schofield (*Engl. Lit. from Conquest to Chaucer*,
London, 1906, 215-17), Sir. I. Gollancz (*Camb. Hist. of Engl. Lit.* (N.
Y., 1907), 1. 366), and Isaac Jackson (*Anglia* 37. 393 ff.).

of *Gawain* is alluding in the account that he gives in the final lines of his poem of the chivalric brotherhood instituted *pro honore Galvani*.[4] Thus the possibility that the poet was alluding to the Garter being definitely "out," and our knowledge of the existence of any other contemporary English order being nil, it would seem wise to inquire whether our author could have had any foreign order in mind.[5]

Now it so happens that the name of Enguerrand de Coucy, Count of Soissons, is connected with an order of chivalry. Indeed, the phrase "connected with" is, to say the truth, putting it somewhat mildly. The *raison d'être* of the Order is vague and uncertain, but all modern historians do unite in naming the Count of Soissons its founder,[6] and the evidence of documents dating from his own time gives them good ground for doing so. The Order in question is that of the Crown (*Ordre de la Couronne*). About its origin, purpose, costume, and ceremonies we know very little. But that little suggests possibilities that tantalize because they are such inviting possibilities, tempting us to leave the solid

4. *Mod. Phil.* 13, 710-14. Though Hulbert has proved that the new Order is not the Garter, he has not driven out of court the possibility that the green lace might have been part of the costume of the lady-associates of the Order during a given year.

5. Hulbert (pp. 714-18) names some twelve orders of chivalry (by no means, as he admits, a complete list) as having been founded in the 14th century. "There is," he tells us, "no reason to suppose that *GGK* must necessarily be connected with an English order." He suggests the possibility that the poet may have been alluding to the Savoyard Order of the Collar, founded by Duke Amadeo VI in 1362 (pp. 716-18). An identification of the order to which the poet seems to be alluding with any of those mentioned is at present impossible, but Hulbert's suggestion is one worthy of consideration. There were a few personal connections between Savoyards and Englishmen at the time that the *Gawain*-poet was writing, and the color of the Savoyard collar was green. Still the most prominent ornament of the continental order was a collar, and that of the order described in our poem a baldric. Furthermore, Hulbert, quite modestly, claims for his suggestion no more than that it is a possibility.

6. Notably G. de Genouillac, *Dict. Hist. des Ordres de Chivalerie*, Paris 1860; J. Moreau, *Notice sur les Sires de Coucy d'après les documents originaux*, 2nd ed. Chauny, 1871, 267.

ground of fact and launch out into the deep. The reader will remember, however, that I have promised to lead him no further than the evidence goes.

Seals of the Sire de Coucy attached to extant documents dated before the year 1379 show (1) a shield of arms barry of six vair (and gules)[7]—Coucy's own arms—or else (2) one in which those arms are quartered with his mother's Austrian fesse (gules a fesse argent). The latter, of course, give plain indication that, at the time that the seal-matrix was made, Enguerrand was advancing his claim to his mother's inheritance in the Duchy of Austria.[8]

Shortly after Coucy's resumption of his French allegiance his seals appear, it is true, with Coucy quartering Austria, but the face of the seal is *semé* with small crowns (*sur champ quadrillé semé de couronnes*).[9] The first document that

7. Since the seal is of red wax, the tincture gules of the Coucy arms is impossible of rendition.

8. Seals of the first type are to be found in Public Record Office, 39E3 *Ancient Deeds* W.S. 576; Collect. Clairambault No. 2838 (*Inventaire* ed. G. Demay, *Collect. Doc. Inédites*, Paris, 1885, 1. 300); PRO 1R2, Museum, Pedestal 6 (E30/1745). The first and third just mentioned are interesting, because No. 1 shows that in 1365 Coucy had not advanced his claim to his mother's inheritance within the Duchy, and No. 3 the possibility that he had, by virtue of a composition with his cousins the dukes of Austria, withdrawn by Aug. 1377 the claims that he had previously advanced; cf. Zurlauben, *Abrégé, Bibl. Mil.* 1709, 2. 332-40. Seals of the second type are to be found in PRO 41E3 *Ancient Deeds*, A. S. 257; British Museum, *Cat. of Seals in Dept. of Mss.* nos. 8998 (A. D. 1369) and 20102 (A.D. 1394). Père Anselme, *Hist. Généalogique* 8. 542, lists a seal of this type attached to a quittance executed by Coucy Nov. 8, 1374, for 6000 frs. d'or given him by the French king. I am greatly indebted to Hilary Jenkinson, Esq., of the PRO. for his courtesy and kindness in sending me, not only full descriptions of the three Coucy seals, but reproductions of two of them as well (the third had been "evacuated" for preservation).

9. Dom. du Plessis (*Hist. de la Ville et de Seigneurs de Coucy*, Paris, 1728, p. 89) admits that the crowns on Enguerrand's seals are upright, but says that those on the seals of Louis, Duke of Orleans, who had purchased the Coucy Lands (circa 1400) from Marie de Bar (née Coucy) are *renversée*, "upside down," and from that statement, frequently repeated by later historians, deductions have been drawn. The kindness of a noted French savant, Mons. Jacques Meurgay, Secrétaire-Général, of the Soc. Française d'Héraldique et de Sigillographie enables me to assure

bears this seal *semé de couronnes* is one dated July 2, 1379,[10] and after that date it appears to have been the only seal that Coucy regularly used.[11]

It has been conjectured by almost all antiquarians and scholars who have studied Coucy's career that the appearance of the crowns upon his seal in 1379 is plain evidence that the *Ordre de la Couronne* was flourishing in that year, and those who are familiar with the punning and allusive spirit of fourteenth-century heraldry will agree that the conjecture is a very likely one. One might even safely go further and say that it is by no means impossible that the Order might have dated from a year earlier than 1379. If such were the case, its foundation would have occurred very close to the time that its founder broke off relations with the English King and resumed his French allegiance.

---

the reader that the crowns that decorate Coucy's seals are not *renversée*. A cast of one of them (Archiv. Natl. Suppl. 2292 A and B) sent me by Mons. Meurgey, shows on either side of the quartered arms of Coucy and Austria a peppering of crowns or coronets of 3 fleur-de-lis right side up. Those examples listed in G. Demay, *Inventaire des Sceaux de la Collect, Clairambault* (*Coll. Doc. Inéd.* 99) 2. 214-15, nos. 8644-8646, and in J. Roman, *Inventaire des Sceaux de la Collect. des Pièces Originales* (*Collect. Doc. Inéd.* 116) 1. 411, no. 3548, do not describe the crowns as upside down. G. Demay (*Le Costume d'après les Sceaux*, Paris 1880, p. 162) explains how the difficulty arose. The *Camail*, the insignia of the order of that name, founded in 1394 by Louis, Duke of Orleans, was mistaken for a reversed crown, and since the Duke purchased in 1400 the Coucy territories, it was believed that he had naturally succeeded to the sovereignty or presidency of Enguerrand's order, and that the insignia of the *Couronne* was a coronet upside down. Demay indicates that the sigillographer Clairambault did a good deal to spread the error.

10. No. 8645 in G. Demay's *Inventaire* 2. 214-15, "quittance de pension."

11. Du Plessis (p. 89) suggests that the crowns that appeared on Coucy's seal might have alluded to the loss of his claim to the crown of Austria in the campaign of 1375-76, and that suggestion has received support from the erroneous belief that those crowns were reversed (see preceding note). It has been repeated over and over again by later historians; see, for example, Tarbé, *Oeuvres Inéd.*, of Deschamps, 2. 55-56. But Zurlauben, *Abregé* (2. 344) shows the impossibility of such a suggestion by pointing out that Enguerrand advanced no claim to the Austrian crown, but only to "les biens mobiliers & allodiaux" of his mother.

Our knowledge of the aims, membership, and fortunes of the Order is of the scantiest. The poet Eustache Deschamps wrote a ballade,[12] and a rondeau[13] in its honor, and makes a fleeting reference to its prosperity in his ballade "Faisant mencion de la Mort de Monseigneur de Coucy."[14] A deed executed by Enguerrand, providing an endowment for the Celestines at Villeneuve to ensure prayers and masses for him and his, proves by its mention of the Order that Deschamps was not referring to some vague and informal association such as that of The Flower, or its companionate and antithetical coterie of The Leaf.[15] And this deed not only assures us of the actual existence of the Order, but proves also that the regulator of its aims and ceremonial was none other than Enguerrand de Coucy himself:—"*Notre Ordre de la Couronne.*"

The existence of the Order, then, is beyond all questioning and doubt. One can only wish that much else about it were equally so. Yet several items of information have survived obliteration by the waves of time. And it is these very items, when one remembers the *Gawain*-poet's story of the new brotherhood founded to signalize his hero's return, that inevitably raise the question whether the poet was not writing with his eye upon the new French order founded by, or

12. P. Tarbé, *Oeuvres Inéd. d'Eustache Deschamps*, 1. 35, "L'Ordre de la Couronne."

13. P. 36: "Aux chevaliers de l'Ordre de la Couronne."

14. *Oeuvres* (ed. G. Raynaud, Paris, 1891), 7. 206. Tarbé (1. 174-75) entitles this poem *chanson royal*.

15. Upon purchase of the barony of Coucy, Louis of Orleans issued letters of confirmation to the Celestines of Villeneuve of those endowments that the last lord of Coucy had given them. These letters, inserted in a cartulary of the Chambre des Comptes at Blois, repeat the words of Coucy's original grant. I quote the relevant portion from *Hist. des Ordres Monastiques* (Paris, 1721), 8. 285:

"Pour avoir prieres perpetuelles pour nous, nos devancieres & successeurs de notre tres chere & amée Compagne Isabel de Lorraine à present notre femme, pour tous les Chevaliers & Dames les Ecuiers & Demoiselles que ont esté, sont & seront de notre Ordre de la Couronne."

in honor of, a knight who had returned to those who had deemed him lost for good.

The first that deserves consideration is the fact, for I think it is a fact, that the *Couronne* had its genesis shortly after Coucy's renunciation of his ties with England. As we have seen above, the first seal that we find powdered with crowns is one attached to a document of July 2, 1379. Even granting the hypothesis that that instance of its use was actually the first, which is granting a good deal, the matrix of the seal would have to have been cut sometime before that date. Furthermore, the intention to have a new seal cut would have had to be in the mind of the owner, or his chancellor or steward, even sometime before the seal-cutter was commissioned to make that new matrix.[16] And such being the case, the decision to have a new seal would more likely have been reached in the year 1378 or even 1377, rather than in 1379. And the earlier the date of the seal, the earlier the date of the foundation of the Order: for of one thing we can be sure, the foundation of the new Order preceded the cutting of the new seal, and not the reverse. The upshot of the matter is that it is quite safe to say that the *Ordre de la Couronne* was founded rather shortly after the Sire de Coucy's surrender of the Garter, and his active resumption of his French allegiance and ties. If, then, there be aught of Enguerrand de Coucy in the poet's picture of Sir Gawain, perhaps his care to inform us of the safe return of his hero and his escape from a situation where he had to be

16. Aug. 26, 1377, was the date when Coucy's *Renunciatio* was authenticated by his seal. That seal, which I have seen, is not *semé de couronnes*. We may feel, therefore, some reasonable assurance that his "Great" and "Privy" seals did not at that date bear crowns. Yet I am chary of drawing closer conclusions as to the date when the new seal appeared, until communication with French sigillographers can be again resumed. That appended to the *Renunciatio* may have been Coucy's principal or official seal, and the others of the new design (listed in footnotes above) only his privy or personal signets for use in travelling or the despatch of urgent business.

slightly false to be greatly true, has more of truth than
poetry in it.

The next fact about the new Order is that to it ladies,
married and unmarried, were admitted. Just what the basis
of selection and the procedure of admission were we do not
know, but as to the fact itself Coucy's own words stand as
warrant: The Celestines of Villeneuve were to pray "pour
tous les Chevaliers & Dames les Ecuiers & Demoiselles qui
ont esté, sont & seront de notre Ordre de la Couronne."
It is, therefore, interesting to observe that the Order described by the writer of our romance has the same provision.[17]
Arthur and his court

> . . . . luflyly acorden
> Þat lordes and ladis þat longed to þe Table,
> Vche burne of þe brother-hede a bauderyk schulde haue.

Finally, we are told by the poet Deschamps that the
Sire de Coucy kept a bounteous and impeccable household for
knights who were constantly with him of his Order and company.[18] And elsewhere he reminds those who take the Order
that it "requiert hauste vaillance et chevaliers de noble par-
enté."[19] It seems quite evident that the *Couronne* was ar-
dently desired and eagerly sought for, since from what Deschamps tells us, its membership rolls appear to have been
always full, and those whose names were written upon them

17. Whether the "ladis þat longed to þe Table" were admitted to full
membership in the Order, or whether they enjoyed only "honorary associate membership," as they did in the Garter, we know not. I suppose
that their enjoyment of full and complete membership rights would
depend on whether the Order was a military brotherhood or one that was
purely social; see note 1 above. Does the adjuration *Armes suiez!* in
Deschamps' *Rondeau* indicate that it was a military brotherhood?

18. Tarbé, *Chanson royal faisant mencion de la mort du monseigneur
de Coucy*

> Hostel tint large et sain
> De chevaliers, qu'il avoit soir et main
> Avecques lui, de s'ordre et compaignie.

Ordre et compaignie, a plain allusion to the Order of the Crown.

19. *Ballade sur l'Ordre de la Couronne*, lines 21-22.

had to be of proven attainment and noble birth.[20] The
Gawain-poet also makes a point of stressing the high standards of admission to the company formed to honor Sir Gawain at the conclusion of his adventure:

> And he honoured þat hit hade, euer-more after.

These few correspondences between the companionage of
fact and that of fiction are interesting—so interesting as to
make us desirous of knowing more about *l'Ordre de la
Couronne*. Perhaps the poet intended his readers to understand that the Order he so tersely described was the Order
that his former lord(?) had established in a foreign land,
but we have no means of finding out that he did so intend.
If it could be discovered that a green baldric was the principal insignia, or even a part of the costume, of a companion of
l'Ordre de la Couronne, then few would hesitate to believe
that the poet was actually describing no other order than the
Couronne. But we have now absolutely no evidence whatever
about the insignia or attire of Enguerrand's Order.

The suggestion has been made that its members wore a
miniature crown attached to the end of a ribbon, or strap,
pendant from their right arm, but there is not one scintilla
of evidence to support such a guess or even to justify its
advancement.[21] As to the green lace, if the knights ever

---

20. Coucy's own words, however, tell something against the glowing
and eulogistic statements of Deschamps. For he distinctly mentions
"Ecuiers" who were, or might be, members of the Order. Apparently
knighthood was no requisite for admission to (some form of) membership in the Order. In medieval times men of proven valor and attainment
sometimes refused knighthood because of its heavier expense, and the
"Ecuiers" of the Crown may have been just such persons. Yet the fact
that in the bequest "Ecuiers" are coupled with "Demoiselles" tells against
the last statement and indicates that there must have been several classes
of membership in the Order. "Chevaliers & Dames" evidently balance
"Ecuiers & Demoiselles."

21. See G. Giucci, *Iconografia Storica degli Ordini* (Roma, 1838), 2.
165-67: "Solo distintivo della loro dignità cavalleresca fosse solamente la
più volte ricordata corona, che pendeva dal braccio diritto" (p. 167).

wore it, they may or may not have worn it baldric-wise.
There is as much likelihood that they did so as that they did
not. Indeed, the poet may be describing some other order
than the Crown. Or—and this supposition seems somewhat
more probable—he may be, in very truth, glancing at that
Order, but also taking care that his description be not too
definite or precise, and deliberately introducing his green lace
not to put us on, but to throw us off trail, conscious that his
function was to stimulate and suggest, not to posit and postulate. If the latter contingency be allowed, it is permissible
to suppose that he was very gently, very tactfully, and with
a charming courtesy reminding his readers that the honor of
the new French order "rooted in dishonour stood." Since
the Count of Soissons, unlike the Count of Ostrevant (for
whose case, see Appendix D), had sent back his Garter, and
repudiated for himself and his vassals the ties it implied, he
had been welcomed back, his past doings minimized, and his
happy return to the French Court signalized by the institution of the new Order. At such goings-on English administrative and aristocratic circles and some members of the royal
family, particularly John of Gaunt or Thomas of Woodstock, might have felt "miffed." The poet who wrote for
their favor or at their behest may have been voicing their
feeling when he pointed out that while the *Couronne* fit-
tingly honored a very gallant gentleman, it also recorded an
event which even he could not remember without regret.

But why

> Vche burne of þe broþer-hede a bauderyk schulde haue,
> A bende a-belef hym aboute, of a bryȝt grene

we know not. And we know as little about the historic order,
if any, that that "bende" betokened. Our discussion of the
preceding paragraph has been but of possibility and surmise.
Possibility and surmise are not fact, as scholars sometimes

seek to make them. But without them, new truth in any field of human endeavor is impossible of attainment; for the possibilities and surmises of today often prove the facts of tomorrow.

Possible Position and Status of the Author of *Sir Gawain*

IF THERE is any connection between the sojourn and marriage of the Sire de Coucy in England and the events that ensued thereupon, on the one hand, and the writing of the romance of *Sir Gawain and the Green Knight,* on the other, what light, as a consequence, is thrown upon the station and activities of its author?

There can be little doubt that the poet grew up in the Northwest Midlands; so much his language[1] and his use of the poetic form native to that region plainly tell us. Residence in London, or elsewhere, may have presented him with opportunities for a more intimate knowledge of men and affairs and a wider range of reading than he could have found in his native county, but his mastery of the alliterative metre could have been attained only if that metre had first mastered him, if its rhythms and phrasings had sung themselves into the tempo of his own life. He may or may not have written or recited his poem outside of Yorkshire or Lancashire, but in the Northwest Midlands, and only there, he had learned how to write it. Wherever else he may have gone, and whomever he may have served, his roots and memories went back into the Northwestern shires.

In a previous essay the reader's attention has been called

1. See Appendices A and B.

to the poet's fairly frequent use of imagery derived from the law. When the vocabulary of a particular pursuit or profession colors a man's speech to a marked degree, it is usually an indication that he has had some experience or training in the profession whose speech betrays him. It is, therefore, a thoroughly sound inference to assume that the poet had had at one time to busy himself with legal affairs. His evident familiarity with the amenities and ceremonial of aristocratic life suggests that his legal duties were carried on within or about a court or nobleman's household rather than independently, i.e., as a lawyer who haunted the parvis of Paul's to pick up clients. His alliterative translation of a well-known French phrase used in chancery documents[2] makes one wonder whether he might not once have been a clerk of chancery. If he were, one may the more readily understand how and why he exhibits some of the interests and habits of thought we detect in his poetry.

The chancery of the fourteenth century was the administrative office of the English government. Through it went the annually increasing mass of royal letters, orders, directions and caveats, pardons, and decisions of the royal council, to the numerous sheriffs, judges, military commanders, and territorial magnates throughout the length and breadth of the kingdom, and back to it came also an annually increasing mass of petitions, acknowledgments, requests for pardons, for permission to go abroad, or for the privilege of crenellation, i.e., of building a castle. As the century grew older, it had begun to be much more concerned in diplomacy and the management of foreign policy, and hard-working members of its staff were not infrequently pulled out from their writing-tables and packed off on embassies headed by some nobleman whose military or social prestige was great but whose experi-

2. Line 267, "For had I founded in fere in feȝtyng wyse" is evidently a paraphrase of "araiez a faire de guerre" of the Chancery documents; see M. D. Legge, "A fuer de Guerre," *Med. Aev.* 5. 121-22.

ence was slight or whose brains small. Thus a chancery clerk, as we shall see more clearly below, not only had to have the ability to read and write, but had trained himself, if he were anxious to get on, in the execution and despatch of all the legal and financial paperwork which underlay the government of his day.

By the time in which our romance was written, the chancery errant was no more. It had ceased to accompany the king on his journeys, because of the enormous swelling of its official records, and the constant need of its clerks to consult them. "It now had headquarters of its own in London, where the clerks lived a sort of collegiate life in common. It kept there its ever-increasing mass of records, and kept them in the very same place where the Public Record Office now preserves the accumulated archives of every great department of state."[3] If the *Gawain*-poet had ever been of "the household of chancery," he would have had to reside in London, and thus we can account for an apparent familiarity with the sights and sounds of a large city shown in *Patience*, *The Pearl*, and *Purity*, and, more specifically, for his writing of the legend of a London saint in or about 1386.

The hypothesis that our poet may have had chancery experience illuminates some of the obscurities and shadows that lie athwart the picture we compose from the reading of his poetry. Professor Tout tells us that the fourteenth-century chancery, as contrasted with the exchequer, where many of the clerks were laymen, was "entirely staffed with clerks," i.e., clergymen. Thus it is easy to understand the poet's knowledge of the Vulgate, of a considerable body of patristic writing on symbolism and theology, and his interest in the question, argued so keenly in his own day, of predestination and free will.

3. T. F. Tout, "Civil Service in the Fourteenth Century," *Collect. Papers* (Manchester, 1934), 3. 197.

And more that Professor Tout tells us makes this possibility a tenable one:

The chancery clerks were, I imagine, both the most important and the ablest of medieval civil servants. Some of them were doctors of the civil and canon law. Among their special spheres was [sic] diplomacy and foreign politics. . . . At home, even more than abroad, there were many fields open to the zealous chancery clerk. Accordingly the chancery was thronged by the academic youth of ability anxious for distinction in the public service. Fourteenth-century Oxford had already marked out this career as its own.[4]

4. *Ibid.*, pp. 202-3. Tout's words on the method of appointment of Chancery clerks deserve quotation (pp. 203-4):
"I have already spoken of the prevalence and of the inconvenience of the hereditary transmission of office. There was only one alternative way to it . . . This other way was the method of nomination, sometimes perhaps by conscientious selection, more often I fear by jobbery, local, family or personal. . . . It was one of the happy results of the clerical element in the medieval service that our celibate clerical officials had not . . . so many opportunities of jobbery for their sons as are vouchsafed to the sages of the law in modern democratic Britain . . . though the cleric's family feeling could find plenty of scope in promoting the interests of his numerous nephews. . . . The commonest of all sorts of medieval jobbery seems to have been 'feudal' and local, rather than personal. The official that had 'got on' planted not only his kinsfolk but his tenants and retainers and their families, in humbler cases the youth of his own village or district, in any posts of which he had the patronage. In the same way the king, as the ultimate fountain of office, always bestowed special favour on men sprung from manors on the royal domain. . . . Nor was this method of selection merely the result of favouritism. The close personal tie of lord and vassal was, under fourteenth-century conditions, the strongest possible guarantee of faithful service."
Had the *Gawain*-poet ever worked as an official of Chancery, it is probable that he owed his job to just such "local" connections and feudal "pull" as Professor Tout describes. Birth on the Coucy estates, and the influence of the Earl and Countess of Bedford, could very well have gotten him the job he held or was promoted to. Cf. on this possibility R. H. Gretton, *The King's Government* (London, 1913), p. 9:
"Since the position of a King's clerk, with its comparative security of livelihood and prospects of advancement, would naturally attract capable men, the increasing complication of business would fall into hands adequate to deal with it; and probably the tendency of certain necessary acts of government to become formalised would be actually hastened by the existence of this class of experienced clerks."
Space forbids further quotation from this book but I refer the reader

In the light of this quotation we can learn something of how the *Gawain*-poet may have come to be the man we know to-day—a skilled artificer of narrative and a poet of sensitivity and genius.

The belief that our author had once worked in the chancery, or some other office of the royal administration (the wardrobe is a possibility), in no way conflicts with a belief expressed in the first essay of this book that he may have served in the household of some great landholder of his native region, the Duke of Lancaster or the Earl of Bedford. For clerks of chancery were readily transferable from one area of the administrative machine to another. "The administration of the lands and franchises of the king's kin was correlated with that of the crown. The clerks of the king's wife and sons [one might add, 'and of his daughter too'] were also the king's clerks. They belonged to a single official service and expected the same rewards."[5] Had the *Gawain*-poet ever been a clerk in chancery, there would have no difficulty whatever about his being transferred from the care of the King's records to those of his daughter Isabella.[6]

Yet the assumption that the *Gawain*-poet must have necessarily been an official of the wardrobe or chancery is not the only explanation of how or why he wrote as he did. We can see that in the cases of the king's household and that of his eldest daughter public and private business and affairs overlapped, or rather had become hopelessly indistinguishable. One experienced in the management of a medieval household, even though he had never spent an hour in

to p. 17, where the author shows that the King's clerks owed their support either to (1) their holding of ecclesiastical livings, or (2) the fees paid them by litigants or claimants who sought their services at the chancery, exchequer, or wardrobe, or (3) by virtue of their being members of the household of the King, the Queen, or one of the royal children.

5. T. F. Tout, *Admin. Hist. of Med. Eng.* 3. 253-54.

6. "The princess had also her central administrative office, including 'her receipt' at Westminster"; *ibid.,* 3. 253, note 1.

chancery or exchequer, would soon have been as astute and practiced in medieval paperwork as any official of either of those offices. "He would already be fully acquainted with the system of tallies, with writs of 'liberate' and 'allocate,' letters patent and close, and the varying significance of a great and secret seal. . . . Men who represented their masters before the king himself, in the exchequer, the Court of Common Pleas, or who maintained the whole defence of a Quo Warranto plea . . . can hardly have been untrained."[7] So the poet may have come up from Craven or Lancashire to enter directly the household of one of the monarch's sons or daughters. I shall not attempt to locate him more precisely. He may have served the Countess of Bedford (and there seen and fallen under the spell of her attractive husband); or, and this is equally plausible and probable, her influential brother, duke and autocrat of the palatine county of Lancaster, John of Gaunt. The Duke, we know, was fond of his sister and the niece who resided with her in England, and probably also of his brilliant brother-in-law who had tarried so briefly and left so soon. A compliment paid to any one of them or to several, by a retainer of his would have been pleasing to him as well.

And yet I cannot but indulge the thought that the poet may have come up from the Coucy lands in Westmoreland or Lancashire, taken service in the household of the Earl and Countess of Bedford, tarried there, after the Earl's departure for his native land, as an approved and trusted dependent, and lived on to serve in his age the daughter whose mother he had served in early or middle manhood.

For such a fancy there is naturally no direct supporting evidence. Yet a couplet written above the second of the manuscript illustrations of *Gawain* (fol. 125) teases one who

7. N. Denholm-Young, *Seignorial Administration in England* (Oxford, 1937), pp. 162-63.

would know more of these hidden matters. It it written down in a hand contemporary with, and perhaps in the same hand as, that which penned the manuscript:

> My minde is mukel on on þat wil me noȝt amende
> Sum time was trewe as ston & fro scham couþe hir defende.[8]

It is quite possible that the author of the poem did not write the couplet (the manuscript is probably several removes from his original copy), and not unlikely that it was not inscribed on the original copy, for the illustration on whose upper margin it appears is probably later than the text it illustrates, and may be later than the couplet. Who wrote it we may never know.

Yet obscure as the lines are in origin and meaning, they have a close and remarkable applicability to the lot of the Countess of Bedford, and that of her daughter the Duchess of Ireland as well. The writer's memory (*minde*) is much on one who could not now assist or succor him (because she was dead?). Once she was true as stone, and knew how to (couþe) defend herself from slander. Does the second line refer to the possibility that slanderous tongues had wagged against Isabella, Countess of Bedford, because she and her husband had parted, and affirm the writer's belief in her innocency and rectitude? Or does the couplet refer to an

---

8. See facsimile of MS Cotton Nero A. x., Introduction (EETS. 162, 1923, p. 11), Gollancz remarks, "The handwriting seems to be the artist's; the lines themselves have all the characteristics of the poet." Of this statement, W. W. Greg, in a review of the facsimile (*MLR* 19. 227, note 1) comments, "What can have suggested to the editor that 'the handwriting seems to be the artist's' I am at a loss to guess." Greg is correct; there is no evidence at present known that would warrant the tone of assurance in Gollancz's words. Of the lines Greg remarks (p. 227), "at the head of fol. 125[a] stands an isolated and enigmatical couplet. It is said to be in a different hand from the preceding text, and I agree that this is probable. In that case it is certainly later, though the interval may not have been long. But the illustration is clearly later than the couplet which it avoids." As against Greg, C. Brett believes, upon the authority of J. P. Gilson, that the couplet is written down perhaps in the same hand as that of the MS; see *MLR* 22. 452.

event of later years, the shameful repudiation of the Countess of Oxford by her husband Robert de Vere, and voice the indignation of someone who had been in some way connected with the last English Coucy? We do not know. Yet among other possible explanations of the couplet this one is valid— until disproved: a connection of some sort, sanctified by tradition, between the tenants of (or sojourners upon) the English ancestral lands of the house of Coucy-Guines, and the romance of *Sir Gawain and the Green Knight*.

A Note

The reader will be interested in the facts given below concerning a middle-class family active in the business and government of the county of Lancashire in the fourteenth century, and connected closely with the house of Coucy-Guines. I do not suggest that our poet was a member of that family, but if we are to find him, I would emphasize the need of combing more assiduously than has yet been done parish and family records of the Northwest Midland counties. I, for one, do not give him up as irrecoverably gone. Some lucky find in an English library or a hitherto unconsulted collection of family papers may give him to us, but I am disposed to the belief that he is more likely to emerge as the result of protracted and patient local gleanings over the fields where once he may have walked.

A searcher through the *Register of John of Gaunt*, the *Calendars of Close, Patent, and Charter Rolls*, and unpublished material in the Public Record Office on the Duchy of Lancaster in the fourteenth century, finds frequent mention of members of the Lancashire family of Hornby. The family, apparently of North Lancashire origin, followed the fortunes of John of Gaunt and his close kinsfolk, and profited by doing so.

A John de Hornby in 13 Ed. II was possessed of free-warren in Ireby (Lancs.); *Cal. Rot. Chart,* p. 153. Ireby is

part of Thornton parish (Yks.). The township is situated
east of Whittington (Lancs.). Whittington Manor and the
advowson of Thornton church were part of the Coucy hold-
ings. John Hornby purchased land in N. Lancs. in 35 Ed.
I (*Lancs. Fines*, Part II, p. 41, note 1). An Edmund de
Horn(e)by held three oxgangs of land in Claughton-in-
Lonsdale in 1346 (*Vict. Hist. of Lancs.* 8. 211). The
Hornby who seems to have made the family fortunes was
William, a trusted servant of John of Gaunt. He had also
served in the Hanaper (Dept. of Enrolling and Sealing) of
the royal chancery ("clericus Hanaperii regis et ducis," D.
King's Rememb. 32, Append. 1, 354, *Roll of Fines, Letters
Close and Pat., and Charters*). He must have been a notable
pluralist, for he had been rector of the church at Ribchester
(1349-64, *Vict. Hist. of Lancs.* 7. 41, note 45) and was holding from 1367-88 (*ibid.*, p. 265) the church of St. Michaels-
on-Wyre (*Cal. Close Rolls* 1369-74, p. 54). Enguerrand de
Coucy's Nether Wyresdale lordship included a large part
of Wyresdale parish (*Vict. Hist. of Lancs.* 7. 300). The
reference from the *Close Rolls* cited a short while ago also
tells us that Hornby had at one time been granted possession
of land and rent in Whittington, a manor held either wholly
or in part by Coucy (*Vict. Hist. of Lancs.* 8. 242-43). One
wonders whether he had secured his grant through the favor
of the Earl or Countess of Bedford, or by virtue of Gaunt's
influence with his sister. He was receiver for the Duchy of
Lancaster in John of Gaunt's household by August, 1371
(*Reg. of John of Gaunt 1372-76*, no. 780), and in 1383
chancellor of the Duchy exchequer (*Reg. of John of Gaunt
1379-83*, 1. xxii-iii). Tenure of these evidently
gave him opportunity to grow wealthy, for we find frequent mention of his name in agreements or deeds concerned with the holding or transfer of lands in the county
(see indices to *John of Gaunt's Reg.*, contemporary *Calen-*

dars of Pat. and Close Rolls, and *Vict. Hist. of Lancs.* 7).
Recognizance deeds of D.K.R. (32, App. 1, p. 362) show
that he was in the custom of making loans to the smaller
landholders of his county. The fact that he is named as one
who had an interest in a lawsuit over a moiety of the manor
of Winmarleigh in Garstang, formerly held by William de
Coucy (was it granted again to Enguerrand after his appearance in England?), shows that he had connections within the
area of the Earl of Bedford's landed interest; see *Vict. Hist.
of Lancs.* 7. 306, note 11.

More interesting than William is a certain Robert de
Hornby. In 1358 he mainprizes John de Ditton, king's
clerk; see *Cal. Fine Rolls* 1356-68, 7. 57. He is mentioned
as a king's clerk in 1360 (*op. cit.* 7. 125-26). On June 1,
1365, he was appointed, along with William de Wykeham, as
an attorney for Enguerrand de Coucy for two years (*Cal.
Pat. Rolls* 1364-67, p. 105). Appointment was doubtless
made because as a Lancashire man he must have been thoroughly familiar with Coucy's holdings in that county. Is he
the same Robert de Hornby to whom, and to his wife
Margery and son William, Gilbert de Kighley granted in
1357 his share of the stream and fishing of the river Wyre
between Crossford and Skepulford (*Vict. Hist. of Lancs.* 7.
277, note 8)? It is interesting to note that the lordship of
the territory mentioned above had belonged to William de
Coucy. Between 1366 and 1371 a certain Thos. de Rigmaiden demised Wedacre in Garstang (a Coucy lordship)
to his son John, if he married Margaret, dau. of Robt. de
Hornby (*Vict. Hist. of Lancs.* 7. 316). Is this last Robert
identical with the preceding one, or with Robert the king's
clerk?

A certain William de Hornby (evidently not John of
Gaunt's receiver) appears to have risen high in the last years
of Richard II. He is mentioned as king's attorney (*Cal.*

Close Rolls 1389-92, pp. 114. 267) and apparently attained
the high dignity of sergeant of the law (*Cal. Pat. Rolls* 1396-
99, p. 28) in 1396. A William de Hornby, a yeoman of the
livery of the crown, was appointed on April 22, 1397, keeper
of Rysebank Castle near Calais (*Cal. Pat. Rolls* 1396-99,
p. 112), but he may have been a relative of William the attorney. In 1387 Sir Richard de Hoghton demised his lands
in Great Sowerby—part of the Wyresdale lordship belonging to the Guines family in 1324—to William de Hornby
the younger for life. Whether this William be the William
last mentioned (or the king's attorney, if that official be
not the "yeoman of the livery"), I have as yet not been
able to find out, but it is noteworthy that a Hornby is again
mentioned in connection with the Coucy lands.

On May 10, 1391, pardon is granted a Richard de
Hornby for illegally crossing the sea with the dowager
Countess de Vere, Philippa de Coucy's mother-in-law, to see
her son (*Cal. Pat. Rolls* 1388-92, p. 407). Was this the
same Richard who in 1372 was indicted for robbery committed in Lancashire (*Cal. Pat. Rolls* 1370-74, p. 217)?
Finally, in a letter patent dated June 2, 1377, Sheen, mention is made of a Wilkin de Hornby as "a former servant of
the Earl of Bedford" (*Cal. Pat. Rolls* 1374-77, p. 477).

It is, then, possible that the last name of the *Gawain*-
poet might have been prosaic Hornby, though it is impossible to find a single piece of direct evidence that justifies us
in the surmise. If it be objected that it would have been
unlikely that such busy and hard-headed men of affairs as the
Hornbys wrote or had time for poetry, we must not forget
Chaucer. Professor S. Moore (*Library*, N.S., 4. 369) wisely
reminds us that the "mediæval writer was not a professional,
but an occasional author. He gave to literary work only a
part of his time, and did not depend upon it for a living; the
making of books was not his vocation, but his avocation."

I do not care to carry the matter further. There is no proof whatever that the *Gawain*-poet lived in the Coucy household or that of John of Gaunt, or that of Chancery, or that he had connections with the royal family or administration. My duty is to suggest possible leads. If they end in blind alleys, we shall know that they are valueless. But we shall not find the identity of this unknown author unless we make an attempt to do so.

APPENDIX L

Coucy's Letter of Resignation, August 26, 1377

Treshonnoure et trespoissant Seigneur:

Vostre noble et grant Seignourie scet et congnoit assez l'aliance, que, de la grace et bonte de, trespoissant et bon Roy, mon treshonnour, et tresredoubte Seigneur et Pere, le Roy, derrainement trespasse (que Dieux face merci) a pleu que j'ai en aly et au encore avec vous; dont treshonnoure Seigneur je vous mercie tant comme je puis et scai.

Or est il avenu que la guerre est entre le Roy de France, mon naturel et Souverain Seigneur, d'une part, et vous d'autre.

Dont il me desplait plus que de chose qui puist estre en ce monde, se admender le peusse.

Et m'a commande et requis qui je le serve et acquitte mon devoir, comme je y sui tenus, au quel, comme vous savez bien, je ne doy desobeir, si le servirai a mon poir, comme je le doy faire.

Et pour ce, treshonnoure et trespoissant Seigneur, que on ne puist, en aucune manere, parler ne dire chose qui fust contre moy ne mon honnour, vous fais assavoir les choses dessusdites, et vous renvoie tout ce que je pourie tenir de vous en foy et hommage.

Et aussi, treshonnoure Seigneur, mon tresredoubte Seignur et Pere dessusdit vuolt moy ordonner et mettre en la tresnoble Compaignie et Ordre du Jartier; si plaise vestre tresnoble et poissant Seignourie de pourveoir, en lieu de moy, tel ou ainsi que il vous plaira, et moy tenir pour excuse en ce.

Car, treshonnoure Seigneur, si en autre maniere vous me voliez aucune chose commander, je le feroie de tout mon pooir.

Treshonnoure et trespoissant Seigneur, je prie a Messire qu'il vous dont bonne vie et longue.
Escript le xxvi jour d'Aoust

Locus Sigilli
Le Sire de Coucy[1]

1. Printed in Rymer's *Fœdera* (London, 1709), 7. 172-73. I have altered in several places Rymer's punctuation in the interests of clarity and consistency, and normalized his system of capitalization. The seal of red wax shows a shield barry of six vair and gules (see Appendix J, note 7).

Bibliography

THE FOLLOWING bibliography is highly selective. It records only those books and articles which have been instrumental in presenting the figure of the *Gawain*-poet—still very much of a torso—as it appears today. Since *Sir Gawain and the Green Knight* is the *pièce de résistance* of the book, the reader will find that the bibliography is centered upon that romance; though all poems supposedly written by this anonymous author, *Pearl* in particular, that furnish materials for his portrait have been laid under contribution. For very good reason I have not swollen it by listing every book or article about the poet or his work. There is no need to rechronicle the earliest attempts to ascertain his identity or to determine his writing methods. These, where rightly directed, are now incorporated in later and more accurate scholarly writings, and, where discredited or overthrown, require no second refutation.

ABBREVIATIONS

Cal. Chart Rolls	(*Calendar of Charter Rolls*, Public Record Office)
Cal. Close Rolls	(*Calendar of Close Rolls*, PRO)
Cal. Fine Rolls	(*Calendar of Fine Rolls*, PRO)
Cal. IPM	(*Calendar of Inquisitions Post Mortem*, PRO)
Cal. Pat. Rolls	(*Calendar of Patent Rolls*, PRO)

EDD	(*English Dialect Dictionary*)
EETS	(Early English Text Society)
IPM (Rec. Com.)	(*Calendarium Inquisitionum Post Mortem.* Published by the Record Commission. London, 1806-28. 4 vols.)
JEGP	(*Journal of English and Germanic Philology*)
LTLS	(*London Times Literary Supplement*)
Med. Aev.	(*Medium Aevum*)
MLN	(*Modern Language Notes*)
MLR	(*Modern Language Review*)
Mod. Phil.	(*Modern Philology*)
NED	(*New English Dictionary on Historical Principles*)
Phil. Quart.	(*Philological Quarterly*)
PMLA	(*Publications of the Modern Language Association*)
PRO	(*Public Record Office*, London, England)
RES	(*Review of English Studies*)
Vict. Hist. Lancs.	(*Victoria History of Lancaster.* Edited by W. Farrer and J. Brownbill. London, 1906-14. 8 vols.)
Vict. Hist. Yks.	(*Victoria History of Yorkshire.* Edited by W. Page. London, 1907-13. 3 vols.)

NOTE: In titles where the danger of misunderstanding is absent, the name of the poem is represented by *GGK*.

FACSIMILE

Facsimile of MS Cotton Nero A. x. Introduction by Israel Gollancz. Publications of Early English Text Society, 162. 1923. Reviewed by W. W. Greg. *MLR* 19. 223-28. (Indispensable).

EDITIONS OF *SIR GAWAIN AND THE GREEN KNIGHT*

Morris, R. EETS 4. 1864; rev. 1869; rev. Gollancz, 1897, 1912

Bibliography 221

Tolkien, J. R. R., and E. V. Gordon. Oxford, 1925. Rev.
1930, 1936. Reviewed by: Brett, *MLR* 22. 451-58; Emerson, *JEGP* 26. 248-58; Grattan, *RES* 1. 484-87; Hol-
thausen, *Angl. Beiblatt* 36. 162-63; Hulbert, *Mod. Phil.* 23.
246-49; Menner, *MLN* 41. 397-400. (Questions as to
the authorship and dialect of the poem insufficiently discussed
in Introduction. Text, notes, and glossary are generally good,
though the first is one of unmarked emendations, and the
second suffers from over-condensation and some neglect of
the work of previous scholars.

Gollancz, Sir I. Re-edited from MS Cotton Nero A. x., with
introductory essays by Mabel Day, D.Lit., and Mary Serjeantson, M.A., D.Phil. EETS 210. 1940. Reviewed by
Savage, *MLN* 59. 342-50

EDITIONS OF OTHER WORKS ASCRIBED
TO THE *GAWAIN*-POET

Morris, R. *Early English Alliterative Poems.* EETS, 1864.
Rev. 1869. (Contains *Patience, Pearl, Purity.*)
Bateson, H. *Patience.* Manchester, 1912. 2nd ed. 1918
Gollancz, I. *Patience.* London, 1913. 2nd ed. 1924
———— *Pearl.* London, 1891. 2nd ed. 1921
Osgood, C. G. *Pearl.* Boston, 1906
Chase, S. P., and members of the Chaucer course in Bowdoin
College, *Pearl.* Boston, 1932
Menner, R. J. *Purity.* New Haven, 1920
Gollancz, Sir I. *Cleanness.* London, 1921 (Glossary and illus-
trative texts of this edition issued 1924)
———— *St. Erkenwald.* London, 1922
Savage, H. L. *St. Erkenwald.* London, 1926
NOTE: The introductions to the several editions of *GGK* and
those in the editions of the other poems ascribed to the *Gawain*-
poet are indispensable for one who seeks more information on the
subject-matter treated in the present study.

BIBLIOGRAPHY BY CHAPTERS
CHAPTER I

1. *For the dating of the poem,* see

Hamilton, G. L. " 'Capados' and the Date of *GGK.*" *Mod. Phil.* 5. 365-76

Oakden, J. P. *Alliterative Poetry in Middle English.* Manchester, 1930. 1. 86-87

Savage, H. L. "A Note on *GGK.* (700-2)." *MLN* 46. 455-57

Steiner, A. "The Date of the Composition of *Mandeville's Travels.*" *Speculum* 9. 144-47

See also Appendix C of this volume.

2. *For the locality and dialect of the author,* see

Hulbert, J. R. "A Hypothesis Concerning the Alliterative Revival." *Mod. Phil.* 28. 405-22

———— "The 'West Midland' of the Romances." *Mod. Phil.* 19. 1-16

Knigge, F. *Die Sprache des Dichters GGK., der Sogennanten Early English Alliterative Poems, und De Erkenwalde.* Marburg, 1886

Kullnick, M. *Studien über den Wortschatz in GGK.* Berlin, 1902

Menner, R. J. "*GGK* and the West Midland." *PMLA* 37. 503-26

Oakden, J. P. *Allit. Poetry in ME* (cited above). 1. 72-87

Serjeantson, Mary S. "The Dialects of West Midlands in Middle English." *RES* 3. 54-67, 186-203, 319-31

See also Appendix B of this volume.

3. *For the status, interests, and personality of the poet,* see

Cargill, O., and M. Schlauch. "*The Pearl* and Its Jeweler." *PMLA* 43. 105

Emerson, O. F. "Notes on *GGK.*" *JEGP* 21. 363-410

———— Review of Tolkien-Gordon's edition, *JEGP* 26. 252-54

Oakden, J. P. *Allit. Poetry in ME* (cited above). 1. 257-61; 2. 46-47; 2. 67-78

Osgood, C. G. *The Voice of England.* New York, 1935. Pp. 93-99

Savage, H. L. "*GGK* 1704." *MLN* 44. 249-50

————— "Fnasted in *GGK* 1702." *Phil. Quart.* 9. 209-10

————— "Notes on *GGK*." *PMLA* 46. 169-76

————— "Hunting in the Middle Ages." *Speculum* 8. 30-41

————— "A Note on *GGK,* 1700." *Med. Aev.* 4. 199-202

————— " 'Scrape' in *GGK*." *LTLS* Sept. 26, Oct. 31, 1936

————— "Brow or Brawn." *MLN* 52. 36-38

Wright, E. M. "*GGK*." *JEGP* 34. 157-79, 339-50; 35. 313-20

————— "Notes on *GGK*." *Engl. Stud.* 36. 207-27

————— *Rustic Speech and Folk-Lore.* London, 1913. Pp. 68-71

See also Appendix K of this volume

4. *For matters of craftsmanship, metrics, and style,* see

Brink, A. "Stab und Wort in *GGK*." *Stud. Engl. Phil.* 59. Halle, 1920

Fischer, J. *Die Stabende Langzeile in den Werken des Gawain-dichters. Bonner Beiträge* 11. 1-64

Fuhrmann, J. *Die Alliterierenden Sprachformeln in Morris' Early English Alliterative Poems und im GGK.* Hamburg, 1886

Kaluza, M. *A Short History of English Versification* (trans. by A. C. Dunstan). New York, 1911. Pp. 191-223

Kuhnke, B. *Die Alliteriende Langzeile in der Mittelenglischen Romanze GGK.* Berlin, 1900

Kullnick, M. *Studien über den Wortschatz in GGK.* Berlin, 1902

Luick, K. "Die englische Stabreimzeile im XIV., XV. und XVI. Jahrhundert." *Angl.* 11. 393-443, 553-618. See also his study of the alliterative line in Paul's *Grundriss der Germ. Phil.* 2nd ed. 2.2. 160-68

Oakden, J. P. *Allit. Poetry in ME* (cited above) 1. 53-93, 234-41; 2. 85-101, 104-11, 166-68, 179-93, 267-312, 344-50, 381-401

Reicke, C. *Untersuchungen über den Stil der ME . . . Gedichte Morte Arthure, The Destruction of Troy, The Wars of Alexander, The Siege of Jerusalem, GGK.* Konigsberg, 1906

Schmittbetz, K. "Das Adjectiv im Verse von *GGK.*" Bonn diss., 1908. A much fuller treatment in *Angl.* 32. 163

Thomas, J. *Die Allit. Langzeile des Gawain-Dichters.* Coburg, 1908

CHAPTER II

1. *For accounts of the animals hunted in medieval times and the etiquette and practice of hunting them,* see

Art of Hunting, The. (Text and English translation of Twici's *Le Art de Venerie*) Ed. with notes by H. Dryden, 1843; ed. revised by Alice Dryden. Northampton, 1908
William Twici (spelled also Twiti, Twyty) to whom *Le Art de Venerie* has been ascribed, was a huntsman in the service of King Edward II.

Master of Game, The. Written by Edward, second Duke of York. Ed. W. S. and F. Baillie-Grohman. London, 1909

Neilson, Miss N. "The Forests," *The English Government at Work 1327-1336.* Cambridge, Mass., 1940. Chap. IX of Vol. 1. Pp. 394-467

Savage, H. L. "Hunting in the Middle Ages." *Speculum* 8. 30-41

Venery de Twety, Le. In Wright and Halliwell's *Reliquiæ Antiquæ.* London, 1841. 1. 150
See also the bibliography of Chapter I, subsection 3, above.

2. *For elucidation of the "symbolism of heraldry,"* see

Guillim, J. *A Display of Heraldry.* London, 1724 (1st ed. 1610)

3. *For the poet's use of color,* see

Eagan, J. F. "The Import of Colors in *GGK.*" *St. Louis Univ. Studies,* Series A, Vol. 1 (November, 1949)

4. *For the poet's knowledge of and interest in Heraldry,* see
Appendix G. of this volume

CHAPTER III: PART I

1. *For information on the family of Coucy and Enguerrand, the seventh Sire of the house,* see

Anselm, le Père. *Histoire généalogique et chronologique de la Maison Royale de France, des Pairs, Grands Officiers de la Couronne et de la Maison du Roy, et des anciens Barons du Royaume* . . . 3e éd. Paris, 1726-33. 8. 542-45

L'Art de Vérifier les Dates. Paris, 1818. 17. 219-49

Cokayne, G. E. *Complete Peerage.* London, 1912. 2. 69-70

Du Chesne, André. *Histoire généalogique des Maisons de Guines, d'Ardes, de Gand et de Coucy.* Paris, 1631

Green, Mary A. E. *Lives of the Princesses of England.* London, 1851. 3. 198-228

Hardy, B. C. *Philippa of Hainault and Her Times.* London, 1910

Lacaille, Henri. "Étude sur la vie d'Enguerran VII, Sire de Coucy, Comte de Soissons (1340?-1397)." *École Nationale des Chartes: Positions des Thèses.* Mâcon, 1890. Pp. 83-91

Mazas, Alex. *Vies des Grands Capitaines Français du Moyen Age.* 2e éd. Paris, 1838. 3. 1-143

Savage, H. L. "Enguerrand de Coucy VII and the Campaign of Nicopolis." *Speculum* 14. 423-42

Zurlauben, Baron de. *Abrégé de la Vie d'Eng. VII, du nom, sire de Couci, avec un détail de son expédition en Alsace et en Suisse. Bibliotheque Militarie, Historique et Politique.* Paris, 1760. 2. 146-402. (A precis of this appeared in the *Histoire de l'Acad. Royale des Inscriptions et Belles Lettres,* Paris, 1769. 25. 168-86

CHAPTER III: PART II

1. *For the English territories of the house of Coucy,* see titles listed in Appendices A and F of this volume: in particular the following:

Calendar of Inquisitions Post Mortem 8. 306 (no. 462)

Green, Mary A. E. *Princesses of England* (cited above), 3. 443-49

2. *For titles dealing with the poet's place of origin, the date at which he wrote, and the occupation he followed,* see Appendices B, C, and K in this volume

3. *For Coucy's membership in the Order of the Garter,* see

Beltz, G. *Memorials of the Order of the Garter.* London, 1841. xxv-lii, 1-376 (particularly pp. 150-53)

Cargill, O., and M. Schlauch. "*The Pearl* and Its Jeweler." *PMLA* 43. 118-23

Cokayne, G. E. *Complete Peerage* (cited above). 2. 527-36, 591-93

Fellowes, E. H. *The Knights of the Garter*. London, n.d. Pp. 7-16, 75, 102-3

Gollancz, Sir I. *Cambridge History of English Literature*. London and New York, 1907. 1. 366

Jackson, I. "*GGK* Considered as a 'Garter' Poem." *Angl.* 37. 393-423

Nicolas, Sir N. H. *History of the Orders of Knighthood of the British Empire*. London, 1842. 1. 1-46

For other bibliography on the Order of the Garter, see Appendices D and L

4. *For the historic background of the period,* see

Armitage-Smith, S. *John of Gaunt*. New York, 1905

Champollion-Figeac, A. L. *Lettres des rois, reines, et autres personnages (Doc. Inéd. sur l'Histoire de France)*. Paris, 1847. Vol. 2

Delisle, Leopold. *Mandements divers de Charles V (Doc. Inéd. sur l'Histoire de France)*. Paris, 1874

Froissart, J. *Chroniques*. Ed. Kervyn de Lettenhove. Bruxelles, 1870-77. See particularly references to the family of Coucy in *Table analytique des noms historiques*, Vol. 21, pp. 38-45

Hardy, B. C. *Philippa of Hainault and Her Times*. London, 1910

Rymer, T. *Fœdera*. London, 1704-35. 20 vols. See particularly vols. 6 and 7

Tout, T. F. *Chapters in the Administrative History of Mediæval England*. Manchester, 1920-33. 6 vols.

Of special importance are the volumes of the following *Calendars*, which document the history of Coucy, his first wife, and their daughters over the period 1350-1405:

Calendar of Charter Rolls
Calendar of Close Rolls
Calendar of Fine Rolls
Calendar of Inquisitions Post Mortem
Calendar of Patent Rolls

The *Issue Rolls,* from which I have culled much useful information, still remain almost entirely unpublished. For the two published by Frederick Devon and for extracts that he made from a number of others, see bibliography of publications on the "Exchequer" in V. H. Galbraith, *An Introduction to the Use of the Public Records.* London, 1934. See also Appendix F of this volume.

CHAPTER III: PART III

1. *For discussion of the meaning of the Pentangle,* see

Beschoff, E. *Geheime Wissenschaften, Die Mystik und Magie der Zahlen.* Berlin, 1920

Dacier, B. J. "Recherches hist. sur l'établissement et l'extinction de l'Ordre de l'Étoile." *Mem. de Lit. tirés des Registres de l'Acad. Royale des Inscriptions et Belles-Lettres.* Paris, 1777. Vol. 39, pp. 662-88

Friedensburg, F. *Die Symbolik der Mittelaltermünzen.* Berlin, 1913

Pannier, L. *La Noble-Maison de Saint-Ouen.* Paris, 1872

Prinet, M. "Les Usages Héraldiques au XIVᵉ Siècle." *Annuaire-Bull. de la Soc. de l'Hist. de France.* 1916

For other bibliography, see Appendix E of this volume.

CHAPTER III: PART IV

1. *For the foundation of the Order of the Crown,* see

Hist. des Ordres Monastiques, Religieux, et Militaires, et des Congregations Séculieres. . . . Paris 1721. Vol. 8, pp. 285-86

Hulbert, J. R. "Sir Gawain and the Grene Kniȝt." *Mod. Phil.* 13. 707-21

Oeuvres Complètes d'Eustache Deschamps. Ed. G. Raynaud. Paris, 1901. Vol. 10, p. 181

For other bibliography, see Appendix J of this volume.

CHAPTER III: PART V

1. *For heraldic problems raised by the poem,* see my treatment of them in Appendix G of this volume. For an understanding of the matters treated in that Appendix, the reader will find the following helpful and authoritative:

Barron, O. "Heraldry." *Encycl. Brit.* 11th ed.

Dewick, E. S. *Coronation Book of Charles V.* Henry Bradshaw Society, Vol. 16. London, 1899

Menestrier, le Père. *Nouvelle Méthode Raisonné du Blazon.* Lyon, 1780 (a new ed. of Menestrier's *L'Art Héraldique* by M. Lemoine, archeviste du chapitre de Lyon)

Norris, H. *Costume and Fashion.* New York, 1927. Vol. 2, pp. 317-33

Planché, J. R. *The Pursuivant of Arms.* London, 1852

Spener, P. J. *Insignium Theoria.* Frankfurt-am-Main. 2nd ed. 1717. (*Pars Generalis* [or vol. 2] of Spener's *Operis Heraldici* has the title given above.)

Truman, N. *Historic Costuming.* London, 1936

Wagner, A. R. *Historic Heraldry of Britain.* London, 1939

Chapter III: Part VI

1. *For discussion of the possibility that lines 642-50 of Sir Gawain and the Green Knight refer to the war cry of the house of Coucy,* see Appendix H of this volume.

Index

Index

Ainsty, Wapentake of, 148
Aire River, 130, 131, 132, 133
Albert, Duke of Austria, 76
Albert, of Bavaria, 172
Albert I, Emperor of Holy Roman
    Empire, 52
Albret, Lord of, 58
Alexander III, King of Scotland, 67
All Souls' Day, 27
Alsace, 76, 77, 81, 82
Amiens, France, 174
Amounderness Hundred (Lancs.),
    132, 133, 135, 136, 137, 138
Ancestor, The, 189
Aquinas, St. Thomas, 13, 14
Aretino, Leonardo, 61
Armitage-Smith, S., 154
Armorial de la Toison d'or. See
    London, H. Stanford
Arthur, King, 15, 102, 108, 161,
    195, 203
Ashton (Lancs.), Manor of, 125,
    133
Ashton with Stodday (Lancs.), 134
Austerfield (Yks.), 149
Austria, Duchy of, 52, 199

Baillie-Grohman, William A., 31,
    33
Bailly, Harry (Host in *The Pro-
    logue to the Canterbury Tales*),
    50
Baker, Sir Samuel, 31
Ballad of the Green Knight, 142
Banastre, Sir Thomas, 146, 148
Barante, A. G. P. B., 156
Barbary, Africa, 149
Barron, Oswald, xi

Barton, parish of (Yks.), 134
Bastin, J., 128
Bath, Order of the, 143
Baugh, A. C., 127
Bawtry (Yks.), 149
Bayazid, Sultan of Turkey, 194
Bedford, Countess of, 73, 91, 92, 98,
    127, 135, 154, 211, 212, 214
Bedford, Earl of, 11, 13, 67, 85, 88,
    91, 94, 98, 114, 127, 135, 139,
    154, 210, 211, 214, 215, 216
Belshazzer, 6
Beltz, G., 155
Bercilak, 23, 26, 27, 33, 34, 35,
    36, 143, 176
Black Prince, Edward, Prince of
    Wales, 86
Blackburn Hundred (Lancs.), 132
Blois, Guy, Count of, 74
Boccace (Boccaccio), 128
Book of the Duchess, 11, 25
Boulogne, 85
Bourbon, Louis II, Duke of, 149
Boxmer MS, 128
Braybroke, Robert de, Bishop of
    London, 8
Brétigny, France, 49, 54
Bruges, Flanders, conferences at, 82,
    85, 87
Brusa, Turkey, 118, 194
Buren in Argau, Switzerland, seign-
    iory of, 82
Burton-in-Lonsdale, Manor of
    (Yks.), 151

Cabus in Garstang (Lancs.), 135
Caerlaverock, Siege of. See London,
    H. Stanford

Calais, France, 174
Camelot, 26
Canterbury Tales, 16, 24
Cargill, O., 143, 144
Carnforth (Lancs.), 125, 134, 138
Cartmel (Lancs.), 134
Cauchon, Jean, 87, 88
Chancery, household of, 207-11, 214, 217
Chandos, Sir John, 146
Charles IV, Holy Roman Emperor, 76
Charles V, Regent and later King of France, 53, 76, 77, 78, 81, 82, 83, 84, 85, 89, 95, 118, 157, 163, 164, 166
Charles VI, King of France, 156, 172
Chartres, France, 49, 194
Chateaumorand, Jean de, 173
Chaucer, Geoffrey, xv, xvi, 10, 11, 14, 16, 24, 25, 28, 149, 150, 165, 216
Cheshire, County of, 7, 8, 10, 21, 113, 129
Chesterfield, Philip Stanhope, Lord, 13
Chin, Sire de, 187
Christmas, 139, 140, 143
Circumcision, Day of the, 27
Claughton-in-Lonsdale (Lancs.), 214
Clifford, Sir Lewis, 149, 150
Clifford, Roger, Lord, 149
Cockerham, parish of (Lancs.), 135
Cockersand (Cumberland), 130, 134
Collins, S. M., 185
Complete Peerage, 189
"Completion and Unity." *See* Pentangle
Coniston Water, 14
Coronation Book of Charles V, 181
Corsham, Manor of (Wilts.), 126
Cotton Nero A. x. Manuscript, 3, 5, 7, 16, 28, 137, 138, 141
Coucy, Catherine de, 52, 76
Coucy, Enguerrand IV, Sire de, 124, 189
Coucy, Enguerrand VII, Sire de, Earl of Bedford, Comte de Soissons, xiii, 11, 50, 52-54, 59-61, 63-67, 70, 72-97, 102-07, 109-11, 113, 114, 116-18, 123-28, 133-41, 151, 154-57, 164-69, 172-75, 186-90, 192-95, 198-206, 214, 215, 217
Coucy, Mary de, Countess of Bar, 73
Coucy, Philippa de, Duchess of Ireland and Countess of Oxford, 74, 114, 118, 141, 153, 168-75, 212, 213, 216
Coucy, Raoul de, 53
Coucy, Robert de, 68, 124
Coucy, William de, 67, 68, 70, 124, 125, 133, 215
Coucy, house of, 51-53, 95, 114-16, 133, 188, 191, 213, 214; territory of, 52, 129, 211
Coucy-Guines, house of, 51, 69, 71, 114, 154, 190, 213. *See also* Coucy
Coucy-le-Château, France, 52, 53, 76, 92
Coupland, Joan de, 71, 135, 169
Coupland, John de, 71
Craven, Yorkshire West Riding, xi, 9, 11, 147, 149, 150, 151, 211
Crossford (Lancs.), 215
Crown, Order of the, 109, 116, 196-205
Cumberland, County of, 67, 69, 71, 129, 138

Dante, 113
Day, Mabel, 179, 180
Dee River, 7
Derby, County of, 9, 21, 113, 129, 149
Deschamps, Eustache, 128, 150, 192, 201, 203
Despenser, Edward, Lord, 148, 149
Destruction of Troy, 130
Dies Iræ, 27
Dinnington, Manor of (Yks.), 151
Dordrecht, city of, 172
Dorling, E. E., 188-90
Ducange, Charles Du Fresne, 192
DuChesne, Andre, 76, 95, 133
Du Guesclin, Bertrand, 81

Eccleston, Great (Lancs.), 136
Eccleston, Little (Lancs.), 136
Edmund, Earl of Cambridge, later Duke of York, 86, 151-53, 174
Edward III, King of England, 13, 54, 55, 57, 59, 64, 66, 67, 69, 70, 71, 73, 74, 78, 80, 81, 85, 86, 89, 93, 105, 106, 133, 140, 143, 145, 146, 155, 168, 186
Ekwall, E., 136
Eltham, 13, 74
Emerson, O. F., 127, 178, 179
"Endless Knot." *See* Pentangle
Enghien, Louis Antoine Henri de Bourbon, Duc de, 171
Erkenwald. *See* St. Erkenwald

Farnesius, probably Henri Farnèse (1550?-1616) of Pavia, 43
"Five Joys" (of the Virgin), 159, 191
"Five Wounds" (of Christ), 159
Flanders, Count of, 57
Flanders, Marguerite of, 79
Freemasonry, 159
Froissart, Jean, 53, 54, 60, 61, 76, 77, 79, 81, 82, 86, 87, 94, 95, 128, 149, 155, 156, 166, 167, 171, 174, 175, 187
Furness (Lancs.), 130
Furness, Abbey of (Lancs.), 10

Garstang, parish of (Lancs.), 135, 136, 215
Garter, Order of the, 64, 76, 90, 97, 102, 104-06, 108, 114-16, 139, 142-49, 152, 154-57, 161, 175, 182, 186, 197, 198, 202, 205
Gascony, France, 49
Gaunt. *See* John of Gaunt
Gawain, 18, 20, 21, 26, 27, 31, 33, 36, 37, 38, 41-45, 99-105, 108, 109, 116, 117, 140, 143, 144, 145, 150, 157, 158, 159, 160, 162, 166, 167, 176-80, 182-87, 190, 193, 195-97, 202, 204
Gawain and the Green Knight, Sir Gawain, Gawain, 5, 7, 9, 12, 14-16, 21, 22, 25, 31, 39, 46, 47, 99, 106, 110, 111, 113, 114, 117, 128-31, 138, 139, 140, 141,

143, 144, 145, 148, 151-53, 176, 198, 206, 211, 213
Gawain-poet, xv, 6, 7, 8, 10-12, 14, 16, 19, 22, 28, 29, 32, 47, 104, 105, 112, 113, 133, 135, 137, 141, 146, 152, 158, 166, 176, 181, 182, 186, 201, 204, 208, 210, 216, 217
Gevaert, E., 38
Ghent, Flanders, 79
Gollancz, Sir Israel, 137
Gloucester. *See* Thomas, Duke of Gloucester
Gordon, E. V., 130, 134, 179
Grasmere (Westmorland), 125
Great Sowerby (Lancs.), 216
Green, Mary A. E., 64, 66, 74, 91
Green Chapel, The, 27, 38, 99, 101
Green Knight, The, 15, 27, 99, 102, 150, 160
Gregory XI, Pope, 61, 79
Guichard d'Angle, 64, 87
Guienne, France, 49
Guillim, John, 40, 41, 43, 46
Guines, Alix de, 67
Guines, Gynes, family of, 67-69, 115, 123, 188-90
Gynes, Guines, Enguerrand (Ingelram) de, 67, 68, 123, 135, 189

Hainault, County of, Flanders, 172
Hanaper, The, 214
Hardy, Blanche Christabel, 56, 91
Hautdesert, 26
Havering-at-the-Bower (Essex), 175
Henry IV, King of England, 114, 141, 143, 173
Henry V, King of England, 143
Hoghton, Sir Richard de, 216
Holland, country of, 172
Holm, family of, 41
Horn(e)by, Edmund de, 214
Hornby, John de, 213, 214
Hornby, Margaret de, 215
Hornby, Margery, 215
Hornby, Richard de, 216
Hornby, Robert de, 215
Hornby, Wilkin de, 216
Hornby, William de (servant of John of Gaunt), 214

Hornby, William de (king's attorney), 215, 216
Hornby, William de (yeoman of the livery of the crown), 216
Hulbert, J .R., 106, 198, 197
Huntington, Earl of. *See* Guichard d'Angle

Ingleborough Hill (Yks.), 14
Ireby (Lancs.), 213
Irish Sea, 11
Isabella, Lady de Coucy, Countess of Bedford, and Princess of England, 55, 56, 58, 59, 62, 63, 73-76, 78, 80, 88-98, 114, 118, 139, 168, 172, 212
Isabella, of Lorraine, second wife of Enguerrand de Coucy VII, 96, 118
Isabella, Queen of England, 175
Isabella, Queen of France, 58
Isabelle, of Bavaria, 58
Italy, 79, 97, 128

Jackson, Isaac, 145, 193
Jacquerie, 53, 164
Jean le Bon, King Jean 11 of France, 49, 54, 60, 161, 163, 166
John of Gaunt, 11, 12, 72, 78, 84, 86, 114, 115, 127, 135, 150, 151, 153, 154, 174, 181, 205, 210, 211, 213, 214, 215, 217
"John Peel," 31
Joinville, Jean, Sire de, 91
Jonah, 5, 10, 15, 22
Jones, of Monmouthshire, 40

Kaiser, R. B., 138
Kendal, barony of, 67, 123, 135, 189
Kent, Thomas Holand, Earl of, 81
Kimberworth, Manor of (Yks.), 148
Kirby in Kendal (Westmorland), 125
Kirby Malesart, Manor of (Yks.), 151
Kirkham, parish of (Lancs.), 136
Kittredge, G. L., 104, 145

Lacaille, Henri, 77

La Fère, France, 52
Lamberton (Berwickshire), 123
Lancaster, Duke of. *See* John of Gaunt
Lancashire (Lancaster), County of, xi, 4, 9, 10, 11, 13-17, 21, 28, 67, 68, 69, 71, 72, 113, 114, 126, 129, 132, 133, 134, 135, 138, 147, 149, 152, 153, 157, 189, 206, 210, 213, 215, 216
Lancaster, Duchy of, 214
Lancaster, town of, 130, 134
Langland, William, 113
Laon, France, 50
Leopold VII, Duke of Austria, 52, 77
le Roulx, J. Delaville, 194
Leyland Hundred (Lancs.), 132, 133
Lionel, Duke of Clarence, 76
Lombard, Peter, 14
London, H. Stanford, 185
London, England, 13, 17, 86, 150, 206
London, Treaty of, 49
Lonsdale, North (Lancs.), 132
Lonsdale, South (Lancs.), 132, 134
Loomis, R. S., 107
Louvain, city in Duchy of Brabant, 172
Lydgate, John, 106
Lyndeheved (Lancs.), 125
Lyndsay (Lindsay), Christina de, 67, 123, 189
Lyndsay (Lindsay), William de, 123
Lyndsay, lands of, 71

Mahadia, Crusade of, 118
Maltby, Manor of (Yks.), 148
Malverne, John, 171
Mandeville, John, 14
Mandeville's Travels, 6
Man of Law's Tale, 26
Marle, France, 52
Mary Madeleva, Sister, 10
Master of Game, The, 34, 35, 39
Mazas, Alexandre, 53, 128, 164, 165
Melibeus, Tale of, 24
Menner, R. J., 178-80
Mersey River, 7

"Merveille," of Château de Coucy, 50, 191, 192

Mezières, Philippe de, 194

Middleton by Multon (Yks.), 125, 134

Midland(s), Northwest, 113, 126, 129, 130, 138, 206, 213

Minds and Manners of Wild Animals, The, 39

Monkton on the Moor, Manor of, 148

Montreuil-sur-Mere, 85

Moore, Samuel, 216

Moorman, F. W., 17, 18

Morgarten, Battle of, 52

Morice, Boniface, 89

Morris, R., 177

Mour(e)holm (Lancs.), 125, 133, 134, 138

Mowbray, Thomas, Duke of Norfolk, 151, 152

Napoleon, 171

New Year's Day, 27, 101, 140

Nicopolis, Battle and Crusade of, 118, 175, 192, 194

Nidau, in Argau, seigniory of, 82

Nimrod, 38

Nineveh, 15

Noah, 10, 15, 30

Norris, H., 144

Northwest Midland, dialect of, 147

Oakden, J. P., 129, 131, 132, 137, 154

Oisy, France, 52

Osgood, C. G., 13

Ostrevant, Count of, 156, 205

Pardoner's Tale, The, 24

Paris, Gaston, 25

Paris, France, 76, 163, 164

Parliament Roll of 1312. See London, H. Stanford

Parmes, James de, 89

Parson's Tale, The, 24

Pas de Calais, France, 67

Patience, 5, 6, 17, 20, 24, 25, 142, 208

Pearl, 5, 7, 13, 14, 19, 20, 22, 46, 47, 108, 112, 142, 148, 208

Pearl-poet, 47

Pedro, of Castile, 56

Pendle Hill (Lancs.), 14

Pentagram, Pentalpha. *See* Pentangle

Pentangle, The, 116, 158-60, 163, 166, 167

Perrers, Alice, 59

Pétrarque (Petrarch), 128

Philippa, Queen of England, 55, 59

Philippe le Hardi, 79, 156

Picardy, France, province of, 53, 69, 78

Pieres, John, 127

Poitiers, France, 49, 163

Potier, Jean, 88

Prague, Bohemia, 76, 77

Prinet, Max, 166

Proust, Marcel, 112

Purity, 5, 6, 12, 13, 14, 20, 24, 25, 142, 208

Pye, Richard, 75

Pythagoras, 158

Radcot Bridge, 172

Reynard, 27, 34, 36, 37, 46

Ribble River, 11, 113, 130-34, 136, 151

Ribchester (Lancs.), 214

Richard II, King of England, 40, 87, 90, 96, 115, 127, 146, 150, 156, 169-72, 175, 186, 215

Richard the Redeles, 40

Richmond (Yks.), 11, 12

Rigmaiden, Thomas de, 215

Round Table, The, 161, 196

Rymer, Thomas, 173

Rysebank, Castle of, 216

St. Augustine (of Hippo), 194

Sainte Chapelle, 163

St. Erkenwald, 7, 19, 20, 24

St. George, 161

Saint-Gobain, near Coucy-le-Château, 92

St. Inglevert, tournament of, 149

St. Mary's Holm, 125

St. Michael's (Lancs.), church and parish of, 135-36, 214

Saint-Ouen, La Noble Maison de, 163
St. Paul, 61
St. Paul's Cathedral, 8, 207
Salford Hundred (Lancs.), 132
Salisbury, Countess of, 105, 155
"Salus," 159
Savoy, Duke of, 79
Savoy, palace of the, 12
Scarsdale, 15
Schlauch, Margaret, 143-44
Scotford, Manor of (Lancs.), 125
Second Nun's Tale, 24
Selous, F. C., 31
Seneschal d'Eu, The, 150
Serjeantson, M., 129
Shakespeare, William, 151
Sheen, 13, 167, 216
Skepulford (Lancs.), 215
Skiddaw (Cumberland), 14
Skipton, Castle of, 149-50
Soissons, Count of, 74, 198, 205
Solomon, 116, 158
Spener, P. J., 184
Spenser, Edmund, 47, 107, 112
Spurgeon, C., 18
Star (of the Magi), 160, 163, 167
Star, Order of the, 161, 163-64
Strafforth, Wapentake of, 149
Switzerland, 76, 81-83, 97

Talleyrand, Charles Maurice de Talleyrand—Perigord, 171
Terrier de Loray, H., 165
Thomas, of Woodstock, Duke of Gloucester, 86, 171, 205
Thornton-in-Lonsdale (Yks.), 125, 134, 214
Three Kings (the Magi), The, 161
Tickell, Wapentake of (Yks.), 149
Tolkien, J. R. R., 130, 134, 179
Toussaints du Plessis, Dominus, 95
Tout, T. F., 208-09
Tyrrell, Sir Thomas, 73

Ughtred, Sir Thomas, 115, 147
Ulvereston (Ulverston), (Lancs.), 125, 133, 134, 138
Upton, Nicholas, 41

Valentine, Duchess of Orléans, 58

Vere, Dowager Countess of, 216
Vere, Robert de, Earl of Oxford, Duke of Ireland, 118, 151, 154, 168-72, 213
Versailles, Palace of, 119
Virgil, Polydore, 105, 155
Virgin, The, 161, 191-94
Visconti, Bernabo, 79
Vulgate, The, 208

Wales, 99
Wappenbuch von den Ersten, 185
Wappen-Rolls (of Zürich), 185
Warton, parish of (Lancs.), 134
Wedacre in Garstang (Lancs.), 215
West Derby Hundred (Lancs.), 132, 133
West Midland(s), 146, 147, 151, 153
Westmorland, County of, 14, 15, 67, 68, 71, 125, 129, 133, 134, 138, 153, 211
Whalley (Lancs.), 130, 132
Whalley, Abbey of (Lancs.), 10
Wharles (Lancs.), 137
Whittingham (Lancs.), 137
Whittington, Wardship of (Lancs.), 125, 133, 134, 138, 214
William of Palerne, 26
Winandermere (Westmoreland), 125
Windsor Castle, 12, 62, 63, 115, 119, 166, 167
Winmarleigh, Manor of, 215
Wirral, forest of, 7
Woodstock, 55
Wykeham, William de, 215
Wyre River, 215
Wyresdale Manor, Parish of, (Lancs.), 125, 133, 135-37, 214, 216

York. *See* Edmund, Earl of Cambridge
Yorkshire, County of, 9, 11, 14, 17, 21, 67, 71, 72, 126, 133, 147-49, 151, 153, 189, 206
Yorkshire, West Riding of, 28, 113, 114, 126, 129, 132, 149, 151-53

Zeeland, County of, 172